Dychweler y llyfr hwn erbyn y dyddiad isod, neu
pan elwir amdano gan y Llyfrgellydd.
Dirwyir unrhyw ddarllenydd a fetho ddychwelyd y
llyfr mewn pryd.

This book must be returned on or before the date
shown below, or when required by the Librarian.
A fine will be imposed on any borrower failing
to return the book in time.

AARON V. CICOUREL

Method and Measurement
in Sociology

THE FREE PRESS
A Division of Macmillan Publishing Co., Inc.
NEW YORK

COLLIER MACMILLAN PUBLISHERS
LONDON

To MERRYL

The Free Press
A Division of Macmillan Publishing Co., Inc.
866 Third Avenue, New York, N.Y. 10022

Collier-Macmillan Canada Ltd.

Library of Congress Catalog Card Number: 64–16964

Printed in the United States of America

printing number
8   9   10

PREFACE

IN THE PAGES THAT FOLLOW I have attempted to set down some of the ideas and problems that have been sources of both guidance and difficulty during graduate work, the teaching of an introductory course in methodology, and my research experiences. The book seeks to codify and present systematically material that is known, but seldom published, by students of methodology and researchers concerned with the measurement of social process. The typical problem of measurement in sociology is, on the one hand, one of implicit theories with vague properties and operations tied in unknown ways to measurement procedures which, on the other hand, have explicit quantitative properties wherein the operations permitted can be defined concisely.

The book has a programatic flavor because it offers no "solution" in the sense of showing precisely how we can construct better measurement procedures. My answer to those readers who dislike programatic statements is that a practical solution requires certain theoretical and meta-methodological clarifications, clarifications not entirely programatic, that are linked explicitly to concrete methods of social research. I have attempted to specify the problems that sociology must address if researchers are to achieve a more basic level of interaction between theory, method, and data. As opposed to the quest for "better" and more "rigorous" measurement techniques, it would be more fruitful to eliminate many sociological attempts at measurement and to seek an explanation of theories and concepts that would clarify what, if any, numerical properties are suggested or can be generated by present sociological theories. A clarification of sociological theory vis-à-vis corresponding arithmetical properties, relations, and operations must be linked to a disentanglement of the sociological language used by investigators, and the common-sense language and meanings used by the sociologist's actor and the "man in the street." Present categories of data are ordered and/or quantified independent of explicit links to theories, while our methods simultaneously rely upon common-sense meanings and procedures for achieving *after the fact* connections between theory and data.

My interest in writing this book began at U.C.L.A., while a student of W. S. Robinson. His lectures on methodology were basic for the views expressed in the following chapters. Particularly stimulating for me were Robinson's lectures on validity and reliability because of the general point that the sociological researcher must rely upon the "folk concepts" of his subject, judge's or coder's ratings and his own personal interpretations of events and data, in order to "make sense" of results and to achieve any sort of systematic codification. Robinson's related observation that seldom in sociology can we maximize both validity and reliability with present techniques of investigation stimulated my interest in seeking more explicit links between theory and measurement.

A two-year period of collaboration with Harold Garfinkel introduced me to the work of Alfred Schutz and clarified my understanding of the role of theory in method and measurement in sociology. This collaboration proved valuable in understanding how formal sociological theories are tied ambiguously to the subject's and researcher's common-sense language and thinking. My debt to Schutz' work and Garfinkel's exposition of it will be evident in the pages that follow. The present work began after my association with Garfinkel and may depart significantly from his own ideas about the same or similar topics. I have not had the benefit of his criticisms, but have sought to footnote his ideas

contained in published and unpublished works within the limits
of not being given permission to quote from them directly.

I have benefited from discussions with former colleagues at
Northwestern University and wish to acknowledge specifically
Donald T. Campbell, Scott Greer, Mitchell Harwitz, Herbert
Hochberg (now at Indiana University), John Kitsuse, and Norton
Long. On the Riverside Campus of the University of California
I have profited from discussions with Egon Bittner, Thomas
Morrison, Stanley Stewart, and Howard Tucker. During summers
on the Berkeley Campus of the University of California I have
learned much from conversations with John Gumperz, David
Matza, Sheldon Messinger, William Petersen, June Rumery, and
Harvey Sacks.

Many persons read various drafts of part or all of the manuscript and their helpful suggestions were incorporated into the
final draft. I want to acknowledge specifically the help of Howard
S. Becker, Gerald Berreman, John Gumperz, Mitchell Harwitz,
David Harrah, Peter McHugh, William Petersen, Stanley Stewart,
Arthur Stinchcombe, Howard Tucker, and Robin M. Williams,
Jr. William Petersen's devastating but always constructive and
valuable criticisms were particularly important in revising chapters I and IX, and also stimulated a general revision of the manuscript. Mrs. Aline Pick Kessler, formerly of The Free Press, was
especially helpful in her editorial suggestions and made numerous important contributions to style and substantive clarity.
Mrs. Donna Lippert provided timely and dedicated typing assistance. I wish to thank the Dora and Randolph Haynes Foundation for a fellowship during the summer of 1961 which enabled
me to draft some of the preliminary chapters of the manuscript.
I also wish to thank the various publishers and individuals for
permission to quote from their published works.

A.V.C.

Buenos Aires
January 1964

CONTENTS

INTRODUCTION

CONCERN FOR THE FOUNDATIONS of social science research should require the continual examination and re-examination of its first principles. In this book I hope to strengthen sociological research by critically examining the foundations of method and measurement in sociology, particularly at the level of social process. This work shares the assumption of R. M. MacIver's *Social Causation* that ". . . the social structure is for the most part created." "Unlike the physical nexus," the social type of causal nexus, "does not exist apart from the objectives and motives of social beings" and requires a methodological strategy that fits the distinctiveness of social events.[1] I am concerned, therefore, with the problems of method and measurement that arise when sociologists seek to study what Max Weber describes as "meaningful behavior" or "social action." [2]

I assume first that methodological decisions in social research always have their theoretical and substantive counterparts; second, that the theoretical presuppositions of method and measurement in sociology cannot be viewed apart from the language that sociologists use in their theorizing and research. My basic assumption is that the clarification of sociological language is important because linguistic structure and use affects the way people interpret and describe the world. Since sociologists have evolved their own theoretical terminologies and frequently discuss, on the one hand, in these often varying terms the language and substance of each other's theories and on the other hand the language of persons in everyday life whose behavior they are interested in explaining and predicting, it is quite likely that the syntax and meaning of these languages will become entangled.[3] Sociological research and measurement require something like a "theory of instrumentation" and a theory of data so that we can disentangle the observer's presence and procedures from the material he labels "data." The confounding of sociological language about sociological theories, social events, and the language used by subjects under study is a basic problem in field research and other research methods such as content analysis and laboratory experiments. The role of language, especially everyday language and para-linguistic forms of communication, in social research is a major focus of the book.

Another focus is the questionning of mathematical and measurement systems currently used in social research. I do not wish to imply that sociocultural events cannot be measured by existing mathematical formulations, but that the fundamental events of social action should be clarified before imposing measurement postulates with which they may not be in correspondence. In arguing this point I have often set up a straw man: asking for measurement conditions which are seldom attainable with our present state of knowledge.

Finally, the book attempts to present a preliminary specification of the elements of social action presupposed in many of the methodological decisions sociologists make in the course of social research.

◄§ *A Brief Overview of the Contents*

In Chapter I, the problem of measurement is taken up in some detail. The difficulties of establishing equivalence classes in sociological theorizing and research are discussed, and attention is devoted to some of the peculiar problems involved in measuring sociocultural events. The central thesis of the chapter is that present measurement devices are not valid because they represent the imposition of numerical procedures that are external both to the observable social world empirically described by sociologists and to the *conceptualizations* based upon these descriptions. Carried to the extreme, this view might seem to suggest that because the concepts upon which sociological theories are based have inherently no numerical properties, we can not know which numerical properties to look for in the correlative observables, whatever they may be.

An inspection of chapters II through VIII will reveal that I do not adopt the extreme position just described. The chapters on participant observation, interviewing, fixed-choice questionnaires, demographic method, content analysis, experimental research and linguistics do not propose that sociologists stop all further research and measurement until the basic categories of daily life have been clarified and their numerical properties ordered axiomatically. The chapters on various research methods seek, instead, a clarification of sociological equivalence classes at the level of basic and substantive theory, not "better" measurement systems. My efforts are consistent with current attempts to strengthen the methodological foundations of sociological research. The two strategies which have appeared seem to proceed as follows:

1. Present theorizing and research operations seek to clarify the measurement and theoretical foundations of the discipline by treating each research project and theoretical paper as both substantive endeavors and attempts to explicate theory and measurement.[4]

2. Miniature models are developed for particular areas of interest (such as small group research) which can be axiomatized. And from such small-scale projects we seek to learn whether a delimited area can receive numeric treatment without being totally distorted.[5]

Neither program can escape an implicit specification of a model of the actor which is presupposed in the formulation and carrying out of the research. The second program requires an explicit concern for what constitutes literal measurement in sociology as opposed to measurement by fiat.[6] If sociologists adopt the first approach, measurement will be vague and seldom literal because most of the efforts will be devoted to a clarification of everyday language and expression, sociological language about everyday life, and a meta-language about concepts which deal with sociological language about daily life.

Chapter IX presents some elements of social action and my conception of what the sociologist's model of the actor should include initially, that is, before specifying the substantive problem under study. This final chapter—which some readers might prefer to read first since much of its content is assumed throughout the book—is, then, intended as a preliminary statement of the kinds of "basic" theoretical material which is presupposed in methodological decisions.

✦§ *Measurement, Science, and Sociological Research*

By insisting that sociologists do not devote enough attention to the study of "subjective" variables, especially those which contribute to the contingent character of everyday life, I hope to stress the importance of constructing models of social action which specify typical motives, values, and course-of-action types within the context of an environment of objects with common-sense properties as originated by Weber. Such formulation provides for a model of the actor which does not reduce social action to psychological variables and assumes that equivalence classes, at least at the conceptual level, can be specified, thereby leaving the problem of measurement open. The assumption is that it is possible to establish equivalence classes at the conceptual level which correspond to correlatives of an observed environment.

I have side-stepped the question of whether sociology is a "science" and its subject-matter definitely amenable to some kind of quantification by implicitly assuming both are reasonable goals. My reasons are as follows: Since we do not at present have theoretical systems that can be meaningfully axiomatized so that they will generate numerical properties that correspond to (and presumably be isomorphic with) , for example, the integers or real numbers, we can seldom measure social events rigorously. I will argue that sociology's present concern for the label "science" and its insistence on "quantitative findings" obscures nontrivial prediction and explanation because measurement is accomplished by fiat. While the physicist has measurement problems that are also tortuous, he can point to replicable experiments leading to nontrivial verification of important predictions. Sociology's theoretical concepts remain ambiguous and divorced from their measurement in research situations. Current measurement in sociological research may be of value in providing intuitive knowledge about the structure of theory and the proper sets of relations between elements of the theory but the measurements and the theories to which they are supposed to be related remain ambiguous because they are not related by what Nagel calls "explicit rules of correspondence." [7] Rather than spend so much time and money doing studies that only achieve measurement by fiat, we should spend more time clarifying our theories and seeking correlatives in a world of observables. The approach suggested would not avoid empirical research; it would avoid findings that are deemed worthwhile only because they are forced into a set of categories which will "scale" or will provide for a test of significance.

Arguments about whether sociology is a "science" or its theories and findings amenable to quantification are premature if we cannot agree on what is theory and whether our theories can be stated so that they generate numeric properties that will have correlatives in an observable world.

I

MEASUREMENT

AND MATHEMATICS

THE RESEARCH TECHNIQUES and measurement scales of any science can be viewed as a problem in the sociology of knowledge. At any given time knowledge depends on the particular state of methods in use; future knowledge will depend on the development of today's methods. It is important to ask whether claims to knowledge are based on methods in correspondence with the theories and the data collected, or whether the research techniques and measurement scales on which these claims are based have little more than a metaphorical or synecdochical relationship to the same theories and data.[1] If our empirical interest in the problem of social order is dependent upon such methods, and if such methods are not being used literally, then the *study* of research techniques and measurement scales becomes critical for understanding what will be considered "knowledge" in any given era. Consider the following questions:

1. What theoretical presuppositions are contained in methods of sociological inquiry that seek to measure the properties of social action?

2. Do the theoretical presuppositions generate measurement properties that fit the observables produced by given methodological procedures?

3. What are the necessary conditions for establishing literal and rigorous measurement in the study of social process?

These three questions suggest the basic theme of the book:

the relation of methodology and measurement to theory. Any attempt to show the theoretical implications of methodological and measurement procedures in sociology requires a digression into current conceptions about measurement. The digression is necessary because social scientists use a much broader and often attenuated form of measurement than do natural scientists. Therefore, the study of measurement in sociology requires some preliminary technical background with which sociological practices are to be compared.

✑§   *Some Technical Background*

We begin with a few remarks about axiomatic systems.[2] It is convenient to distinguish between *uninterpreted* and *interpreted* axiomatic systems. An abstract, formalized axiomatic system containing only logical terms like "or," "and," "not," and arbitrarily chosen marks such as $, %, #, is an uninterpreted system.[3] Such systems are useful because they permit deductions and proofs in explicit steps and thereby guard against mistakes that often accompany the use of descriptive (interpreted, meaningful) terms.[4] Mathematical systems, when uninterpreted, consist of mere marks, logical truths or tautologies. Thus, a formalized axiomatic system is one which has no necessary reference to the empirical world.

An interpreted axiomatic system contains descriptive as well as logical terms. Replacing the marks and logical truths of an abstract uninterpreted axiomatic system by descriptive terms and empirical statements leads to an interpreted system.[5] The axioms or postulates of an uninterpreted axiomatic system may become scientific laws in an interpreted system. Thus, interpreted axiomatic systems require that a correspondence be demonstrated between the elements, relations, and operations of the mathematical and substantive systems in question. The empirical consequences require that the measurement properties of the theoretical events be specified. For example, Zetterberg's illustration of an axiomatic system containing ordinal properties implies that in Durkheim's theory of suicide the substantive properties are limited to the ordinal properties of the measurement system.[6] Whereas such restrictions can be severe in their limitation of the measurement scale used, they also raise the question of whether such a scale is appropriate to the measurement of the social processes intended in Durkheim's theory.

Implicit and Explicit Theories. Not all theories are axiomatic in nature. When a theory consists of a set of laws and definitions that are deductively interrelated it is an axiomatic system.[7] Not all axiomatic systems are theories. It is useful, at least temporarily, to distinguish between two kinds of theories. The first type, implicit theory, may be defined broadly as a set of descriptive statements and definitions that is not axiomatic in form and therefore not to be taken as a set of interrelated laws. This is not to say that such theories may not contain laws or that interrelationships among its descriptive statements and definitions do not exist. The point is that various implicit theories may contain unknown amounts of ambiguity, "unknown" unless otherwise indicated by whoever develops or uses them. The ambiguity refers to the lack of systemization within the conceptual structure and to external criteria. The "sophistication" of many implicit theories in sociology rests upon the use of various kinds of typologies, paradigms, and similar devices. Theories in sociology are primarily of the implicit variety with occasional islands of systemization and measurement. An explicit theory is an interpreted axiomatic system as defined above.[8] Explicit theories are virtually nonexistent in sociology. However, there are several attempts to "simulate" such formulations.[9]

To summarize, we note that mathematical systems *per se* are uninterpreted (abstract, formalized) axiomatic systems containing uninterpreted signs and marks and tautological statements, while some theoretical systems contain empirical axiomatic systems or explicit theories. If the axioms of a mathematical system have the same structure as the laws of an explict theory, such that (1) the axioms of the mathematical system can be "translated" into the laws of the explicit theory so that (2) there is a one-to-one correspondence between the terms of the two systems and their statements; and (3) logical connections between the axioms and the laws, respectively, are preserved, the two systems are *isomorphic.* The relevant question here is how are such isomorphisms presupposed by sociologists building or using "mathematical models" and "measurement models" with implicit theories, and what are the consequences for theory and method that follow?

Can we generate propositions from implicit theories that are amenable to rigorous measurement? Must we have axiomatic theories for measurement to occur? I do not have explicit answers to these questions but I will touch upon them in subsequent discussion.

Measurement. Much of what is written on measurement in psychology and sociology is taken from the work of the physicist Norman Campbell. Recent books by Torgerson and Churchman and Ratoosh [10] provide excellent coverage of various discussions of measurement and their mathematical foundations. Much of the work on measurement in sociology has been in the areas commonly called social psychology and demography and has concentrated upon the development or use of mathematical systems for describing small group interaction, measuring attitudes, and analyzing demographic data.

Campbell defines measurement "as the assignment of numbers to represent properties" (or more generically, of numerals to represent properties).[11] Nagel refers to measurement as "the correlation with numbers of entities which are not numbers." [12] Stevens points out that, generally speaking, it "is the assignment of numerals to objects or events according to rules. And the fact that numerals can be assigned under different rules leads to different kinds of scales and different kinds of measurement." [13] For Coombs "Measurement in the physical sciences usually means the assigning of numbers to observations (a process called 'mapping'), and the analysis of the data consists in manipulating or operating on these numbers. The social scientist, taking physics as his model, has, frequently, attempted to do the same. It is the thesis . . . that the social scientist who follows such a procedure will sometimes violate his data." [14]

Torgerson takes the position

that measurement pertains to properties of objects, and not to the objects themselves. Thus, a stick is not measurable in our use of the term, although its *length, weight, diameter,* and *hardness* might well be. . . .

Measurement of a property then involves the assignment of numbers to systems to represent that property. In order to represent the property, an isomorphism, i.e., a one-to-one relationship, must obtain between certain characteristics of the number system involved and the relations between various quantities (instances) of the property to be measured.

The essence of the procedure is the assignment of numbers in such a way as to reflect this one-to-one correspondence between these characteristics of the numbers and the corresponding relations between the quantities.[15]

Numerals may be simply an ordered set of elements in one-to-one correspondence with the number system. Number and numeral are not always interchangeable as implied in the quotes from Campbell and Stevens. Reese notes that "numerals, by which is meant simply a group of conventional signs or marks on a piece of paper, obtain their order by convention." [16] Many authors fail to clarify the distinction between numerals and numbers when discussing measurement. Reese quotes Campbell on this point:

"In discussing the assignment of numerals it is well to stress again that it is numerals that are assigned and not numbers. As Campbell says, '. . . it would be difficult to avoid the impression that the conception of number and the rules of arithmetic were concerned in the matter. Of course, they are closely connected with measurement; but if we fail to recognize that they are not essential we shall not understand the connection.' " [17]

This distinction is important in order to clarify the significance of assigning numerals to objects without specifying which algebraic system governing operations on numbers is applicable. It is possible to develop a mathematical system that utilizes numerals to represent a substantive theoretical system but does not specify whether the mathematical operations developed or implicit in the system refer to any particular number system. The mathematical system may be developed without specifying a number system, leaving the question of postulates of measurement unclear. A formal mathematical model, an interpreted system, may be developed which says nothing about how the observable events stemming from the interpreted system would be measured. Many formal uses of mathematical systems have little connection with an empirical social science. Unless useful deductions can be made which lead to empirical consequences, such developments remain intellectual exercises of questionable unknown importance.

The general problem of measurement has been stated by Churchman:

The qualitative assignment of objects to classes and the assignment of numbers to objects are two means at the disposal of the measurer for generating broadly applicable information. But which means is better? The striking consequence of the proposal is that measurement is a decision making activity, and, as such, is to be evaluated by decision making criteria.

In this sense, i.e., measurement taken as a decision activity designed to accomplish an objective, we have as yet no theory of measurement. We do not know why we do what we do. We do not even know why we measure at all. It is costly to obtain measurements. Is the effort worth the cost? [18]

A more serious problem has been raised by Coombs. Consider the following remarks:

The method of analysis, then *defines* what the information is and may or may not endow this information with certain properties. A "strong" method of analysis endows the data with properties which permit the information in the data to be used, for example, to construct a unidimensional scale. Obviously, again, such a scale cannot be inferred to be a characteristic of the behavior in question if it is a *necessary* consequence of the method of analysis.

It therefore becomes desirable to study methods of collecting data with respect to the amount and kind of information each method *contains* about the behavior in question as distinct from that *imposed*. Similarly, it becomes desirable to study the various methods of analyzing data in terms of the characteristics or properties each method imposes on the information in the data as a necessary preliminary to extracting it.[19]

This statement of Coombs in juxtaposition with the following of Torgerson, concerning measurement in the social sciences, presents a paradox. Discussing different kinds of measurement, Torgerson notes:

A second way in which those characteristics might obtain meaning, after a fashion, is simply by arbitrary definition. We might call this *measurement by fiat*. Ordinarily, it depends on *presumed* relationships between observations and the concept of interest. Included in this category are the indices and indicants so often used in the social and behavioral sciences. This sort of measurement is likely to occur whenever we have a prescientific or common-sense concept that on a priori grounds seems to be important but which we do not know how to measure directly. Hence, we measure some other variable or weighted average of other variables presumed to be related to it. As examples, we might mention the measurement of *socio-economic* status, or *emotion* through use of GSR, or of *learning ability* through the number of trials or the number of errors it takes the subject to reach a particular criterion of learning.[20]

Torgerson's statement sanctions the very practice that Coombs warns us about. Implicit in Coombs' work, however, is the assumption that *some* forms of scaling methods are appropriate. This assumption presupposes some definition of measurement quoted earlier. Coombs implicitly assumes that sociopsychological events are amenable to measurement by the axioms of arithmetic or some derivation thereof. The assumption can be stated as follows: that the events of interest to the sociologist have the same properties mathematically that physical properties have and, therefore, that social events are amenable to the same kinds of measurement theories, if only the "right" combination or derivation of the axioms of arithmetic can be found along with "adequate" data that fit the model used. Coombs has pinpointed a good deal of this problem in the statement:

> Almost anyone is willing to say that any given set of data contains some error, but just what is to be classified as error depends a good deal on the level of measurement assumed to hold in the data.
>
> The social scientist is faced by his dilemma when he chooses between mapping his data into a simple order and *asking* his data whether they satisfy a simple order. By selecting a strong enough system, the social scientist can always succeed in constructing an unidimensional scale of measurement, commonly an interval scale, thus requiring a portion of the data to be classified as error. By not *requiring* a strong system, the social scientist permits the data to determine whether a simple unidimensional solution is adequate. Unidimensionality, obtained by a method of analysis which guarantees it, obviously cannot thereby be shown to be a characteristic of the behavior in question. This is merely a special case of a more general principle that no property of data can be said to hold unless the methods of collecting and of analyzing the data permit alternative properties to exhibit themselves. The problem of the social scientist, in blunt terms, is whether he knows what he wants or whether he wants to know.[21]

These comments by Torgerson and Coombs indicate the dilemma of the sociologist: (1) If his theoretical concepts are not sufficiently precise to tell him what forms of measurement systems are adequate for measuring his data, then he may well be deluding himself by imposing methods that force incongruous relationships and false interpretations on his theory and data; and (2) the very measurement devices employed are inappropriate by the nature of their construction and so lead to measurement by fiat rather than to literal measurement.

Examples of such measurement are numerous. Virtually all scaling devices, as Torgerson's comments imply, are subject to measurement by fiat, for example, the measurement of attitudes in studies of voting, mass media, and prejudice, among others.

◂§ *Measurement in Sociology*

What are the appropriate foundations for measurement in sociology? The literature discussed above implies that with our present state of knowledge rigorous measurement (in the literal sense which obtains with the use of explicit theoretical systems) cannot be obtained in sociology for properties of social process. The precise measurement of social process requires first the study of the problem of meaning in everyday life. Social inquiry begins with reference to the common-sense world of everyday life. The meanings communicated by the use of ordinary day-to-day language categories and the nonlinguistic shared cultural experiences inform every social act and mediate (in a way which can be conceptually designated and empirically observed) the correspondence required for precise measurement. The literal measurement of social acts (which implies that conceptual structures generate numerical properties corresponding to existing or constructable measurement systems) requires the use of linguistic and nonlinguistic meanings that cannot be taken for granted but must be viewed as objects of study. In other words, measurement presupposes a bounded network of shared meanings, i.e., a theory of culture. The physical scientist alone defines his observational field, but in social science the arena of discourse usually begins with the subjects' preselected and preinterpreted cultural meanings. Because the observer and subject share cultural meanings interwoven with the language system they both employ for communication, the shared everyday meanings and the particular language used by the sociologist form a basic element of the measurement of social acts. The "rules" used for assigning significance to objects and events and their properties should be the same, i.e., the language systems should be in some kind of correspondence with each other. But in sociological discourse the "rules" are seldom explicit even though there is a concern for precise definition and operational criteria. The "rules" governing the use of language and the meanings conveyed by linguistic and nonlinguistic utterances and gestures are unclear and remain an almost untouched problem for empirical research. If the "rules" governing the use of language to describe objects and events in everyday life and in sociological discourse are unclear, then the assignment of numerals or numbers to the properties of objects and events according to some relatively congruent set of rules will also reflect a lack of clarity.

In the writings of Paul Lazarsfeld we may find implicit acknowledgment of the lack of literal measurement in sociology where he notes that the problem of singling out relevant properties is a major one and is revealed by the language we use to denote properties *per se*.[22] The properties of social objects and events are sometimes called "aspects" or "attributes" rather than "variables." Lazarsfeld indicates the looseness of measurement in sociology when he remarks that "The attribution of properties is interchangeably called description, classification, or measurement." [23] He proceeds to specify four steps in the establishment of "variables" in the measurement of complex social objects: "an initial imagery of the concept, the specification of dimensions, the selection of observable indicators, and the combination of indicators into indices." [24]

The notion of "imagery" refers to the researcher's creation of a vague image or construct about some set of regularities he is trying to explain or understand. Or, it may be the perception of several types of phenomena and the analyst thinks there are underlying characteristics in common. Attempts to define or delimit the concept then move from the imagery to a specification of its "components," its "aspects," or "dimensions," or something similar. Lazarsfeld says that "the concept is shown to consist of a complex combination of phenomena, rather than a simple and directly observable item." [25] He views the breaking down of the concept into a "reasonable" number of dimensions as essential for translating the concept into some kind of operation or measurement.

After making some choice about the dimensions the concept will assume, the researcher is led to finding appropriate indicators. Lazarsfeld does not provide a set of rules for selecting indicators. The lack of explicit rules is a reflection of the inadequate state of sociological theory, and the reduction required to translate abstract theoretical statements to concepts with specifiable dimensions is probably the most difficult task facing research-oriented sociologists. To illustrate this difficulty Lazarsfeld presents concepts that are assumed to be obvious to the reader and to need little conceptual clarification as to a larger body of theory (e.g., the efficiency of a production team in management) and demonstrates the many meanings these may have. The essential point to be learned from Lazarsfeld's discussion of indicators and their selection is that by "breaking down" the concept into a variety of "meanings," the researcher is forced to clarify his theoretical ideas.

In discussing the formation of indices, Lazarsfeld must again assume that our knowledge of the theoretical concepts we wish to measure is sufficiently precise to enable us to talk meaningfully about each individual indicator's probability relation to "what we really want to know." His discussion of the relevance of theory for the combining of indicators leaves us with the following: "To put the matter in another way, we need a lot of probings if we want to know what a man can really do or where he really stands" on an issue.[26] The discussion then shifts to how we put many indicators together into one index and how these indicators are related to one another. This discussion is oriented more to the mechanics of combining indicators rather than to the relevance of theory for specifying their combination and interrelations. Lazarsfeld is concerned with deriving mathematical ideas from the interrelations of indicators so that we can speak of the "power of one indicator, as compared with another, to contribute to the specific measurement one wants to make."[27]

In moving on to the discussion of the interchangeability of indices, Lazarsfeld reveals a basic procedural device that will require continual discussion throughout the book: how responses to questionnaire items rather than explicit theory provide the basis for deciding the relevance of indicators. The fact that most of Lazarsfeld's work and ideas about measurement in sociology stem from his interest in and commitment to survey research methodology—particularly since such methods take language and meaning as self-evident—cannot be ignored if we are to understand how sociology's measurement problems are confounded and have been linked to conventional measurement procedures in the natural sciences.

The general procedures Lazarsfeld suggests are particularly well adapted to field research conditions where the investigator is unable to specify clearly and precisely what variables are relevant for translating his concepts into a set of operational activities that will produce data to support or discredit his conjectures. In moving from the initial imagery through the development of indices, both implicit and explicit inferences and deductions are made, based in part upon the general kinds of data to which the imagery directs the researcher, and, more important, on how the data are manipulated by various classifications and crosstabulations which then lead to continuous inferences about the substructure of the initial imagery. The latter inferences provide the field researcher with both an expanded form of imagery or theoretical framework and the sense of his data, i.e., their relevance for the theoretical imagery used. As Lazarsfeld notes, "Classifications in social research are mainly used to establish relations between a number of variables. The crucial question, therefore, is whether these relations, the empirical finding we are looking for, are much affected if we interchange one reasonable index with another." [28] What is not clear here is whether the theoretical imagery dictates the initial relations, and the attempt to impose some form of measurement crystallizes the "variables" in question, or whether the classification of responses by some arbitrary coding rules or "natural" breaks in the results produces the quantitative sense of the "variable" and also informs the initial imagery. Presumably our "variables" should be specified by theoretical translations of our concepts so that their domain of relevance, the range of the values and the numerical properties they should take on, are all derivable from the theory. Except in cases where data are produced (and occasionally take on natural numerical properties) by agencies of the society for their own bookkeeping purposes, most sociological research that requires contacts with subjects always involves implicit theories that are a long way from hypothesis-testing before the fact. Our often arbitrary classifications of data become the basis for establishing some form of quantification. Since the classification is after the fact, the validity of our measurement is relative to the arbitrary classification and makes replication and the possibility of rigorously obtained knowledge remote at this time. The most serious problems of measurement, then, arise when we deal with qualitative "variables."

References to "qualitative variables" assume that ". . . there is a direct line of logical continuity from qualitative classification to the most rigorous forms of measurement, by way of intermediate devices of systematic ratings, ranking scales, multidimensional classifications, typologies, and simple quantitative indices." [29] This in turn assumes, first, that the arbitrary and variously informed classifications that the sociologist uses are operational approximations to elusive concepts whose properties are not easily ascertainable by direct inspection at our present stage of development; second, that the materials we label "data" and to which are assigned either a dichotomous or more refined measure correspond to the concepts under study. Moreover, sociological research seeking to order materials through field research must assume that the measurement by fiat generated by currently used procedural rules are unique classifications for each research project and, further, that their justification is to be found ultimately in the theoretical concepts used to explain the findings. Finally, there is an implicit assumption or belief that such concepts have the same structure as the natural science concepts that generate numerical properties corresponding to the measurement systems successfully used by the natural sciences.

If we are faced with the choice of using measurement systems modeled on natural science or on simple description, we should in both cases be informed about the sequence of steps that leads to "acceptable" measurement procedures. By careful retrospective examination of the assumptions built into the classification procedures and imposed upon our concepts, we can better evaluate the extent to which our efforts at measurement, theoretical elaboration, and general substantive and invariant findings are mutually distorting or clarifying. The fact that we cannot demonstrate a precise or warranted correspondence between existing measurement systems and our theoretical and substantive concepts but must establish the link by fiat, means we cannot afford to take research procedures and, therefore, the conclusions based on them for granted.

By assuming that the fundamental events and concepts of sociology do correspond to existing measurement and mathematical systems, Lazarsfeld and Barton can proceed to the basic problem of subsuming some set of experiences or identifiable objects under some category. For example:

How does one go about forming such categories in the first place? Why pick out certain elements of the situation and not others? Why combine them in just these categories?

It can properly be argued that one cannot lay down a set of handy instructions for the categorization of social phenomena: such instructions would be nothing less than a general program for the development of social theory. One cannot write a handbook on "how to form fruitful theoretical concepts" in the same way that one writes handbooks on how to sample or how to construct questionnaires.[30]

Ideally, then, the categorization of social phenomena requires the development of general social theory, but as Lazarsfeld and Barton imply this cannot be done in sociology today. The authors suggest a set of more practical procedures that begins with the following substantively delimited questions focusing on descriptions of what occurs in given situations, e.g., "What do young people do when making up their mind about choosing a career? What kinds of reactions do people have to unemployment? What are the channels of information about public issues in an American community?" [31] The practical solution, then, requires that the researcher ask general questions on specific substantive issues, questions that can be operationally translated into both theoretically relevant and common-sense lines of thinking. The lack of a developed social theory forces all researchers in sociology to employ common-sense concepts that reflect common knowledge known to both sociologists and the "average" members of the community or society. By assuming from the outset that the social scientist and his subjects form a common culture which each understands in more or less the same way, the "obvious" meanings of the operationalized questionnaire items on which the indicators are based, will incorporate properties only vaguely defined in social theory but nonetheless taken for granted as relevant to the research project.

Thus a culture common to sociologist and subject and a theory of social order are implied in the Lazarsfeld and Barton discussion of qualitative measurement. For example, they note four "requirements" as necessary for ". . . a good classification system for free responses. . . ." The authors imply that the requirements—"articulation," "logical correctness," "adaptation to the structure of the situation," and "adaptation to the respondent's frame of reference"—involve easily understood rules of procedure which are self-evident." [32] The numerous decisions which must be made presuppose an implicit correspondence between the following:

1. The indicators by which the man in the street identifies meaningful objects and the indicators used by the social scientist for identifying meaningful objects and events.

2. The actor's point of view—the language and meaning categories the actor uses to describe and subsume observations and experiences—and the observer's point of view—the language and meaning categories the observer uses to describe and subsume observations, responses, and documents about the social scene.

3. The normative rules governing the actor's perception and interpretation of his environment and the theoretical and methodological rules governing the observer's perception and interpretation of the same environment of objects.

Underlying the practical procedures described by Lazarsfeld and Barton are cultural and subcultural differences, which they assume to be easily determined and handled. The necessity of relying upon a common-sense definition of the world which the observer shares with the actor is revealed in the following quotation:

Suppose we want to classify the reasons why women buy a certain kind of cosmetics. Women have a great many comments on their reasons which are hard to group if one takes them at face value. But visualize a woman buying and using cosmetics. She gets advice from people she knows, from advertising, and from articles in mass media; in addition, she has her own past experiences to go on. She has her motives and requirements: she uses cosmetics in order to achieve various appearance values so as to impress others—one might find out whom—and perhaps to impress herself. The cosmetics have various technical qualities which relate to these desired results. She may also worry about possible bad effects on health or appearance. There are problems of applying the cosmetics. And finally there is the expense. All of the women's comments might be related to the following scheme: "channels of information," "desired appearance values," "prospective 'audience,'" "bad consequences," "technical qualities," "application problems," and "cost."

The reason the comments would fit is that the scheme of classification matches the actual processes involved in buying and using cosmetics. These are the processes from which the respondent herself has derived her comments; the classification, so to speak, puts the comments back where they came from.[33]

The classification problems described are easily resolved by the authors' use of the common-sense meanings they seek to classify. The researcher relies upon his common-sense knowledge of how persons would respond and assumes that their actual responses will correspond to the expectations based on this common-sense knowledge. The assumed correspondence provides him with an implicit model of the actor. The observer begins with unstated common-sense procedures for defining the problem, then relies upon operational measures of formalized common-sense categories for obtaining his indicators (interrogating the subjects and classifying their "answers" and "comments") for treating the subject's "obvious", i.e., apparently self-evident and easy to understand responses as literal reflections of their perception and interpretation of their environments. He then further assumes that each subject is responding to the same environment and stimuli, and on this assumption he begins to combine and order indicators into tables and summary measures.

The researcher's particular sensitivity and intuition to the world around him provide the basic clues for his success in making up questions and possible response patterns. The "rules" governing this sensitivity and intuition are not a problematic issue for the researcher and are not contained in explicit delineations of methodological procedures such as those four given by Lazarsfeld and Barton for establishing a "good" classification system. Our lack of methodological sophistication means that the decision procedures for categorizing social phenomena are buried in implicit common-sense assumptions about the actor, concrete persons, and the observer's own views about everyday life. The procedures seem intuitively "right" or "reasonable" because they are rooted in everyday life. The researcher often begins his classification with only broad dichotomies, which he expects his data to "fit," and then elaborates on these categories if apparently warranted by his "data." Finally, he may employ classification procedures which conform to the progression (from rating and ranking scales to interval or ratio measures) mentioned by Lazarsfeld and Barton. Although some "rules" exist for delineating each level of classification, our present knowledge seldom permits us to link category and thing according to theoretically and substantively justified derivations; instead, the coupling between category and observation is often based upon what are considered to be "obvious" "rules" which any "intelligent" coder or observer can "easily" encode and decode. Each classification level becomes a more refined measurement device for transforming common-sense meanings and implicit theoretical notions into acceptable "evidence." The successive application of classificatory operations produces "data" which assume the form of conventional measurement scales.

The present state of sociological method makes difficult the adherence to Coombs' earlier remarks about mapping data into simple or strong measurement systems because the correspondence between measurement scale and observed and interpreted objects or events is imposed without our being able to ask—much less determine—if it is appropriate. Once imposed, the measurement framework "translates" or "transforms" the common-sense responses into "data." The logic of the measurement operations assures the necessary transformation for producing the desired product. Fixed-choice questions asked of respondents are designed to elicit common-sense meanings from the subject and also to provide an automatic basis for generating responses that will fit into two or multivalued categories. The form of the question is an integral part of the classification procedures which follow. We thus have a formalization of the questions and responses through "obvious" or "reasonable" coding procedures and thereby manage, through progressive classification operations, to keep one foot in the common-sense world of everyday life and the other foot in quasi-acceptable (in a practical sense) measurement procedures. The realities of measurement in sociology include short-run practical difficulties and long-range hope. This quotation from Lazarsfeld and Barton illustrates the difficulties involved:

It should be possible to systematize the procedure for classification in terms of sociological concepts so that (1) researchers can be trained in a reasonably short time to perform classification with a high degree of agreement, (2) research procedures can be communicated to others, and (3) investigations can be duplicated and extended. In any given situation, the research worker using systematic procedures may be unable to compete with the innately gifted and long-experienced artist in the field; in the long run, however, the cumulation and refinement of research knowledge should carry us further than art and intuition.[34]

Lazarsfeld and Barton acknowledge the difficulty of communicating the indicators upon which the classifier's decisions are based. In the words of the authors, we are presumably now operating with the "innately gifted" and "long-experienced artist," and will hopefully proceed to the "objective" social scientist who ideally ". . . would reduce a complex concept to such clear and unambiguous indicators that the classification procedure would become practically mechanical; anyone with the same set of instructions could duplicate the observations and judgments of any other observer."[35] To further illustrate the point, the authors make an analogy with the judging of draft horses:

> The reader who is unfamiliar with draft-horse judging will be aware that these are hardly instructions which anyone could follow and come to the same judgments; the rules work only where there is a common body of understanding as to what is meant by the various terms and what represents good and bad characteristics. Nonetheless, the adoption of this segmentation results in agreement within one or two points between experienced raters using the full hundred-point scale.[36]

Reliance upon a "common body of understanding" is required to systematize the correspondence between empirically based indicators and theoretically derived categories. Initial open-ended pretests provide the researcher with clues for setting up categories for subsuming fixed-choice questions and responses assumed to be based on "obvious" meanings held in common. The authors do note that more detailed indicators for a given area can lead to greater reliability and less reliance upon "an unstated body of common knowledge." But they add: "If, however, there is seldom any serious disagreement about an indicator, one can leave it without further definition. At some point one has to stop defining one's terms and rely on a common understanding of the language."[37] Measurement in sociology—or more appropriately, observation, classification, and labeling—is rooted in the "common body of understanding" and "common understanding of the language" in everyday life. Thus, sociologists must operate "from inside" the society, using its native language (syntax and vocabulary) and its many undefined cultural meanings. Acquiring an "insider's" point of view means learning or assuming the native's common culture. But there is a strong tendency among sociologists to take the common culture and language for granted particularly when studying their own society. The difficulties of taking language and cultural meanings for granted are obscured but not eliminated when a measurement system is arbitrarily imposed upon "data" into which are built language usages, implicit and explicit grammatical rules and cultural meanings, whose correspondence with the measurement properties is unknown. Since almost all sociological measurement, particularly in the study of social action, is arbitrary, we cannot afford to ignore the three media—language, cultural meanings, and properties of measurement systems—through which we formulate theoretically derived or *ad hoc* categories and link them with observable properties of objects and events. Thus, any serious interest in sociological measurement requires the study of separate and interrelated elements of language, cultural meanings, and measurement postulates.

Each of the three medias acts as a "grid" for defining and letting certain forms of "data" through to the observer.[38] Each "grid" becomes a "filter" for what we come to perceive and interpret as referent, its significance, and its logical status as a datum. Each "grid" or medium shapes or influences our perception and interpretation of our common-sense and scientific experiences.[39] We begin with the notion of measurement as a "grid" or "filter." The problem of establishing equivalence classes necessary for measurement cannot be conceived as independent of the problems of language and cultural meanings. Logical equivalence, as a critical precondition for measurement, has its own language forms, but is also linked with the language and meanings of everyday life and consequently of sociological investigation. If we are to understand how implicit theory and method are transformed into the status of formal measurement, we must study the link between common language and the language of logical equivalence.

◄§ *The Language of Measurement*

Current measurement systems have their foundations in formal logic, set theory, and derivations therefrom. An understanding of the axioms and definitions used to construct measurement scales can be found in the references cited earlier. Here I will touch upon a few elementary properties of measurment systems to illustrate how our description and study of social events are influenced by the language of measurement.

The progression from dichotomous truth values to real numbers (from nominal scales to ratio scales) forms the basis for measurement as it is conventionally known. Through the use of a binary operation it can be shown how conjunctions can be formed so that in addition to p or q, taken separately, p-and-q taken together can also be formed, together with various other connectives. Notions like property space or attribute space can be shown to be either simple statements or compound propositions built out of elementary propositions and the use of binary or higher order connectives. Thus, two attributes X and Y may be linked to the presence or absence of some properties or dichotomies like high or low income, high or low religious involvement. The dichotomy, of course, can be generalized, as indicated earlier, to a multiproperty type of classification corresponding to p-valued logic and multidimensional attributes. This amounts to setting up a correspondence between the laws of propositional calculus and sociocultural events.

Two notions of this logical system are especially critical for how measurement is introduced in sociology. The *first* concerns the compound proposition, because the proposition itself may be "true" regardless of the truth value of its constituent parts. For example, constructing a class of objects that is labeled by some attribute "republicanism" or "democratic viewpoint," and placing objects or persons in the category even though it is known that they are not homogenous, are not identical in how "republican" they are, that is, how much they "believe in" or have "faith in" the "principles" or "policies" of the Republican party. The *second* notion is obviously an extension of the first. It provides for the notion of *logical equivalence* or simply *equivalence*.[40] The setting up of equivalence classes reifies the environment of objects under study by assuming its boundary and hence its elements are known, but the establishment of equivalence classes also permits us to order the events to be counted, described, classified, or measured. Our everyday language is full of presumed equivalence classes. For example, when we speak of persons as social types we often use such terms as "dull" or "interesting," "exciting" or "boring," "hip" or "square," and so on. The use of such terms implies that the class of objects called "persons" can be partitioned into a set of equivalence classes according to some criteria or "rules." The procedures of Lazarsfeld and Barton assume that it makes sense to formulate a correspondence between the social categories used by subjects and the logical relations employed in establishing equivalence classes necessary for classification and measurement. Recall the Lazarsfeld and Barton assumption of a "logical continuity from quantitative classification to the most rigorous forms of measurement." The properties of everyday social interaction, according to Lazarsfeld and Barton correspond to the laws assumed in logic and set theory. For example:

1. If we wish to develop laws that would correspond to the ways in which actors go about managing their daily affairs (i.e., the "rules" and values which orient their conduct, the processes involved in taking the role of the other, defining the situation), then we must show that the three properties which define logical equivalence (reflexivity, symmetry, and transitivity) are applicable to everyday social relations without distorting their theoretical and substantive sense.

2. Our theories should generate the logical properties assumed to hold for logical equivalence classes. The categories we use to classify empirical properties of our constructed actors are limited (as to the finite all-or-none deterministic) values they may take on. The logical properties assumed applicable to and imposed upon conceptions and data define the limits of the "truth value" or significance of a given property attributable to the actor.

3. The three laws necessary for equivalence determine the conditions under which we may be permitted to count. They state the conditions under which the equivalence of objects and events in the social structures may be assumed and therefore

placed in correspondence with the natural numbers so that a counting operation is possible.

4. But the three assumptions for equivalence do not provide for the temporal character of sociocultural objects and events. Does A equal A invariantly under a changing social scene, a changing social environment, a changing definition of the situation? Clock-time is dependent upon experienced time, in the sense that clock-time t_1 and clock-time t_2 may be defined differently by the actors of the social scene, even though an outside observer may define the two situations as identical with respect to some set of structural and locational variables.

5. Definitions, counts, measurements of the number of births, deaths, marriages, divorces, crimes of a particular type all presuppose the three logical assumptions necessary for equivalence classes, and these logical relations are presupposed in the official recording of a set of social actions subsumed under a sociolegal category. The sociological relevance of these categories should be decided on theoretical and methodological grounds; their status as data is not automatic. Yet it is clear that conditions exist, irrespective of the sociologist and his theories and methods, whereby sociolegal categories in everyday life permit equivalence relations and literal counting operations. These conditions assume some knowledge of and/ or reliance upon a shared common culture.

6. But the events and objects counted in sociolegal categories are compound propositions in the sense that not all elements in their assembled form are identical, that is, have the same truth value, and this is particularly true of marriages, divorces, and crimes. It is a fact that we can treat each marriage, divorce, and some crimes as equivalent under limited conditions even though many would question the theoretical and substantive utility of certain combinations or groupings. Sociologists clearly recognize that a two-valued logic is inadequate. They begin to ask whether the ages of the couples or offenders are different. Are there differences in religion, occupation, education, and so on. These additional questions qualify the initial equivalence relation which is imposed by treating each divorce or marriage or crime as identical for counting purposes in sociolegal activities. But without more explicit theoretical and substantive ideas to guide our actions,

the language of measurement forces us to employ equivalence classes which may reify or distort our ideas and findings by fiat.

7. If we assume that the actor's perception and interpretation of some set of events or environment of objects varies by the unique and patterned conditions of social encounters and taking the role of the other during the course of interaction, then we cannot automatically assume the existence in our theory and data of equivalence classes which satisfy the reflexive, symmetric, and transitive laws. The notion of role-taking as being both a function of what the actor brings to the social scene and some set of contingencies which unfold in the course of social action requires that we distinguish between equivalence classes that have a static quality (e.g., questionnaire studies which elicit data on ethnicity, occupation, income, etc.) and emergent processes (e.g., ideas and courses of action produced in the course of social action itself and controlled according to unfolding conditions of the social scene). Public commitment to common-sense ideas, values, or ideologies may occur throughout the course of action, but these commitments may not reflect the actor's private thoughts nor be reflected in the responses that can be produced via a fixed-choice questionnaire. One common procedure is to correlate structural and locational variables with attributes of social process. For example, age, sex, residence, income, or education on the one hand, with attitudes toward ethnic groups, or political preference on the other. It is the language of measurement (in its generic sense) which imposes the necessary equivalence classes, not the theoretical concepts.

8. One dangerous consequence of measurement by fiat is that the measurement scales assume logical relationships which may not correspond to our implicit theories. Ideally, we would like our theories to generate numerical properties that would correspond to the measurement scales and their postulates. Our implicit theories do not generate numerical properties except after they have been transformed into explicit theories: after the language of measurement has imposed some measurement scale or set of logical relationships or some set of arbitrary or semitheoretical categories upon them.

9. Another consequence of present classification procedures and the selection and combination of indicators is to be found in the progressive refinement of classification categories and indi-

cators such that the data are progressively transformed or given a quantitative appearance. Each operation is calculated to transform the data into a comparative set of equivalence classes which, in the language of survey research, can be "partialed," some "variables" can be "washed out," and the like. The vocabulary is intended to convey the notion of rigorous measurement even though the researcher is usually fully aware of its arbitrary character. The danger remains, however, that the vocabulary will displace the search for the theoretical rationale for classification that assumes reflexiveness, symmetry, transitivity, and the other properties basic to measurement systems. Every methodological decision presupposes some theoretical equivalent even though our present state of knowledge may not be adequate for determining precisely what the correspondence is.

◆§ The Measurement of Social Facts
versus Social Action

Sociologists are accustomed to distinguishing between structure versus process, social structure versus social action, institutionalized norms versus changing definitions of the situation, and the like. Attributes such as age, sex, births, death, income, education, size of city, geographical dispersion of industry or agriculture or population, the amount of in- and out-migration, and so on, are typically viewed as "obvious" and easily measured even though problems of a technical nature may produce varying amounts of error. Similarly, the anthropologist often studies kinship, particularly in its formal sense via diagramatical social organization, in the same way; it is assumed to be "obvious" and easily analyzed. Certain types of "dominant" values and norms or "themes" or belief systems are also viewed as patterned and fairly stable such that their classification is not viewed as problematic in relation to the conditions of social action. The empirical determination of kinship and dominant values and norms is often a function of questions posed in static terms which do not make the practiced and enforced character of norms and values problematic.

Serious problems of measurement arise when the sociologist's interest in the more easily measured variables is coupled with an interest in showing the relation between the structural or locational variables and cultural attributes (to which it is difficult to order and assign numbers). Difficulties occur when he attempts to employ the measurement scales used in studies of the distribution and change in births or deaths, chronological age, income, etc., for the study of reference groups, role-taking, attitudes, values as held by the actor, the actor's definition of the situation, the actor's political ideology, a collective's values and ideology, behavioral and verbal attributes of conformity, attitudes toward family size, conceptions about migration or residence location, and the like. Lazarsfeld's work assumes that what is true for more readily quantified variables is also true for the qualitative or cultural attributes. There is little doubt that, if one insists on conventional measurement scales to measure the properties of both qualitative and quantitative objects or events, Lazarsfeld is correct and his suggestions an essential part of sociological research.

Problems of measurement also arise when the sociologist decides to assign certain factual conditions the status of cultural attributes. For example, we may wish to view age as an attribute imputed by one or more actors to some other actor, where the imputations are based upon physical appearance, verbal and nonverbal gestures, and cultural definitions of youthfulness. We might view income the same way; as an attribute imputed to others or projected as a personal aspiration. The same can be said for education, sex (imputations of virility or homosexuality) , intelligence, race, color, the perception of population density, residence location, illegitimacy, incest, and so on.

The measurement of social facts often assumes that certain behavorial, value, or ideological attributes are operative. Thus, we assume that cross-tabulating friendship choices (primary-group membership) with voting patterns of individuals will show the influence of the former on the latter. We also may correlate income with voting, religion with voting, income with fertility, age with religion, some measure of class with ideological commitments, expressed values or aspirations, or with indicators of patterned social action whose status is not problematic. The assumption that social facts can be correlated with social action is both reasonable and necessary under a variety of research conditions.

To assume otherwise would preclude any form of systematic study. On the other hand it might be useful, for certain purposes, to discard the assumption, and assign factual or structural or locational variables or conditions a problematic status. An example can be found in Bennett Berger's paper "How Long is a Generation?" [41] which views chronological age as a cultural attribute, thereby generating a new set of problems. An important rationale for discarding the *a priori* assumption of patterned or invariant social action as determining factual or structural or locational variables is that the more complex and varied a society or system of social relationships, the more pluralistic are its values or ideologies or norms, and the less likely will such variables operate in a deterministic way. This is particularly important if the acceptable measurement systems assume a deterministic axiomatic base.

If we assume that factual conditions can be described as (empirically researchable) patterned social action with invariant properties or invariant biological properties, and if we can view structural or locational variables as products of this (empirically researchable) patterned social action—products, accordingly, whose probability of recurrence is very high—then we cannot escape addressing the theoretical, methodological, and empirical conditions under which we assume that factual, structural, locational, and cultural variables are to be assigned either deterministic (which would include probabilistic) or emergent status. It may be appropriate to ask whether there is a larger class of measurement systems which would not have its basis in logic and set-theoretic operations, but where these latter types of deterministic conditions would be a subset of some more general conception of measurement.

Logical systems and higher mathematics dealing with finite structures assume the *law of contradiction* and the *law of the excluded middle,* or what Weyl briefly calls the *finite rule.*[42] The basis for measurement in the natural sciences rests on mathematical structures which assume *consistency* in the axioms (that both *a* and not-*a* will not obtain) and *completeness* (that either *a* will obtain or not-*a* will obtain), but for these structures completeness, says Weyl, is not simply a matter of ". . . the establishment of such procedural rules of proof as would lead demonstrably to a solution for every pertinent problem." [43] Instead, the deductive procedure has to be discovered and rely upon construction; it is not predesigned. But what about systems of mathematics which do not consist of symbols in a game played according to fixed rules?

The possibility of alternative mathematical systems or more general theories, of which the axiomatic approach might be merely one among many systems, was opened by Brouwer in his work on "intuitionism" versus "formalism." [44] Consider these statements by Weyl:

The classical logic of propositions as formalized by G. Frege, and later by Russell and Whitehead in the *Principia Mathematica,* is based on the assumption that a proposition puts a question to some realm of reality whose facts answer with a clear-cut yes or no, according to which the proposition is either true or false. Up to the time of the *Principia Mathematica* everybody believed, or at least hoped, that mathematical propositions were of this nature, leaving no room for indeterminacies expressed by the modal words "possible," "may be," and the like.[45]

The basic assumption of the strict alternative of true and false, characteristic for classical logic, leaves no room for bridging the abyss by "perhaps" or "possibly." However, the major part of statements in our everyday life which have a vital meaning for us and our communicants are not of this rigorous nature. A given hue may be *more or less* gray instead of pure black or pure white. We may find it too arbitrary or even impossible to set exact boundaries in a continuum. By far the most important examples are provided by statements about the *future.* A question of this sort, say: "Will a large-scale European war break out within the next year?" does not point to a verification by any reality, and is nevertheless discussed and judged right now, under such aspects as possible, likely, inevitable, rather than true or false.[46]

By challenging the law of the excluded middle, Brouwer provided a basis for going beyond a completely formalized mathematical system and still permit the development of models that would correspond to the indeterminacies of everyday life. Weyl discusses the possibility of using different mathematical systems depending upon the structure of—in this case—the physical world. He cites the example of quantum physics:

Again we encounter in the symbolic set-up of a discipline, here quantum physics, a certain part which may justly be said to be its *logic.* Each field of knowledge, when it crystalizes into a formal theory, seems to carry with it its intrinsic logic which is part of the formalized symbolic system, and this logic will, generally speaking, differ in different fields.[47]

If history ever becomes ripe for the stage of theoretic symbolic construction, it would not be surprising if in symbolic form this possibility inherent in our very existence, on which I dwelt before in Section II, and the depth of which resounded in the last quotation from Heidegger ["Die Möglichkeit als Existenzial ist die ursprünglichste und letzte positive ontologische Bestimmung des Daseins," or roughly translated, "Possibility as (a kind of) existence is the most original and last affirmative ontological definition of being"], would play a paramount part in an intrinsic "logic of history." But the example of quantum physics should warn us against any attempt to predict *a priori* what a symbolic logic of history will look like—if its time ever comes.

One may also expect the entire situation to change if one passes from a logic of propositions to a true logic of communications. The propositions either are impersonal or involve only an ego from which they irradiate; communications play between an existential I and thou. Promises, questions, commands, will have to be treated in such a logic.[48]

My brief discussion of modalities and the general problem of viewing factual, structural, locational, and cultural variables as deterministic or indeterministic is intended to call sociologists' attention to the possible virtues of modalities as a basis for measurement when our theories remain implicit and social conduct is contingent upon the course of action itself. On the other hand, we cannot avoid the dangers inherent in imposing deterministic measurement systems upon implicit theoretical concepts. Viewing variables as quantitative because available data are expressed in numerical form or because it is considered more "scientific" does not provide a solution to the problems of measurement but avoids them in favor of measurement by fiat. Measurement by fiat is not a substitute for examining and re-examining the structure of our theories so that our observations, descriptions, and measures of the properties of social objects and events have a literal correspondence with what we believe to be the structure of social reality.

ᴇᑐ§ Conclusions

I began this chapter conceiving of measurement as a problem in the sociology of knowledge. There are several ways to express this conception of measurement. Language and cultural meanings can be viewed as problems in the sociology of knowledge which set the conditions for literal measurement in sociology. They remain relatively unexplored media whereby some correspondence is achieved between some set of observables, a set of measurement categories and theoretical concepts. A more detailed discussion of language and cultural meanings viewed as another set of sociological methods will be presented in Chapter VIII. Here I want to restrict my discussion to the possible significance of the Sapir-Whorf hypothesis for the view of measurement as a problem in the sociology of knowledge. Consider the following:

The central idea of the Sapir-Whorf hypothesis is that language functions, not simply as a device for reporting experience, but also, and more significantly, as a way of defining experience for its speakers. Sapir says (1931: 578), for example:

> "Language is not merely a more or less systematic inventory of the various items of experience which seem relevant to the individual, as is so often naively assumed, but is also a self-contained, creative symbolic organization, which not only refers to, experience largely acquired without its help but actually defines experience for us by reason of its formal completeness and because of our unconscious projection of its implicit expectations into the field of experience. In this respect language is very much like a mathematical system which, also, records experience in the truest sense of the word, only in its crudest beginnings, but, as time goes on, becomes elaborated into a self-contained conceptual system which previsages all possible experience in accordance with certain accepted formal limitations. . . [Meanings are] not so much discovered in experience as imposed upon it, because of the tyrannical hold that linguistic form has upon our orientation of the world."

Whorf develops the same thesis when he says (1952: 5):

> ". . . that the linguistic system (in other words, the grammar) of each language is not merely a reproducing instrument for voicing ideas but rather is itself the shaper of ideas, the program and

guide for the individual's mental activity, for his analysis of impressions, for his synthesis of his mental stock in trade. . . We dissect nature along lines laid down by our native languages. The categories and types that we isolate from the world of phenomena we do not find there because they stare every observer in the face; on the contrary, the world is presented in a kaleidoscopic flux of impressions which has to be organized by our minds —and this means largely by the linguistic systems in our minds."

It is evident from these statements, if they are valid, that language plays a large and significant role in the totality of culture. Far from being simply a technique of communication, it is itself a way of directing the perceptions of its speakers and it provides for them habitual modes of analyzing experience into significant categories.[49]

The Sapir-Whorf hypothesis suggests that we view the language of measurement as a derivation from our conception of the physical world and the nature of logical and mathematical systems. Thus, science and scientific method as means of viewing and obtaining knowledge about the world around us provide those who accept its tenets with a grammar that is not merely a reproducing instrument for describing what the world is all about, but also shapes our ideas of what the world is like, often to the exclusion of other ways of looking at the world. Language, then, and the cultural meanings it signifies, distorts, and obliterates, acts as a filter or grid for what will pass as knowledge in a given era. Similarly, cultural meanings about an after-life, causation, physical events, social events, biological events, beauty, ugliness, pain, pleasure, and the like have their own grammar which may be expressed and/or influenced by language.

A more concrete way of indicating how science can become a problem in the sociology of knowledge and influence what passes as measurement can be found in a recent doctoral dissertation by Warren O. Hagstrom.[50] If we share Hagstrom's concern with how science controls the thoughts of its adherents by the way colleagues influence decisions about such matters as which problems will be deemed worthy of study, which techniques should be adopted, how to measure events and conceive of them, how to state and publish results, and which results and theories will be acceptable, then scientific knowledge constitutes one grammar among several for describing and seeing the world. But this also means that when one decides to operate within the scientific community the kind of choice to be exercised is limited by the kinds of controls which Hagstrom describes. Social scientists operating within the scientific community, or at least those who identify with its goals and methods of control, may view an alternative community of scholars as unacceptable and seek to bar them from membership or discredit their writings. Here lies a danger of science that many writers (Hagstrom among others) have described: the control of scientific activities and thought may set limits upon certain kinds of theories, methods, and discoveries because of prevailing methods of control and the imperfect organization of science as a self-correcting and open system of thought.

Measurement in sociology is directly affected by science and modern technology through still another set of activities. Consider the following: The structure of modern society reflects the rationalization of everyday life via its bureaucratic institutions. The idealized goals of efficiency and rationality correspond to the logical-mathematical-physical view of the world; the filing systems and automation facilities of modern bureaucracies epitomize these goals. It is, therefore, no accident that the measurement systems used by sociologists receive their most intensive use when applied to data generated by modern bureaucracies. The very conditions for ordering and reporting the data of large-scale societal activities have built into them the assumptions which insure a quantitative product, irrespective of the structure of the social acts originally observed and interpreted. The social conditions of our time provide a set of definitions—dictated primarily by considerations of efficiency and practicality—for bureaucratic officials to organize the experiences of their everyday work activities.

These definitions are to be found in conventional measurement systems which begin with simple presence or absence and progress to real numbers and ratio scales. Most of the data that sociologists honor as "given," therefore, are largely the product of bureaucratically organized activities, for example, census bureaus, vital statistics bureaus, correctional agencies, welfare agencies, and business agencies. The multitudinous perceptions and interpretations that went into the assembly of such data are invariably lost to the reader or user of such materials. The quantitative features must be accepted by fiat. The fact that even factual data are subject to perceptions and interpretations which may vary with the actor's biography, the occasion of recording, the explicit or implicit rules employed for deciding the sense of the objects or events categorized, and the stated language and unstated meanings which were relevant to the particular observer, means that these are variables to consider in assessing the relevance and importance of such data. Even when these data are used by organizational personnel as "given," as for example when school counselors or administrators honor test scores and classroom grades when evaluating a student's over-all performance in school as a basis for recommending him to a college or university, the significant interest of the sociologist is not merely what correlations or general interrelationships exist among the "objective" data, but how such bureaucratic personnel interpreted *and acted* on them. It is the set of rules employed for interpreting such information that would demonstrate the significance of these data for producing concerted action. Any actual correlations may be artifacts of the imposed quantification procedures. The fact that bureaucratically organized activities invariably employ a system of classification and ordering which stems from two-valued or p-valued logic means that we have already imposed a system of measurement irrespective of what such data might "mean" if such impositions were not made. In Coombs' succinct language, we are caught in the "dilemma" of the social scientist who imposes a strong system of measurement even when he is not sure whether it is warranted. The research sociologist has advertently or inadvertently hidden behind the façade of a set of conditions—bureaucratic organization—which insures that quantitative data will be produced. By taking such data for granted and honoring it for its own sake the sociologist subverts his theories in favor of "rigor" which is assumed to follow automatically from respect for such "data" above all else. This is a curious problem in the sociology of knowledge. The very features of a secularized society, the rationalization of everyday life, have become an object of study for the sociologist, but also a prison for him. He is in the peculiar position of studying the conditions of everyday life, but his data are the product of the conditions.

In addition to language and cultural meanings, the measurement systems themselves, or the controls exerted by the organization of modern science, there is still another problem that many sociologists would dismiss out of hand. I am thinking of whether the sociology of knowledge is itself governed by scientific rules of procedure or whether we should view it as one more kind of ideology. We can view religious dogma and science as both ideologies and bodies of knowledge, each with its own theoretical assumptions, methods, and rules for admitting propositions into its respective corpus of knowledge.[51] The problems of measurement, therefore, can be viewed from the perspective of the sociology of knowledge: the world of observables is not simply "out there" to be described and measured with the measurement systems of modern science, but the course of historical events and the ideologies of a given era can influence what is "out there" and how these objects and events are to be perceived, evaluated, described, and measured.

The remainder of this book focuses upon the problems of everyday language, cultural meanings, and the language of measurement in achieving sociological research; particularly the correspondence between some set of observables and theoretical and measurement categories. In examining various methods I avoid the problem of whether they represent particular ideologies or systems of thought that are scientific or nonscientific, but I view each method as a pragmatic means of attaining some form of knowledge about the social world.

II

THEORY

AND METHOD

IN FIELD RESEARCH

RESEARCHERS IN THE SOCIAL SCIENCES are faced with a unique methodological problem; the very conditions of their research constitute an important complex variable for what passes as the findings of their investigations. Field research, which for present purposes includes participant observation and interviewing, is a method in which the activities of the investigator play a crucial role in the data obtained. This chapter will review some of the literature on field research and critically examine problems of theory and method. In discussing the literature I will assume that some ideal form of field research is attainable. This amounts to establishing something of a straw man. The procedure is not intended as a criticism of the literature for its failings, but merely as an expository device for recommending some ideals rather difficult to obtain in social research. I hope to indicate the kind of basic theory that can be of use to the observer and simultaneously tested in field research. I wish also to direct attention to some of the methodological problems encountered in meeting canons of scientific inquiry in field research and to review some proposed solutions. This chapter will focus upon participant observation; Chapter III will concentrate on interviewing.

⊷§ *An Overview of the Literature*

Anthropologists, using the techniques of field research, have accumulated a vast literature on different cultures. Despite the long history of field research, and the courses given in field techniques, there has been little effort to codify the different researches.

The difference between working in one's own society and in one that is foreign provides a basic point of departure for the conditions within which the observer's perceptions and interpretations take on meaning.

The sociologist who limits his work to his own society is constantly exploiting his personal background of experience as a basis of knowledge. In making up structured interviews, he draws on his knowledge of meanings gained from participation in the social order he is studying. He can be assured of a modicum of successful communication only because he is dealing in the same language and symbolic system as his respondents. Those who have worked with structured techniques in non-Western societies and languages will attest to the difficulty encountered in adjusting their meanings to the common meanings of the society investigated, a fact which highlights the extent to which the sociologist is a particular observer in almost all his work.[1]

The differences between working in one's own society and some other also can lead to differences in how the initial contact is made. Benjamin Paul's comments illustrate the problems of initial contact:

There is no prescription for finding the correct entree into a new community. It depends on the sophistication of the community and the amount of advance information the investigator is able to get. Frequently he can count on a chain of introductions which leads at least to the threshold of his group. By the time he reaches a provincial center or trading post near his destination, he is likely to have learned the names of people who have contacts with the natives. Here on the peripheries he can pick up bits of information which will serve to orient him. The novice who is anxious to obtain the full acceptance of the natives sometimes by-passes regional administrators for fear of prejudicing his reception. But it will do him little good to be well received by the natives, only to be impeded by higher authorities who make it their business to follow the movements of strangers.

In carrying out investigations in a modern community or in an industrial organization, it has been found expedient, and sometimes essential, to establish the initial contacts, with those people who have controlling voices in the community. These may be men who hold status in the power hierarchy or people in informal positions who command respect. Their endorsement of the project can be critical, and they can serve in a useful liaison capacity. This procedure applies equally in the non-occidental community.[2]

Paul notes the importance of convincing those to be observed that the researcher will do them no harm. Those to be observed can be members of some distant tribe or staff men in an industrial organization. The researcher must also avoid the problem of slighting some potentially important figure because of failure to contact him for assistance. As Paul cautions, this can lead to the production of rumors by the offended parties and cause the researcher considerable difficulty.

A common point made by field researchers is the necessity of establishing a role within the group to be studied. Paul states: "In part, the field worker defines his own role; in part, it is defined for him by the situation and the outlook of the natives. His is the strategy of a player in a game. He cannot predict precise plays which the other side will make, but he anticipates them as best he can and makes his moves accordingly." [3] The problem of defining a role or different roles within and between groups raises the general question of what participant observers do and the kinds of roles they develop in the course of their research. Schwartz and Schwartz provide the following definition:

For our purposes we define participant observation as a process in which the observer's presence in a social situation is maintained for the purpose of scientific investigation. The observer is in a face-to-face relationship with the observed, and, by participating with them in their natural life setting, he gathers data. Thus, the observer is part of the context being observed, and he both modifies and is influenced by this context.[4]

An immediate consequence of participating in the group's life is that the researcher inevitably is asked to help make policy decisions which will alter the group's activities. Although many researchers caution the novice not to become "so active" in the group being studied, the practical circumstances of the research setting may not allow the observer much choice. Many times the best he can do is to record carefully the details of the changes he has influenced and attempt to understand their consequences for his research objectives. As noted before, many researchers may become so involved in their participation that they "go native." [5]

Every paper on field research mentions the problem of how the researcher comes to be defined by the natives. The importance of this point obviously stems from the fact that the kinds of activities to which the observer will be exposed will vary with his relationships in the group studied. Most writers stress the theme of "being accepted" by the natives.

I soon found that people were developing their own explanation about me: I was writing a book about Cornerville. This might seem entirely too vague an explanation, and yet it sufficed. I found that my acceptance in the district depended on the personal relationships I developed far more than upon any explanations I might give. Whether it was a good thing to write a book about Cornerville depended entirely on people's opinions of me personally. If I was all right, then my project was all right; if I was no good, then no amount of explanation could convince them that the book was a good idea.[6]

The emphasis that the participant observer be accepted as a "person" can be found in many sources:

A person becomes accepted as a participant observer more because of the kind of person he turns out to be in the eyes of the field contacts than because of what the research represents to them. Field contacts want to be reassured that the research worker is a "good guy" and can be trusted not to "do them dirt" with what he finds out. They do not usually want to understand the full rationale behind a study.[7]

Schwartz and Schwartz indicate similar views for gaining maximum rapport with the subjects to be studied. One of the difficulties in following such advice lies in the lack of more specific procedural rules for achieving the goal of "being accepted." The day-to-day decisions that researchers make while in the field concerning who seems to be a "good person" to approach for certain information or how he will conduct himself in the course of a variety of emergent situations that continually arise, would provide more instructive information for the novice. The problem is managing one's appearance and action before others. The solutions these writers offer are specifications for role behavior before others in the field. The following comments will illustrate this point: "The variable on the continuum of role activity is the degree to which the observer participates in the research situation, the scale extending from 'passive' participation to 'active' participation." [8] Schwartz and Schwartz characterize the "passive" participant observer as being similar to one observing behind a one-way screen. The idea is to interact with the natives as little as possible under the assumption that such behavior will interfere with the group's activities to a lesser degree and provide for a more natural observation of events. The "active" participant observer, in effect, "joins" the group he is studying to the extent that he feels they accept him as one of the group. Frequently this means participating on what Schwartz and Schwartz call the "simply human level" and the "planned role level," that is, as a native *and* a scientist. They provide an example where this dual role system broke down. ". . . we found that without being aware of it at the time the observer tended to withdraw when a patient was withdrawn. Similarly, when low morale was a dominant aspect of the ward context, the investigator discovered that he, too, was functioning less effectively." [9]

The problem of different types of roles that might be assumed has been discussed more formally by Gold: "Buford Junker has suggested four theoretically possible roles for sociologists conducting field work. These range from the complete participant at one extreme to the complete observer at the other. Between these, but nearer the former, is the participant-as-observer; nearer the latter is the observer-as-participant." [10] The four types of roles are defined as follows:

The true identity and purpose of the complete participant in field research are not known to those whom he observes. He interacts with them as naturally as possible in whatever areas of their living interest him and are accessible to him as situations in which he can play, or learn to play, requisite day-to-day roles successfully. He may, for example, work in a factory to learn about inter-workings of informal groups. After gaining acceptance at least as a novice, he may be permitted to share not only in work activities and attitudes but also in the intimate life of the workers outside the factory.

Role-pretense is a basic theme in these activities. It matters little whether the complete participant in a factory situation has an upper-lower class background and perhaps some factory experience, or whether he has an upper-middle class background quite divorced from factory work and the norms of such workers. What really matters is that he knows that he is pretending to be a colleague. I mean to suggest by this that the crucial value as research yield is concerned lies more in the self-orientation of the complete participant than in his surface role-behavior as he initiates his study.[11]

Whyte's study illustrates Gold's point because he describes several incidents in which his middle class social background differed radically from that of the group he studied. One involved taking off his hat when only males were present, the other had to do with the rules for lending money to members of the gang. In both situations, and in numerous others, he was helped by role pretense and by a very important key informant. Gold describes the other three roles:

Although basically similar to the complete observer role, the participant-as-observer role differs significantly in that both field worker and informant are aware that theirs is a field relationship. This mutual awareness tends to minimize problems of role-pretending; yet, the role carries with it numerous opportunities for compartmentalizing mistakes and dilemmas which typically bedevil the complete participant.

Probably the most frequent use of this role is in community studies, where an observer develops relationships with informants through time, and where is is apt to spend more time and energy participating than observing. At times he observes informally—when attending parties, for example. . . .

The observer-as-participant role is used in studies involving one-visit interviews. It calls for relatively more formal observation than either informal observation or participation of any kind. It also entails less risk of "going native" than either the complete participant role or the participant-as-observer role. However, because the observer-as-participant's contact with an informant is so brief, and perhaps superficial, he is more likely than the other two to misunderstand the informant, and to be misunderstood by him. . . .

The complete observer role entirely removes a field worker from social interaction with informants. Here a field worker attempts to observe people in ways which make it unnecessary for them to take him into account, for they do not know he is observing them or that, in some sense, they are serving as his informants. Of the four field work roles, this alone is almost never the dominant one. It is sometimes used as one of the subordinate roles employed to implement the dominant ones.[12]

The various roles described can be related to the importance of learning the nature of the group's experiences. More intensive participation has the advantage of affording the observer a greater exposure to both the routine and the unusual activities of the group studied. The assumption is that the more intensive the participation, the "richer" the data on the one hand, and on the other the greater the danger of "going native" and as a consequence of taking over the group's way of perceiving and interpreting the environment becoming blinded to many points of scientific importance. The solution which I feel emerges from the literature is one of marginality, that is, becoming very conscious of the roles being played and providing for occasions of "leaving the field" for periodic reviews of what has happened and of where the research is going. By this time the reader is probably aware of the difficulties involved in laying down a set of clear-cut procedural rules for engaging in field research. The analytic description of formal roles provides a guide for the researcher and a set of categories for evaluating his work. The actual substantive roles he will choose obviously must vary with the research setting. Certain kinds of information will not be available to researchers who remain too marginal to the everyday workings of the group studied. Intensive participation may make hypothesis testing very difficult, but it may be helpful in uncovering the vernacular of the group studied, the meanings employed by the group when strangers are around. Thus, participating and interviewing in the field can be difficult regardless of whether one is working in his own society or one foreign to him. This problem raises many others. One of the most critical, and the one with which we shall terminate our review of the literature, is that of inference and proof in field research.

Recording information and checking out leads and hunches during intensive participant observation is hard and time-consuming work. The group's activities may not permit the recording of events until considerable time between observation and recording has elapsed. If the researcher's true identity is not known to the group, then he may find it necessary to cultivate some other acceptable occupation or initiate other activities for the purpose of recording information. Such conditions obviously place a strain upon hypothesis testing, for many of the activities observed may be known only in the process of observation. The researcher would need a rather extensive theoretical framework and detailed design for testing hypotheses. It is possible, however, even during intensive participation, to engage subjects in conversation on topics relevant to hypothesis testing. The greatest problem to overcome here is that of the time interval between observation and recording. The following comments by Schwartz and Schwartz are instructive.

What happens in the time interval between the event and its final recording is of utmost importance. In retrospective observation the investigator recreates, or attempts to re-create, the social field in his imagination, in all its dimensions, on a perceptual and feeling level. He takes the role of all the other people in the situation and tries to evoke in himself the feelings and thoughts and actions they experienced at the time the event occurred. . . . What occurs is a type of reworking of the presentation of the phenomenon as initially registered. . . . In this reworking the previous data may be maintained unaltered; they may be added to or changed; significant aspects of the event may appear which were previously omitted; and connections between the segments of the event and between this event and others may appear which were previously unrecognized.[13]

Retrospective observation makes hypothesis testing before the fact impossible. But what basic requirement is not mentioned in the above quotation which accordingly makes retrospective observation appear as a necessity in field research? The writers do not assume that a theory is available which instructs them as to what objects should be observed and the conditions surrounding the observations at different points in time. Without some prior explicit assumptions about the nature of all groups, and the careful recording of events as they were witnessed, there is a danger that because of retrospection changes due to adopting the group's point of view will not be treated as changes. Vidich pinpoints this problem:

The participant who studies change as an observer must therefore maintain a perspective outside and independent of change. Non-involvement helps to prevent the alteration of memory structures and permits the observer to see cumulative changes.

To refresh his memory, the participant observer can turn to his records, but, if his perspective has changed with time, he may disregard or discount early notes and impressions in favor of those taken later. Field notes from two different periods in a project may, indeed, be one of the more important means of studying change. Instead, what probably happens is that the field worker obscures change by treating his data as though everything happened at the same time. This results in a description from a single perspective, usually that held just before leaving the field, but redefined by the rereading of his notes.[14]

The linking of noninvolvement with the study of change and presumably the testing of hypotheses brings us back to the dilemma of "richness" as revealed by intensive participation, or "objectivity" as obtained by noninvolvement. One possible solution might be to participate intensively during the first part of the research and map out the necessary details for hypothesis testing, then use later events, presumed here to be in part recurrences of past events, as the basis for testing hypotheses. The critical question here is whether the observer would be able to detach himself for the later observations and whether his involvement would preclude making the observations necessary for hypothesis testing. If the observer's role is appropriately structured, he could then conduct formal interviews at some later date. The conditions of research that arise in the field do not always permit such proposed solutions. Some type of similar solution would be necessary if we are to achieve the level of formalization needed for testing hypotheses. Howard S. Becker has addresed some of these problems in an attempt to clarify the necessary formalization.

Sociologists usually use this method [participant observation] when they are especially interested in understanding a particular organization or substantive problem rather than demonstrating relations between abstractly defined variables. They attempt to make their research theoretically meaningful, but they assume that they do not know enough about the organization *a priori* to identify relevant problems and hypotheses and that they must discover these in the course of the research. Though participant observation can be used to test *a priori* hypotheses, . . . this is typically not the case. My discussion refers to the kind of participant observation study which seeks to discover hypotheses as well as to test them.[15]

Becker identifies four stages in participant observation: (1) the selection of problems, concepts, and indices and their definition; (2) some estimate of the frequency and distribution of the phenomena under study; (3) the articulation of individual findings with a model of the organization under investigation; and (4) problems of inference and proof.

In the first stage, decisions about problems, concepts, and indicators are made. Becker distinguishes three tests used for checking items of evidence. The first is the "credibility of informants"; it checks on whether the informant might have reasons for lying, concealing information, or for misstating his role in the event or his attitude toward it, and whether the informant actually witnessed the event or is basing his description on other channels of information. In short, the actor's perspective is important. A second test is called "volunteered or directed statements." It questions the spontaneity of the responses, whether they are made to coincide with the observer's interests and to what extent the observer's presence or questions have influenced the respondent's remarks? The third test, "the observer-informant-group equation," takes into account the observer's role in the group—whether his research is done incognito or as an intensive participant—and how this might influence what he will see and hear as an observer.

In the second stage, the researcher decides the frequency and distribution of data relating to problems, concepts, and indicators. What will constitute evidence is determined. The investigator attempts to account for the typicality of his observations, their frequency, and importance in the group studied. Quantitative accounts of the organization are possible in this stage.

The third stage integrates the various findings into a generalized model of the events under study. Becker notes that in this stage the observer seeks a model which best fits the data he has obtained.[16]

In the fourth stage, the observer rechecks and rebuilds, where necessary, the model in accordance with his data. Here he must decide how he will present his findings. As Becker notes, the problem of presenting data after field research has been troublesome to social scientists for a long time. He proposes the following solution: Present a description of the natural history of the conclusions, allowing the reader to follow the evidence as it came to the attention of the observer during the course of the research and as the problem under investigation was conceptualized and reconceptualized over time. The idea of a "natural history" does not mean that every datum will be presented, but the general types of data obtained during each stage of the research. Included would be significant exceptions in the data and their correspondence to the theoretical conceptions utilized. The critical point of Becker's suggestions lies in allowing the reader the possibility of checking out the details of the analysis and giving him the opportunity to examine the basis for any conclusion reached.[17]

There are three interrelated major points which I feel should be stressed to close this section. The first is the importance of linking the problems encountered in field research directly to the reporting of the findings. Such a procedure permits the reader to discern what problems surrounded the gathering of what information and how they influenced the conclusions about the particular findings. The second is the obvious lack of comment by writers on field research concerning the importance of making theoretical assumptions explicit *prior to* engaging in field research and the fact that the very process of successful field research tests both basic theoretical concepts and social process and substantive theories we are interested in explaining and predicting. The third point follows from the second in that it relates to the problem of what constitutes the conditions for testing hypotheses in field research. These three points will now be discussed in the remaining sections of this chapter.

◄§ *Methodological Problems and "Objective" Data*

The problems encountered in observing, interpreting, recording, and deciding the import of data for a relevant theory arise in field research because the observer is part of the field of action. A critical methodological problem that arises here is a consequence of the difference between physical reality as described by the physical scientist, and social reality as described by the social scientist. Schutz states this difference in the following passage:

This state of affairs is founded on the fact that there is an essential difference in the structure of the thought objects or mental constructs formed by the social sciences and those formed by the natural sciences. It is up to the natural scientist and to him alone to define, in accordance with the procedural rules of his science, his observational field, and to determine the facts, data, and events within it which are relevant for his problems or scientific purpose at hand. Neither are those facts and events pre-selected, nor is the observational field pre-interpreted. The world of nature, as explored by the natural scientist, does not "mean" anything to the molecules, atoms, and electrons therein. The observational field of the social scientist, however, namely the social reality, has a specific meaning and relevance structure for the human beings living, acting, and thinking therein. By a series of common-sense constructs they have pre-selected and pre-interpreted this world which they experience as the reality of their daily lives. It is these thought objects of theirs which determine their behavior by motivating it. The thought objects constructed by the social scientist, in order to grasp this social reality, have to be founded upon the thought objects constructed by the common-sense thinking of men, living their daily life within their social world.[18]

If the observer is not part of the field of action, but merely a "disinterested" scientist, then, as Schutz notes, the cognitive interest of the scientist requires that he replace his personal biographical situation with a scientific situation.[19] The social scientist simultaneously must grasp the meaning of the actor's acts, while he retains a disinterested attitude toward the actor and action scene. There is no interlocking of motives governing his relationship with the actor or actors of the action scene he observes. This point emphasizes Schutz's view that the social scientist must attend to the meaning structures employed by the actors of the scene he wishes to observe and describe, while simultaneously translating such meaning structures into constructs consistent with his theoretical interests. The natural scientist does not face this problem. But we have been discussing the ideal situation of a carefully planned experiment or observational situation which does not require the observer's participation in the field of action. How does this complicated situation affect the observer who is part of the field of action?

Before we can attempt to address this question, another more basic one must be mentioned: ". . . the exploration of the general principles according to which man in daily life organizes his experiences, and especially those of the social world." [20]

The observer, as part of the field of action, brings with him a set of relevances or meaning structures which orients his interpretation of whatever environment of objects lies within his visual field. Under such conditions he is faced with the following problems:

1. He must interpret the actions of his subjects (or their reports about their actions) according to the relevance structures of

everyday life. His model of the actor, the typical course-of-action patterns with which he endows his actor, must be coordinated with the observed events (or those told him by the actor).[21]

2. He must maintain simultaneously a theoretical perspective which takes into account the actor's relevance structures while entertaining a separate set of relevances which permit him to interact with the actor. This means that the observer entertains a set of motives which permits him to carry on a sequence of interpersonal transactions.

3. But as Schutz notes of the observer: "He can never enter as a consociate in an interaction pattern with one of the actors on the social scene without abandoning, at least temporarily, his scientific attitude. The participant observer or field worker establishes contact with the group studied as a man among fellowmen; only his system of relevances which serves as the scheme of his selection and interpretation is determined by the scientific attitude, temporarily dropped in order to be resumed again." [22]

Thus, our observer, as part of the field of action, must (a) have some model of the actor which includes the actor's meaning structures as part of his theory of social order; (b) employ a set of procedural rules [23] consistent with the theoretical constructs of his model; (c) use his knowledge of the actor's and his own everyday life experience (which presumably has provided him with the basis for his model) to engage in interpersonal transactions necessary for gathering his data; (d) temporarily drop his use of scientific rationalities, yet maintain the scientific attitude when describing the actor's actions (or the actions described by the actor).

But how does the observer entertain these two different perspectives? According to Schutz the observer must have some grasp of the common-sense constructs of everyday life by which the actor interprets his environment. The field worker cannot begin to describe any social event without some specification of his scientific theory, i.e., his theory of objects, his model of the actor, or the kind of social order presupposed. To do otherwise would lead to a difficult theoretical and methodological problem; namely, how would he know whether the observer's description of an action scene were based upon the common-sense constructs the observer uses in participating in this scene, or whether his description were based upon some theory that employs scientific constructs. Harold Garfinkel refers to this as the problem of "seeing the society from within." [24]

Unless the observer addresses this problem he cannot warrant his findings on scientific grounds. Instead, he is open to the criticism that his findings are not necessarily any different from those of a lay actor in the society. To say that one wishes to take the actor's point of view into account or, as Malinowski states, to describe the culture through the eyes of its members, does not mean that the actor's rules of evidence are to be employed. The methodological impasse should be clear; by specifying his theory of the actor, states Schutz, the observer provides the methodological basis for establishing rules of evidence, of knowledge, and of correct proof. He establishes the basis for a correspondence between his theory of the actor and the events he observes and describes. By adopting the alternative of the actor's rules of evidence, he does not resolve the problem unless he can specify the properties of such rules. But how does he decide the properties?

If we accept the proposition that the first task of the sociologist is to discover the rules employed by the actor for managing his daily affairs, the reader may well raise the following question: Does this mean that we cannot engage in social research until this task has been accomplished? The answer is a qualified "yes." The fact that researchers *are* carrying out research every day is not sufficient evidence for taking the position that going through a set of logical and empirical operations constitutes significant research. The procedural rules employed must be examined. Participant observation, unstructured and structured interviewing, and questionnaire surveys commonly presuppose a community between actor and observer which required the use of common-sense constructs. Although the existence of such rules or constructs may not be acknowledged, they are nonetheless variables in accomplishing the research project. I have been leading up to the following:

1. Even if common-sense rules of interpretation, as used by persons in everyday life, are not known to the researcher, he can contribute to his particular project, general theory and methodology in sociology by being aware of their existence and seek to study their properties and their influence in his research.

2. Researchers, by examining the basis for entering a research

situation, the actions required, the kinds of thoughts generated by the subjects when questioned about their activities, and the rules of procedure they employ as observers, can simultaneously study a given problem area and shed some light on the nature of common-sense constructs.

3. Specifying the unstated details of unstructured questions, forced-choice questionnaires, and casual conversations which elicit information called "data" by the observer become a basis for understanding the elements of common-sense constructs.

4. Knowledge of the steps utilized in securing data is not new to the researcher, but in social science research information about such steps usually is obtained long after one of the most important sequence of events has been accomplished; namely, the social relationships required to establish some kind of community between actor and observer.

Anthropologists have long indicated the importance of this point. Anthropological field reports reveal very little of the initial experiences of the research or of the procedures used for deciding the meaning of a given event. A closer inspection of such activities might well reveal that the researcher, even when studying an entirely foreign culture, relies heavily upon his experiences in his own culture for deciding the sense of the events he witnesses. But few report the raw details of how they enter the research situation, much less how they sustain their work and finally terminate it. One of the most informative recent studies is a monograph by Dalton.[25] His methodological appendix, though lacking in the rich details on which it obviously is based, is one of the most revealing because it considers the kinds of social relationships that would be comparable to those in which an anthropologist in the field might be involved and to the field experiences of certain sociologists or political scientists. Examination of the problems revealed by researchers in obtaining their data would demonstrate that the problems just raised are overlooked or given scant attention. The point is that rather than recognizing such conditions as problematic, researchers make the customary comments about establishing "objective" observations and the nature of the "scientific" problem addressed. Only occasionally does one find references to the procedures employed in obtaining the data.

What social scientists have done with all types of research, including participant observation, is to place such a premium on "objectivity," that the conditions of the present stage of research in the social sciences are explored not for their theoretical and methodological potential but as vehicles for obtaining substantive data. The concern for substantive results has obscured the fact that such results are only as good as the basic theory and methods used in "finding" and interpreting them. The actual research situation, especially in the case of participant observation and similar methods, constitutes an important source of data, for it is just as subject to prediction and explanation as the substantive results sought. Thus, if one is to study a governmental agency and uses participant observation together with extensive unstructured and structured interviewing, then gaining access to subjects in their everyday activities, developing the necessary social relationships with those to be interviewed, and assessing the import of unofficial and official sources of data are all problematic features of the research situation the study of which can contribute both to our knowledge of methodology and theoretical properties of social organization. Consideration of the actual problems that researchers encounter in their activities provides the appropriate basis for a discussion of how the research situation can become both a source of data and a datum itself of comparative methodology.

❧ *Theoretical and Practical Considerations*

A wide variety of important problems are discussed in Dalton's methodological appendix, which provides an inclusive point of departure for covering previous statements of a similar nature. One problem he raises is that of establishing the research situation. Dalton does not believe in formally approaching the higher authorities of any organization to be studied because of the possibility of management setting limits on the research. The complexities of this problem are many. The arguments on the problem of how best to gain entrance to the research situation can be presented as follows:

1. If formal channels are used (let us initially assume the researcher does not have any special influence with outside or inside parties) the possibility exists that the researcher's study will

be restricted or that he might be refused the opportunity to study at all.

2. The use of unofficial channels has the obvious advantage of permitting the exploration of areas upon which higher authorities might place restrictions. Official contacts can be valuable (even Dalton stated they proved helpful to him) in developing leads and hunches which might otherwise be buried.

3. Use of formal channels permits the reader to follow the steps in obtaining entrance to the research situation, but so does a carefully reported unofficial approach. The issue is actually an ethical one. The question is: Should research be public both to the researcher's scientific community (assuming that the anonymity of the subjects is preserved) and the societal community from which the data are obtained? Science, as a set of procedural rules for admitting and eliminating propositions from a body of knowledge,[26] is not concerned as long as the researcher follows the canons of inquiry accepted by his scientific community. It seems clear, then, that the researcher's ethical problem with regard to this particular situation stems from his membership in the lay community.

4. The formal restrictions which authorities might place upon the researcher's activities can be overcome by a research design that takes the restrictions into account by identifying them as variables, these to be treated as complimentary to or as qualifying the substantive ones.

5. In the use of unofficial channels the researcher may have to rely upon a restricted set of subjects who can be consulted only for limited matters, or so informally as to preclude the gathering of systematic data which would permit the testing of hypotheses. This limitation has led to a rather large number of "pilot studies" in the study of complex organizations by researchers committed to participant observation. The data adduced from these studies remain impressionistic. For many sociologists the term "impressionistic data" and "participant observation" have become synonymous. Dalton actually used a combination of participant observation procedures by gaining official status in the organization which permitted him to be around the premises. He then used the official position as the basis for carrying out his unofficial inquiries.

6. By "backing up" to the data via unofficial sources, the participant observer attempts to overcome restrictions which higher authorities may place upon his activities.

What are we to make of the above remarks? A codification of procedures might help. Procedures utilized by the researcher should be made public from the outset. He should establish *a priori* the conditions (e.g., the number of subjects required, the kinds of questions necessary for eliciting particular kinds of information, etc.) for deciding the factual character of his findings. Dalton's comments, and those of others, indicate some of the complexities involved in obtaining data via unofficial channels. By making the intricacies of unofficial contacts explicit, the participant observer can contribute to the formulation of more general questions of theory and method. Theoretically his work would tell us in what roles one may succeed in obtaining unofficial information from suspicious subjects. For example, information as to how he conceived of the subject as a basis for initiating social action, how the subject responded, the influence of sex, age, ethnic background, socioeconomic differences, personal influences, and so on. Social scientists have long acknowledged the importance of such factors, but we must view them as possible contributors not only to their theory but also to their method. Dalton's careful and rich account of his research activities and the highly informative material he provides are not presented in such a way that the reader can appreciate the influence of the operations he employed in obtaining his data, his assumptions about when he had the subject's confidence, when he should take a drink so as to set the subject at ease, what kinds of questions or conversations produced what responses, how he decided that certain responses were to be accepted as "data" and others as misleading, or how many subjects were taken as the basis for a generalization and based upon what kinds of responses, and so on. Material on the context of interaction between researcher and his subject is exceedingly difficult to obtain and record accurately, but it would also provide an important source of data for documenting the social processes Dalton mentions as important for moving up the career ladder, power struggles on the line, relations between staff and line, and so on. Thus, all social scientists engaging in participant observation and interviewing encounter difficulties in achieving and maintaining access to subjects and in discovering leads and unofficial factors. In spite of this, these unofficial factors are often the basis for data but not reported as such, yet parallel the kinds of material researchers report to document statements about the workings of complex organizations.

Dalton's efforts in his appendix to indicate some of these problems become an important methodological contribution precisely because he provides what other studies frequently— whether intentionally or not—bury in reporting their findings. Without a systematic basis for describing his observations as he makes them and interprets them, the researcher is faced with the problem of communicating the "facts" objectively. Thus, he cannot resolve the problem discussed earlier, of "seeing the society from within." From a methodological point of view his findings can be compared only to those of the journalist or the man on the street. In order for comparative data to exist, the methods for obtaining such data must be known and comparable. It is to these methods that Dalton next addressed himself.

He notes that, because of the problem of explaining to his subjects what he was up to and why, he did little interviewing.[27] He does, however, indicate various procedures used to check out the informant's comments, and whether they both employed the same grammar or speech mannerisms. Further, he writes: "In the process of reconstructing interviews, I noted down emphases made, facial expressions, marks of concern and relief, and other gestures—aware that they could mislead—as possible clues to more basic things." [28] Dalton does not tell the reader precisely how such factors as grammar and speech mannerisms, facial expressions, marks of concern, and the like affected his relations with his subjects and entered into the interpretation of what he observed. It is unlikely that anyone could always remember or even be fully aware of such information. An example of this can be found in the following brief account of a critical problem in both Dalton's research procedures and his explanation of the findings:

The subject of Masonry was so touchy at Milo that even some intimates shrank from having a hand in establishing precise membership and the number of Catholics who had become Masons. What seemed like a simple thing to accomplish, aroused fears, and alienated some of my fringe acquaintances whom I had mistakenly counted on for help, and whom I now saw as themselves worthy of more study. These people now avoided me and aroused my fear for success of the research. I learned later that they feared to aid me and feared not to, lest some of my intimates cause them trouble. (What should the researcher do when he disturbs the situation he would like to hold still?) Since the Masons were distributed among numerous lodges, to confirm membership I eventually had to submit lists of doubtful officers to seventeen intimates among the Masons.[29]

Field research could be even more beneficial for others engaging in participant observation if problems of access, interpretation, and the like could be inserted at the place of discussion in the text. On the one hand, many references to contacts with subjects often use terms stated in vernacular not explained to the reader and report material without it being clear as to how the subject's comments were interpreted by the researcher. On the other, many researchers discuss that their subjects "think" or "mean" something without providing the documentation for such statements. This kind of description "at a distance" makes difficult the comparison of the data of different researchers.

Returning to our point, we should note again Dalton's inclusion of material pertaining to his efforts and successes in establishing contacts with various subjects in the organizations studied. The comments, while revealing, are too truncated to indicate what data were obtained by what kinds of contacts, and they are not integrated with the actual reporting. The following comments by Dalton indicate an important approximation to the ideal of participant observation.

Usually expecting guarded talk, I sought when possible to catch men in or near critical situations, and to learn in advance when important meetings were coming up and what bearing they would have on the unofficial aspects of various issues. Experiences with reneging informants (below) prompted me to get comments or gestures of some kind from certain people before their feelings cooled or they became wary. In "interviewing" I usually had in mind a schedule of points to follow. But when the respondent's talk uncovered events of seeming greater importance, I omitted or adapted my prepared questions. Then, or at a later meeting, when I had exhausted the planned questions for a given part of the research, and was sure of the intimate, I asked loaded questions in various directions and followed promising responses.[30]

By indicating precisely at what points specific questions were asked of respondents, their answers, how events of seeming greater importance were brought up, how all of this affected the observer's understanding of the events and his interpretation of them, the researcher approximates something like an experimental setting. The demands of participant observation obviously become much greater than those placed upon other forms of research, providing the researcher is interested in meeting, or rather approximating, the ideal canons of scientific procedure. It may be too much to expect such ideal procedures to be met, but the *actual* procedures should be stated clearly so that the basis for making an inference about a set of events can be known to other researchers, can provide for a comparative base, can be replicated, and procedures improved.

A few remarks should be made about the practical circumstances likely to be encountered in field research, but such "how-to-do-its" should be couched within a framework which stresses the basic features of social interaction, in effect, some basic properties of social order.

The approach to the organization or group to be studied requires an evaluation of the observer's position relative to the subjects to be studied, the means of access and how access will affect his relationships with the subjects. How does one present oneself before others? This becomes a basic question. How does the observer make his initial contact with those persons who obtain access for him, the subjects to be studied, in short, with any person who becomes the object of his study? Goffman, among others, considers this question a critical one for all social interaction.

When an individual enters the presence of others, they commonly seek to acquire information about him or to bring into play information about him already possessed. They will be interested in his general socio-economic status, his conception of self, his attitude toward them, his competence, his trustworthiness, etc. . . .

Let us now turn from the others to the point of view of the individual who presents himself before them. He may wish them to think highly of him, or to think that he thinks highly of them, or to perceive how in fact he feels toward them, or to obtain no clearcut impression; he may wish to ensure sufficient harmony so that the interaction can be sustained, or to defraud, get rid of, confuse, mislead, antagonize, or insult them.[31]

Goffman's theoretical material is concerned with how persons in everyday life go about managing their presence before others. His monograph and related papers provide a framework for describing a wide set of social activities which occur when persons engage in social action. The following quotation suggests a possible approach to many of the problems already discused by presenting a more analytic basis for the field researcher's procedures.

Underlying all social interaction there seems to be a fundamental dialectic. When one individual enters the presence of others, he will want to discover the facts of the situation. Were he to possess this information, he could know, and make allowances for, what will come to happen and he could give the others present as much of their due as is consistent with his enlightened self-interest. . . . Full information of this order is rarely available; in its absence, the individual tends to employ substitutes—cues, tests, hints, expressive gestures, status symbols, etc.—as predictive devices. In short, since the reality that the individual is concerned with is unperceivable at the moment, appearances must be relied upon in its stead. And, paradoxically, the more the individual is concerned with the reality that is not available to perception, the more must he concentrate his attention on appearances.[32]

In earlier writings Schutz made much the same point as Goffman, but he addressed the analytic side of the constitutive features of everyday life. Schutz explicitly points out that, as scientific observers, we must construct a model of the actor, his typical motives, typical actions, typical likes and dislikes, and so on as a basic condition to observing and interpreting the actor's behavior according to the procedural and theoretical rules of our discipline.

In the following pages we take the position that the social sciences have to deal with human conduct and its common-sense interpretation in the social reality, involving the analysis of the whole system of projects and motives, of relevances and constructs dealt with in the preceding sections. Such an analysis refers by necessity to the subjective point of view, namely, to the interpretation of the action and its settings in terms of the actor. Since this postulate of the subjective interpretation is, as we have seen, a general principle of constructing course-of-action types in common-sense experience, any social science aspiring to grasp "social reality" has to adopt this principle also.[33]

The writings of Schutz and Goffman illustrate a fundamental goal in sociology: the search for the basic principles of social interaction. The field researcher, then, is not without a model of the actor to guide him in his observations. Indeed, he can contribute to knowledge on two counts if he treats basic principles of social interaction as problematic: first, he provides a test for basic theory; secondly, he treats such propositions as "given," and uses such "principles" as a basis for entering into social relationships with the "natives" and in ordering his initial contacts and development of roles and interaction.

If it is correct to assume that persons in everyday life order their environment, assign meanings or relevances to objects, base their social actions on the common-sense rationalities, then one cannot engage in field research or use any other method of research in the social sciences without taking the principle of subjective interpretation into consideration. While engaging subjects in conversation during field research, asking them unstructured or structured questions in an interview situation, or using a questionnaire, the scientific observer must take into account the common-sense constructs employed by the actor in everyday life if he is to grasp the meanings that will be assigned by the actor to his questions, regardless of the form in which they are presented to the actor. To ignore this point is to render both the questions (or conversations) and the answers received as problematic and/or meaningless. The researcher, without specifying his theory of objects—his model of the actor—would not be able to attach any more warrant to his propositions than any lay person interested in the same events or merely having "an opinion" of the same events.

To summarize this last point, the scientific observer requires a theory which provides a model of the actor who is oriented to an environment of objects with common-sense features. The observer must distinguish between the scientific rationalities he uses for ordering his theory and findings and the common-sense rationalities which he imputes to the actors studied. Both sets of constructs—common-sense and scientific—are the scientist's constructions, for as Schutz notes:

He begins to construct typical course-of-action patterns corresponding to the observed events. Thereupon he co-ordinates to these typical course-of-action patterns a personal type, namely, a model of an actor whom he imagines as being gifted with consciousness. Yet it is a consciousness restricted to containing nothing but all the elements relevant to the performance of the course-of-action patterns under observation and relevant, therewith, to the scientist's problem under scrutiny. He ascribes, thus, to this fictitious consciousness a set of typical in-order-to-motives corresponding to the goals of the observed course-of-action patterns and typical because-motives upon which the in-order-to-motives are founded. Both types of motives are assumed to be invariant in the mind of the imaginary actor-model.

Yet these models of actors are not human beings living within their biographical situation in the social world of everyday life. Strictly speaking, they do not have any biography or any history, and the situation into which they are placed is not a situation defined by them but defined by their creator, the social scientist. He has created these puppets or homunculi to manipulate them for his purpose. A merely specious consciousness is imputed to them by the scientist which is constructed in such a way that its presupposed stock of knowledge at hand (including the ascribed set of invariant motives) would make actions originating therefrom subjectively understandable, provided that these actions were performed by real actors within the social world. But the puppet and his artificial consciousness is not subjected to the ontological conditions of human beings. The homunculus was not born, he does not grow up, and he will not die. He has no hopes and no fears; he does not know anxiety as the chief motive of all his deeds. He is not free in the sense that his acting could transgress the limits his creator, the social scientist, has predetermined. He cannot, therefore, have other conflicts of interests and motives than those the social scientist has imputed to him. He cannot err, if to err is not his typical destiny. He cannot choose, except among the alternatives the social scientist has put before him as standing to his choice.[34]

Schutz' remarks indicate that the same logic employed by physical scientists is also employed by the social scientist in deciding what is knowledge, though the procedural rules may differ. What is different, of course, was quoted earlier, but warrants repeating:

. . . the structure of the thought objects or mental constructs formed by the social sciences and those formed by the natural sciences. It is up to the natural scientist and to him alone to define, in accordance with the procedural rules of his science, his observational field, and to determine the facts, data, and events within it which are relevant for his problem or scientific purpose at hand. Neither are those facts and events pre-selected, nor is the observational field pre-interpreted. The world of nature, as explored by the natural scientist, does not "mean" anything to the molecules, atoms, and electrons therein. The observational field of the social scientist, however, namely the social reality, has a specific meaning and relevance structure for the human beings living, acting, and thinking therein. By a series of common-sense constructs they have pre-selected and pre-interpreted this world which they experience as the reality of their daily lives. It is these thought objects of theirs which determine their behavior by motivating it. The thought objects constructed by the social scientist, in order to grasp this social reality, have to be founded upon the thought objects constructed by the common-sense thinking of men, living their daily life within their social world.[35]

It should now be clear why Schutz insists that the first task of the social sciences is the exploration of the basic principles by which man organizes his experiences in everyday life. The field researcher has no choice as to whether he will have a model of the actor, implicitly or explicitly, for ordering his observations and deciding their meaning. Something *is* known about the kinds of models that are available, and we also know some of the basic features which are to be taken into account for any model. This is not the place to pursue the notion of common-sense constructs or the conditions which surround their use, but some comments on the "application" of these concepts are relevant.

An important part of field work has to do with the problems of identifying, obtaining, and sustaining the contacts the field researcher must make. For example, given his choice of role or different roles he assumes toward or ascribes to different subjects, what kinds of intimacies should he cultivate? What types of persons should he contact? How should he make the contacts? How should he maintain them? How do they affect the data he obtains? How might particular contacts preclude certain data? These are only a fraction of the questions the field researcher must ponder. To illustrate this point it might prove instructive to contrast the comments of an experienced field researcher, writing about the methodological problems of participant observation, and the statements of someone concerned with describing the basic features of everyday life.

Dean [36] presents an important discussion of several kinds of informants which he considers to be more helpful than the "average" person. He distinguishes between those who are more sensitized to insights in the problem area and those considered "more-willing-to-reveal." The first group is:

—The *outsider,* who sees things from the light of another culture, social class, community, etc.
—The *"rookie"* who is surprised by what goes on and notes the taken-

for-granted things that the acclimated miss. And as yet, he may have no *stake* in the system to protect.
—The *nouveau* status, the person in transition from one role or status to another where the tensions of new experience are raw and sensitive.
—The *"natural,"* i.e., the rare reflective objective person in the field. He can sometimes be pointed out by other intelligent and reflective persons.[37]

The second group is characterized as follows:

—The *naive informant,* who knows not wherof he speaks: either (a) naive to what the field worker represents or (b) naive about his own group.
—The *frustrated person* (rebel or malcontent), especially the one who is consciously aware of blocking of his drives and impulses.
—The *"outs,"* those out of power, but "in-the-know," and critical of the "ins"—eager to reveal negative facts about the "ins."
—The *habitué* or *"old hand,"* "fixture around here," who no longer has a stake or is so accepted that he is not threatened by exposing what others say or do.
—The *"needy" person* who fastens onto the interviewer because he needs the attention and support. As long as the interviewer feels this need, he will talk.
—The *subordinate,* who must adapt to superiors. He generally develops insights to cushion the impact of authority, and he may be hostile and willing to "blow his top."[38]

The quotations from Dean reveal a mixture of common-sense constructs of social types used by persons in everyday life and the observer's categories for dealing with social types, which may or may not be the same as those used by the actors studied. Let us now turn to a discussion by Goffman of persons who learn of "team secrets" and could discredit or disrupt the performances that a group wishes to foster. He refers to persons possessing such information as occupying "discrepant roles."

First, there is the role of "informer." The informer is someone who pretends to the performers to be a member of their team, is allowed to come back-stage and to acquire destructive information, and then openly or secretly sells out the show to the audience. . . .
Secondly, there is the role of "shill." A shill is someone who acts as though he were an ordinary member of the audience but is in fact in league with the performers. . . .
We consider now another impostor in the audience, but this time one who uses his unapparent sophistication in the interests of the

audience, not the performers. This type can be illustrated by the person who is hired to check up on the standards that performers maintain in order to ensure that in certain respects fostered appearances will not be too far from reality. . . . [Goffman uses the term "spotter" for this discrepant role.]

There is yet another peculiar fellow in the audience. He is the one who takes an unremarked, modest place in the audience and leaves the region when they do, but when he leaves he goes to his employer, a competitor of the team whose performance he has witnessed, to report what he has seen. He is the professional shopper—the Gimbel's man in Macy's and the Macy's man in Gimbels; he is the fashion spy and the foreigner at National Air Meets. . . .

Another discrepant role is one that is often called the go-between or mediator. The go-between learns the secrets of each side and gives each side the false impression that he is more loyal to it than to the other.[39]

While the two sets of social types described by Dean and Goffman do not correspond point for point, they indicate the identical concerns of the participant observer interested in obtaining "good" contacts in the field and the social scientist interested in studying basic patterns of social interaction. The participant observer interested in studying ethnic relations in a community, staff-line conflicts in industrial plants, the socialization of physicians, and so on must not only be explicit about the model of the actor to be used in his research but should also be alerted to the possibility of studying basic theoretical concepts while engaged in the mechanics of his research, for both are critical in observing and interpreting the substantive area being studied. Awareness of the social types prevalent in various kinds of groups, how to identify them, enter into relationships with them and engage their support, enables the field researcher to restrict the frame of possibilities in his research design, in short, to attempt to specify and test relevant hypotheses. Dean's paper provides some excellent suggestions for identifying, obtaining, and maintaining contacts. Goffman's writings present a wealth of material which can be used by field researchers for understanding the descriptive details of how persons present themselves before others and manage their appearances in everyday life.[40]

The final point I wish to discuss in this section has to do with terminating the research. The interpersonal relations which develop during field research are not easily terminated by leaving the field of action. The researcher must make his own decisions

about the kinds of "social contracts"—to use Durkheim's phrase—
he will honor. This is particularly the case because such "contracts" will include unstated or noncontractual conditions. There
are problems of whether the material to be reported by the researcher will affect the subjects studied in adverse ways. There is
the further problem of leaving the research setting intact so that
other social scientists will not be discouraged from coming to the
scene. The obligations—assuming they are construed as such—
incumbent upon the researcher in these matters are far from
codified.[41] If every effort is made to insure complete reporting
to the reader on the details of entering, sustaining, and leaving
social relationships during field research, the researcher will have
considerable material available for deciding when to terminate
the study. Researchers have indicated that many field studies
lead to relationships which continue indefinitely. The obvious
drawbacks are the possibility of completely obscuring the value
of the research by "going native" or of a refusal on the part of
the observer even to report his findings, to variations of withholding information because of its possible damage to the subjects. Many students have found that the very requirements of
doing the research preclude the use of certain data. The obvious
but not too helpful conclusion is to be as explicit as possible in
making the necessary decisions. The various descriptions of entering, maintaining, and terminating field research are buried usually within the framework of the particular study done by some
observer and not discussed explicitly, or they are so abstract that
few if any procedural operations are provided.

✺§   *Field Research and Testing Hypotheses*

In this section I wish to focus upon the relative advantages
and disadvantages of participant observation as a method of
social research. My concern is its usefulness in relation to other
methods.

A paper by Becker and Geer and the accompanying comment by Trow, discuss the relative merits of participant observation and interviewing.[42] In field research the two procedures
ideally would be complementary. Intensive participation restricts
the standardization that interviewing permits, but participation

provides a more intimate view of social process. Without some kinds of systematic probes and questions during participant observation the method would be of limited value for testing hypotheses. The importance of systematic theory becomes obvious here if the researcher is to have control over his activities as a participant observer. Otherwise, this method amounts to a continual "pilot study."

Present uses of participant observation and interviewing in field research remain primarily after-the-fact reporting. A recent exception can be found in one study where explicit hypotheses were formulated for testing in field research. This is a study by a group of psychologists and anthropologists on child-rearing practices in different cultures.[43] The papers cited earlier indicate an increasing awareness of the need for social scientists to improve field techniques so that hypotheses can be tested. The chief obstacle remains the lack of precise theory, or at least a willingness on the part of the researcher to make explicit his assumptions about theory.

One position would be that we are not improving our theory and methods of research from participant observation studies, but simply adding a large number of descriptive observations of dubious validity and value to the corpus of social science knowledge. Of course, it might be pointed out that there is nothing wrong with such descriptive or impressionistic knowledge and that every young science has done something similar. But such an argument is meaningless unless it can be demonstrated that we do not have any sufficiently precise theories to specify hypotheses in advance of our research, and further, that it is impossible for researchers in participant observation and interviewing to employ systematic methods of obtaining information (that is, standardized questions that would be flexible to the situation and at the same time permit some pattern to be discerned). But no such demonstration has been made. On the contrary, the papers cited earlier indicate that a great deal of progress has been made toward awareness of the practical and methodological difficulties of participant observation and interviewing, but very little has been done toward the specification of theory which might be translated into operational procedures to be used in advance of obtaining the data.

In the case of interviewing, there has been considerable work done in calling to the researcher's attention the pitfalls and remedies in using this method. But in spite of improvement in interviewing techniques, little has been done to integrate social science theory with methodology. The subtleties which method-ologists introduce to the novice interviewer can be read as proper-ties to be found in the everyday interaction between members of a society. Thus, the principles of "good and bad interviewing" can be read as basic features of social interaction which the social scientist presumably is seeking to study. Any researcher must have, at least implicitly, some command of the basic theoretical features of interaction if he is to observe and interpret them to others. The difficulties encountered in obtaining data through participant observation and interviewing are no different, though devoid of its research implication, than those which persons liv-ing their daily lives would encounter if they were placed in a comparable situation. Moving into a new neighborhood, start-ing work at a new job, applying for a new job, starting school, meeting groups whose customs and language are different from one's own, attempting to befriend someone so as to obtain certain information, trying to sell a customer some merchandise, trying to pick up a girl—any number of similar and divergent social processes include the same features which are to be found in field research. The problems discussed in the above cited papers pro-vide us with two sets of information: a set of propositions about social interaction as social process and a set of rules for seeking data under the various conditions of field research.

To the extent that a field researcher can observe and record his data while being aware of the difficulties noted above, he would be able to specify the grounds for his inferences. To sum-marize:

1. The field researcher should formulate as explicitly as pos-sible what he is seeking to accomplish in his research endeavor, explore some general theoretical propositions, test specific hypoth-eses, map out previously uncharted territory for future research and hypothesis testing, and the like.

2. Any knowledge of the research situation, independent of that which might be obtained in the actual field work should also, if possible, be secured. This means covering the relevant literature, contacting sources which might have information

about the problem to be studied, seeking information on the field setting in which the research will take place, and so on.

3. To the extent that the problem to be investigated or explored permits, the researcher should spell out what kinds of information would be necessary for accomplishing his objectives. This may vary from formulating specific questions to be asked of respondents to simply indicating one's lack of foreknowledge of what will be asked or even of how contact will be made.

4. Becker's "natural history" suggestion can be very helpful regardless of what is known. Keeping careful notes of every stage of the research should reveal procedural discrepancies or congruence between (1) explicit or implicit design, (2) theory and methodology, and (3) changing positions over time. Unless one can specify what is unknown in a given area, it is difficult to see what and how one comes to know anything in that area. It is only by making what they know, assume, and are concerned about explicit that field researchers and others can assess their attempts to test hypotheses.

5. Each step in the "natural history" can be treated formally if the problem is stated precisely enough. Abraham Wald's *Sequential Analysis* [44] provides a formal guide for testing hypotheses when the research is conducted over time and when hypotheses are continually being tested, restated, and retested. Each step would produce data which could be related to later data, in order to improve the theory, the methodology, to clarify the substantive problem and, as Becker and Vidich have stated, to add to our knowledge of change in social process.

6. Whereas a researcher may have started with a very meager research design and vague notions about the problem under investigation, by means of a detailed specification of his methodological procedures as well as of their limitations, he may come to test some very specific hypotheses, if the conditions of the setting permit it. Provided with the natural history of the study, the student can profit by knowledge of the researcher's mistakes and can replicate all or some part of the work.

We have described briefly an ideal set of "recipes" for field research. Some of the realities are:

1. The researcher has an idea of a problem and even of what he expects to find. This may mean that he implicitly goes about

his research in such a way as to find precisely that information to support his initial ideas, however vaguely they may have been conceived. It is one thing to make such ideas public, say in preliminary form, and another to keep them private until the research is being written up. Specifying the design in advance requires that alternative interpretations be provided, but keeping such information private enables the researcher to say he "knew it all along," or "that's the way it was conceived to be in the first place."

2. Many participant observers, then, enter the field situation with some vague notions in mind about previous findings of various studies that have been made and may use these as a basis for "misunderstanding" information obtained. This point is mentioned frequently in the literature cited above. It is often upheld as a virtue of participant observation that the researcher continually is able to modify early conceptions and results, often considered less correct than later observations, in light of subsequent experiences. As Becker has noted, the importance of the "natural history" recording and presentation of data and inferences is to provide the researcher with a basis for studying changes in his views, his data, his methods, and his inferences over time.

3. Most field researchers present their findings so as to best highlight the major points of their study. This frequently means ignoring the changes in the perspectives of the subjects and researcher over time. The fact that being more accepted by the group studied may lead to more detailed information or new information previously unavailable, may also keep the observer from noticing critical distinctions or activities. Distinctions which might have been noticed earlier become discounted. The findings are presented as if the problems of access, maintaining contact, terminating contact, did not influence the finding and interpretation of data. The report, as Vidich notes, has a "timeless" quality.

4. The after-the-fact report is honored by subsequent readers and researchers as "final" knowledge about the group studied. Rather than recognize the problematic character of such results and attempt to then refine basic principles or extend our knowledge and permit comparative study, it becomes common that each succeeding researcher seeks his own unique setting. This procedure presumably would attest to the relative contribution

of the researcher, and it tends to reinforce the view that every group *is* unique, each requiring unique methods, unique theoretical interpretations, and a unique observer. All of this in spite of the regularities claimed for participant observation by the same researchers when discussing various concepts.

5. The tendency has been to stress substantive findings not the development of basic theory. "General theory" often consists of a few general propositions that are difficult to translate into procedural rules and are treated as "constant" in that they are not made problematic in field research, but are simply to be "applied" for explaining the findings of the study.

⌇§ *Summary*

The growing literature on participant observation, interviewing, and field work in general has served to codify our knowledge about these research methods. The information reported provides a set of instructive "how-to-do-its" and "what-to-look-out-fors" in field research. I have touched upon interviewing only tangentially, reserving more detailed comments for the following chapter. The literature contains a number of important statements on establishing contact with the group to be studied, identifying relevant subjects, entering social relationships, becoming too involved with the subjects, recording data, making checks on findings, and so on. The point I have stressed is that running through this rich information on field research are the elements of basic concepts in social science. Rather than entering the research setting with an explicit theoretical scheme and design, the field researcher frequently develops his "theory" during the study or after the data have been collected and while writing up the findings. I have tried to show that a great deal is known about the problems of field research that can be found in material on basic theory. If the kinds of assumptions presupposed in his interpretations of what is observed are not specified, the researcher has no way of recommending the factual character of his findings, except on common-sense grounds. Accordingly, the researcher frequently uses his own common-sense to interpret his observations. The researcher, who says on the one hand that he is following scientific procedures but on the other that there is no theory available with which to do field research, suggests that he does not wish to make explicit the bases of his observations and interpretations. Without such specifications the reader cannot distinguish between scientific description of a set of events and those that could be obtained by consulting any lay member of the group studied. The fact that the common-sense constructs of everyday life are basic to any study of social order requires that explicit attention be given to this problem. Finally, field research provides an excellent setting both for using and testing basic theory and for the study of how such theory enters into our knowledge of substantive areas.

INTERVIEWING

STUDENTS OF SOCIAL RESEARCH recognize that every social encounter is potentially an interview situation and that interviewing can elicit or stimulate a wide range of responses. There are
a variety of strategies currently in use for orienting the interviewer to the subject of interviewing. My interest here is not to
catalogue all these strategies, but to discuss the theoretical presuppositions implied in them as a group and to present some
brief remarks about two outstanding recent works on the subject.
A discussion of the theoretical presuppositions underlying interviewing strategies entails showing how such methodological decisions in the use of the interview correspond to theoretical
assumptions.

The various forms of the interview can be discussed under
three headings. The extent to which (1) they can approximate
the testing of hypotheses; (2) their successful use presupposes a
knowledge of variable and invariant elements of basic and
substantive sociological theory; and (3) their use constitutes
cumulative tests of basic theory. By basic theory I mean those
properties of action scenes without which communication could
not take place and that are invariant to the substantive features
of the setting or the particular actors present.

✑ Interviewing and Social Process

To ask how the interview situation influences the data as a
result of the difficult social encounters into which the interviewers
and respondents must enter is to seek the relevance of common-

sense knowledge for general social interaction. Observers concerned with making the interview a more precise and reliable instrument in social research often seek a number of incompatible objectives. For example, standardized questions and answers yet focused and unfocused probes; "good rapport" yet detachment of respondent and interviewer from the social impact of the interview; avoiding role prescriptions and role conceptions that are irrelevant to the data but necessary to complete the interview; assuming that the interviewer's ideology may never affect the subject's responses, and so on. The attempt to make the interview a more valid and reliable instrument cannot be performed without consideration of basic theory because such theory is a built-in feature of every interview and therefore presupposed in its very conduct. Three well-known books that seek to make the interview a more valid and reliable instrument are *The Focused Interview, Interviewing in Social Research,* and *The Dynamics of Interviewing.*[1] These books describe the subtleties of interviewing and can be read for their accounts of basic social process even though their primary interest lies in perfecting the interview as an instrument of social research. Attempts at perfecting the interview assume that this form of data gathering can achieve literal hypothesis testing. Their primary concern is with describing and improving the intricacies of this particular tool of social research. Attention is not always given to the theoretical assumptions required for its use or to how its very procedures constitute a test of basic theory.

Hyman *et al.* begin their book on interviewing with a chapter devoted to interviewer error. They cite many studies which attest to the amount of error present in interviewing by experienced social researchers. The evidence appears convincing. Conceive of the error as evidence not only of poor reliability but also of "normal" interpersonal relations; of the ways in which persons come to interpret each other as social objects in the course of social interaction. The failure of any one set of interviews to provide identical or consistent results might be viewed as evidence of the situational indeterminancy of social interaction described in Chapters I and II. Such "errors" can be read as instances in which situational factors altered the ideal criteria or standards which were formally to govern the interchange. A high degree of statistical reliability may be achieved while the conditions under which the results were attained, the set of procedures producing particular responses and social relationships, remain unstated. Put another way, in spite of the problem of interviewer error, "somehow" different interviewers with different approaches produced similar responses from different subjects. The question then becomes one of determining what was invariant or, more precisely, how were invariant meanings communicated despite such variations?

When Goode and Hatt state that interviewing is "a process of social interaction"[2] and when Hyman *et al.* notice that the data obtained in the interview are "derived in an interpersonal situation," we are reminded again that basic social process is necessarily a part of all interviewing. These and other writers stress the importance of the interviewer's "perception" or perceptiveness, his "insight," playing some role, developing rapport, and so on. The interviewer, through his intuition, must develop a community with the respondent that will enable him to elicit frank answers with the questions of the study. The interviewer must have the ability to evaluate moods and such feelings as anxiety, suspicion, and sincerity so as not to "lose" the subject. A double responsibility is imposed on the interviewer; he must simulate spontaneous participation while evaluating the subject's views toward the interview, the observer, and their relationship. Meanwhile the respondent is doing something identical or similar, but he may not be as committed to sustaining the interaction and therefore have the more advantageous position. One often implied solution to this difficult task is "programing" the interviewer's actions in advance; giving him an interview guide or standardized schedule which tells him how to anticipate moods, anxiety, hostility, and so on. Such a view assumes that "naturalness" is always in some sense contrived and, therefore, runs the risk of being detected. The "programs" are designed to meet contingencies, but the interpretation of such problematic situations remains for the interviewer to determine. The "naturalness" of the subject's environment is affected by the conditions of the formal interview. The moment-by-moment interpretations the interviewer must make while at the same time attempting to communicate a positive, "friendly," "sincere" relationship compromise him at the outset. The subject may take his time "testing" the interviewer for his "sincerity," "friendliness," importance, and the like, while the observer must immediately demonstrate an unguarded interest in the respondent. Such interaction may be likened to that between a car salesman and a prospective buyer or the door-to-door salesman and the housewife, because it is not reciprocal. The social positions of the interviewer and respondent will assume variable status in that the subject may or may not view the interview situation as one he wishes to pursue, while the observer must avoid communicating any sense of status inequality in the course of the interview. Except perhaps for the obtaining of face-sheet information, interviewing is complex and difficult because it necessitates presenting, establishing, and maintaining appropriate and possibly conflicting roles. The range of possible relationships is wide indeed: we might find everything from a relationship of two "strangers" to that of two potential "lovers."

The remainder of the chapter will present critically and in some detail material from the books by Hyman *et al.* and Kahn [5] [7] and Cannell as examples of data on basic social interaction in everyday life and of the problems of using the interview as a research tool. This discussion of interviewing as both method and object of social study from the theoretical orientation of this book will attempt to show how common-sense knowledge and everyday language and meaning enter into the role-taking process of the interview; how common-sense interpretations must be used as technical knowledge by the interviewer for deciding how the information obtained from the respondent is to be interpreted.

✑§   The Problem

Errors arise in interviewing because the researcher and the actual questions are both potentially misinterpreted and misinterpreting, respectively. The concern with reliability stresses the instrument as invariant to the researcher and the data as invariant to the respondent's perception and interpretation of the interviewer. Hyman *et al.* point to a more general problem: "whether or not interviewers differ in the results they obtain, there is also the problem of whether any or all of them obtain accurate results, results that approximate some true value." [3] In their discussion of approaches to interviewing and the strategies employed to avoid low reliability and validity, Hyman *et al.* state:

> In developing a model interviewing procedure, one must somehow balance the gains in reduction of inter-interviewer variability that come from standardization against the possible loss of validity due to the inflexibility of the procedures for the range of circumstances, the constraints placed upon the interviewer's insight, and the loss of informality. One can array various approaches in the literature along the continuum of the freedom allowed the interviewer. Depending on the position of this continuum, one notes that the validity component has presumably been maximized through the exercise of great freedom in interviewing, or that the reliability component has been maximized through standardization of procedure. One can also note whether or not *alternative* procedures are developed to treat which-ever component has been neglected.[4]

The problem is clear. The more the interviewer attempts to sustain a relationship with the subject which he feels will reveal valid responses, the more he feels the interview is "successful." The more standardized the interviewers are in their relations with the subject, the more reliable the data presumably become. Hyman *et al.* propose the usual solution: systematic controls built into the study design in order to avoid having the interviewer assume the burden of handling the problems of reliability and validity. This would be resolved by research designs which anticipate situations of "deeper meaning," and "difficult rapport." Such problems as managing role relationships, occasions of intimacy in the questioning, and so on might conceivably be resolved by having interviewers exhibit standardized facial gestures, tonal expressions, and physical spacing for all interviews. These problems assume interviewers can be trained to present themselves in standardized ways. But this does not guarantee that the necessary responses from interviewer and interviewee will always be forthcoming. The general solution to the problem of reliability and validity discussed by Hyman *et al.* takes the following form:

> The needs to be covert, to dissemble the research purpose, to describe the richness of a complex attitude structure do not have to be entrusted to the whims of the interviewer. Such requirements can be met within the framework of standardized procedure by systematic attack upon

them. Projective questions and covert approaches can be adopted *routinely* and solve the problem that the lack of disguise is not conducive to reports of private feeling. Open-ended questions or complex batteries of polling questions can be used systematically by every interviewer and provide insurance that neither validity nor reliability will be sacrificed.[5]

Clearly, Hyman *et al.* are in a dilemma: at once, they advocate a sophisticated and systematic solution to problems of reliability and validity, while presupposing a theory of the actor which makes it difficult to achieve literal hypothesis testing. Though the underlying theory is never indicated explicitly, it emerges in certain general remarks and references cited. The solution achieved does not hold for a class of cases which could be treated as "identical" for statistical purposes, but it does support the reliability and validity of each interview taken separately. Their implicit assumption is that the theory presupposed could be spelled out and applied directly to the excellent material and procedures they have collected and reported. The critical material for the solution is contained in their chapter on "The Definition of the Interview Situation" and the appendix that goes with it. This material is important since it (1) contains hints at an implicit theory of the actor and interpersonal transactions, and (2) presents some imaginative descriptions of attempts to study experienced interviewers and their routine biases, biases which are seldom made explicit in research reports. The reader should note the similarity between interviewer-subject interaction and the interaction between methodologist and professional interviewers as described by Hyman *et al.,* and general social interaction described in Chapter II of this book.

Hyman *et al.* begin by asking what is perhaps the most important question of all: What is the implicit or explicit model or theory which is employed or presupposed about the interview situation? They correctly note that this model or theory frames the basis for what may be distinguished as error. If the model directs our attention only to certain things, then many errors may go undetected and others may be called "data," all because the model does not take them into account as such. The extent to which the model or theory remains unclear, unexplicated, is the extent to which many errors will go undetected, to which data remain useless or unknown; both because errors may not be discovered and once discovered their significance not recognized. The authors ask where one should obtain such a model. They examine a few implicit models available and point to some of their basic difficulties, such as not having any empirical basis or logical coherence. Then they adopt what amounts to a *method* of viewing interviews. The method proposed is the phenomenological approach described by MacLeod.[6]

What do Hyman *et al.* indicate as the value of the "phenomenological approach"? In their preliminary discussion leading up to a mention of "phenomenological inquiry" in the interview, they comment:

Cognitive factors in the interviewer deriving from other sources, such as his belief about the respondent's true sentiments, were not noticed because such concepts were less prominent in influential bodies of theory. Prevailing theory and conceptions of the interview must be at least temporarily suspended while we go about examining the situation in its complexity. Lundberg rightly remarks in discussing the Interview Method that "it is not possible here to enter into a detailed consideration of the intricate interstimulation and response which are the structure and content of the interview. The fact is that there are very few scientific data available on the subject, although research in this field lies at the very foundation of sociology." A sound conception of the interview, which in turn would guide future research on interviewer effects into appropriate directions, would seem best achieved through empirical study. Then we might check whether the interview actually conforms to our preconception of it, and broadens our views, where necessary, to accord with reality.[7]

This quotation approximates Schutz' view that the social scientist's first task is to study the common-sense categories of thinking in everyday life. The well-conceived interview, complex as it may be, must have its roots in the categories of common-sense thinking, for without a knowledge of such roots the interviewer could not establish the necessary community for conducting his research. This means a recognition and understanding of how the respondent-interviewer interaction involves overlapping social worlds. According to Schutz, relevances necessary for the synchronization of meaning are presupposed. The respondent's and interviewer's stock of knowledge at hand and their definition of the situation will determine their mutual reaction to the questions posed. The relevances not related to the substance of the interview *per se* will also determine the amount of "extra-interview" bias or error which enters. This is a necessary consequence of not treating each other only as objects for rational consideration; their attractiveness or unattractiveness to one another, their bodily presence, the social, physical, and role distance, all produce bias and error *naturally* because these are basic to the structure of everyday conduct. If the goal of the interview is to achieve some measure of "naturalness," then reliability cannot be achieved by the same procedures for all subjects, but only for each subject taken separately. Standardized interviews are altered by the demands of validity and the data obtained are not uniform in the sense of the ideal experiment where every subject is given the same stimulus or exposed to the same stimulus equally and simultaneously. Empirical studies of "successful" and "unsuccessful" social interaction are necessary if we are to estimate how the interviewer's communication of the same schedule to different subjects may alter the standardized character of the questions.

Our argument (beginning on page 78) appears to indicate that every case is a unique event. A carefully designed study should make it possible to transcend some of the inevitable situational factors which permeate every social event and to predict the form of invariant properties, but also some of the situational variables. We may not be able to make precise predictions; pinpointing exact outcomes may be difficult or impossible given our present knowledge of social process. What we know of social process at this time makes it difficult to talk about precise measurement because we really do not know the structure of social action well enough even to predict or indicate with precision what form the measures would take. All social research includes an unknown number of implicit decisions which are not mirrored in the measurement procedures used. The abstraction process required to describe a set of properties, regardless of the measurement system, automatically imposes some amount of reification. The effect of reification, however, can be "controlled" by knowing it occurs and being able to indicate how it transforms the data. The reification, in this case, would be a direct consequence of forcing measurement properties on data which are produced by common-sense meanings given "self-evident" status.

Each interview constitutes a unique event in the sense that

the identical conditions will not exist again for eliciting the properties called data. In a statistical sense, the uniqueness of such events precludes our calling a set of data identical measures of the same property of different objects. The uniqueness of the single interview or observation means that the very process of measurement *imposes* the comparability which allows each frequency in a given cell to be treated as identical and, hence, subject to statistical manipulation. The measurement process imposes the reification as a necessary condition for extracting the information required for comparative or statistical analysis.

The lack of common or standardized denominators for the measurement of social events in field settings stems from our inability to specify the structure of common-sense meanings in everyday life and to incorporate them into a model which also provides for their observation and transformation into theoretically relevant data. Overcoming uniqueness of interviews in field research requires that we examine our cases for invariant properties which are not affected adversely by the noncomparable character of present decisions for assigning meanings to observations and extracting the data. The model for deciding what is observed and what the observation means to us within the framework of our theory must view some part of the world of everyday life as a system of invariant relevance structures. Studies of interviewing procedures and common-sense "rules" of everyday life are essentially studies on the same phenomena: the same model will explain the data of both kinds of study.

◄§ *Two Approaches to Interviewing*

An account of features universally considered as "necessary" of interviewing cannot be found in any one volume. There exists no uniform set of propositions to which everyone would subscribe. However, an examination of textbooks on methods shows some agreement on a wide range of factors that are felt to be associated with "good" interviewing. The following discussion is limited to the work by Hyman *et al.* cited above. The material is not intended to be exhaustive. The point of departure is a set of problem areas on interviewing taken from Hyman *et al.*

✍ *Detachment of Respondent and Interviewer from the Social Impact of the Interview* [8]

Here the authors describe the reactions of experienced interviewers toward their respondents in order to show the negative feelings that can exist even though they make every effort to convey interest and positive feelings. Nothing is said about how interviewers felt they appeared to respondents, but we are told that one respondent viewed an interviewer favorably and told the researcher that she might "like" him. The authors conclude for one case that the respondent was not aware of the underlying hostility felt by the interviewer toward him, and that the interview was not affected by this negative feeling. In other cases interviewers indicated that private thoughts existed that were very hostile or negative but were never revealed to the respondents. The respondent obviously may also reveal what seems necessary but withhold what he feels might be viewed as hostile or otherwise unfavorable. The interviewer may have the upper hand in that he or she will probably be more experienced in this kind of exchange and because he may have learned to control emotional outbursts, having more to lose should he fail to do so. Interviewers and respondents will vary in the extent to which they maintain detachment both publicly and privately. Goffman, in *The Presentation of Self in Everyday Life*,[9] describes this phenomenon as "impression management." The notion of the separation of public and private dialogues is contained in Schutz' writings and can be found in other works within and outside of social science. Interviewers and respondents both should have had experience in maintaining detachment from the social impact of the interview, because this is often expected during many forms of interaction in everyday life. The following quote from Hyman *et al.* on fragments of what an experienced interviewer stated illustrates this point:

Of course I simply smiled—I don't think I showed my reaction. That bothers me—the necessity of remaining sweet as pie all the time—I'm not a blank thing. I'm a person with very strong opinions of my own. I have to make some sort of effort to keep myself out (of the interview). I have schooled myself. When the person expresses an opinion, no matter what it is, I look like I approve. You can't remain blank—that's impossible. . . .[10]

In everyday life persons are continually confronted with situations that are similar to if not identical with the one described above. Depending on the topics covered, in casual exchange between two persons or between an interviewer and respondent, the concern with revealing oneself can vary tremendously. It is difficult to know whether the respondent is not playing the same game as the interviewer—withholding feelings and conceptions both about the other and about the topics covered. The following running account between one of the respondents and one of the authors about the reinterview indicates a striking use of common-sense interpretations.

He began the session with some negative comments to the interviewer about public opinion polls. When asked later why he wanted to be interviewed, he said: "I didn't want to be interviewed. Naturally, if she's walking her feet off I'll help her out." But he added: "Not that I saw any point in the interview." This apparent note of sympathy for the interviewer is the only suggestion of any positive response to her as a person.

The cynicism and hosility and complete detachment may be best indicated in his summing up of the experience. He said: "This here interview thing's a bunch of ——. I think it is a back-door way of getting information for a commercial outfit. A congressman is still going to vote for whoever he wants to."

What about the impact of the experience:

This is best indicated by his answer to the question asked of him several days later, as to whether he remembered the interview pretty well. He replied: "Almost forgotten it" and comments—"I don't know —it was in one ear and out the other—a conversation like any others. I wouldn't be improving my mind any to try and remember." When asked what impressed him most about being interviewed, he replied, "Nothing about it impressed me at all. She came at a time when we were busy and I had to answer between customers, on questions I'd have to think six months about."

As to the impact of the interviewer:

In reply to a question as to whether the interviewer created an initial favorable or unfavorable impression, he says: "Neither, no impression" and remarks, "I wasn't concerned. I've seen better looking dames." [11]

The authors, in referring to this last quoted reinterview, state that the interviewer did not appear to influence the respondent in such a way as to bias his answers, and add that if the respondent's hostility is viewed as bias it is diffuse and would have been present with any other interviewer. The question of validity still remains. The authors imply that the respondent's answers could still be honored because of the lack of interviewer bias, but the question of whether the answers would have been different given a male interviewer with whom the respondent might feel more comfortable, or a female interviewer who might interest the respondent for "other" reasons, remains an unexplored issue. The excellent material collected by Hyman *et al.* shows not only the importance of common-sense decisions during the interview but also that a set of interviews could be distributed like the variety of interpersonal exchanges that occur in everyday life. For example:

1. Have the actors revealed private feelings advertently or inadvertently to each other?

2. Were the private and public conceptions and feelings masked, and, if so, did one or the other "see" through them?

3. Is there any recourse for the respondent or interviewer when one or the other feels that the "truth" is not being revealed and that the other party is not being "sincere"? (This is perhaps exemplified in the last case cited by Hyman *et al.* above when they note that the respondent "in answer to the explicit question as to whether the interviewer seemed satisfied with his answers, 'Yes, she had to be.'")

4. If friendly relations develop which permit both subject and observer to "feel relaxed" during the questioning, does this affect the form, substance, and length of the responses?

5. Do hostile relations develop which lead the interviewer to go through the interview as quickly as possible and not probe some questions at all or too deeply? Can the same be said for the interviewee?

6. Is it possible for the respondent and interviewer to be neither friendly in an intimate or spontaneous way nor hostile, but view the questions as routine, nothing more, nothing less, so long as the topics appear "reasonable"? Descriptions of the interviewer and respondent as "reasonable," "relaxed," "cool," "interested," "truthful," etc., are common-sense expressions in

that they are neither explicitly defined nor easily classified as uni-dimensional traits or observable entities.

In order to achieve better validity, the interviewer might control himself and his manner and approach if he were to change roles within each stage of the interview or with each new interview occasion. Notice what this would mean. Each subject might perceive the interview (or some part of it) as a new situation and this presumably would call for a new role. Depending on the versatility of the interviewer, such procedures can dominate most interviews. Nevertheless, comparability will be difficult unless the interviewer presents the same stimuli and the same definition of the situation to the entire sample of subjects interviewed. The rules of evidence employed by the respondent are as important as those employed by the interviewer for determining what will be said next, how it will be stated, how much information will be given, and in what manner it will be presented. The "phenomenology of the interview" suggested by Hyman *et al.* is an excellent step toward understanding the nature of interviewing, but it should include a theory which addresses the subject's and the interviewer's rules of evidence within the same conceptual scheme.

►§ *"Good Rapport" in Relation to the Opinion-Giving Process*

Hyman *et al.* considered the case just described as departing from traditional conceptions of what "good" interviewing should be like and the way in which bias is introduced and conveyed. This in spite of the extensive past experience of the interviewers. In describing the problem of rapport they present a situation where everything appears almost ideal.

The affection was definitely reciprocated. Both parties reported that they would like to know each other better. The interviewer said of the respondent, she "was so sweet and friendly she had no impulse at all to refuse a chat with a stranger." She also commented about the respondent: "While not mentally stimulating, her innate kindness and optimism is most attractive." The respondent, in describing her initial reaction and motives in being interviewed, said, "Just because she came to the door and seemed like a nice person and had some questions to ask me." [12]

Further quotes revealed positive rapport as well established but not to the point of seeming to bias the interview. Then the authors present the following which might suggest that there was some bias:

According to the interviewer's remarks there was no bias: "She asked me what I thought of sending food to Russia. I did not reveal my opinion." But while the respondent said, "She didn't *try* to change my opinion," she also said: "Once in a while I asked her how she felt and we seemed to agree on our ways of feeling." She also reported that the interviewer agreed with her opinions, as indicated by "just her way of talking. Now it may be that she didn't but she didn't let on that she didn't." [13]

The authors note that this case appeared to have all the traditional virtues of "proper interviewing." Which for them means:

. . . no marked disparity in group membership, excellent rapport, no hostility or sharp divergence in ideology, considerable social interaction, willingness of the respondent to assume her role and the requirements of the survey seriously yet not special insecurity about her opinions, explicit communication of biasing tendencies, and insightful handling by the interviewer [yet in conclusion they note:] What then is wrong with it? It was too good! The identification with the interviewer was too great; the rapport was too much and the respondent seems to have been biased in the direction of compatibility with the interviewer's sentiments.[14]

The authors further report that bias through overidentification occurs because we have traditionally tended to overemphasize the problem of "rapport," mistaking it for "love." Interviewers have probably overstressed the value of rapport and should perhaps put a little more emphasis on a "business-like" detachment or something similar. While we can certainly agree with this important point, it may be that in some situations the respondent may simply not respond to a very detached interviewer. But we have no idea of what the distribution of types of respondents would be like if we were to ask the question as how many demand "love," how many "require detachment," how many prefer "hostility"? Hyman *et al.* conclude this section with an interesting and, in my opinion, correct view when they say:

The third case history of an interview and related material from the interviewers again suggest some modification of the usual view. Some degree of sociability on the part of the interviewer is obviously needed. Some degree of rapport is obviously called for. But there needs to be some clarification of dimensions and types of rapport and of desirable forms of sociability. Sociability that is predicated on intrusiveness may increase the orientation of the respondent to the interviewer, to the point where bias is more likely.[15]

Though they do not mention it, they imply that both interviewers and respondents can be viewed as social types and that they treat each other as such. Thus, though certain subjects and some observers can control the imputations attached to others, they cannot always control their actions or suspend the relevance of the imputations for the purpose of the brief encounter. We find that continuous situational imputations, strategies, and the like occur which influence how actors treat each other and manage their presence before each other. Now, these are precisely the conditions found in everyday life. Yet these problematic conditions remain virtually unexplored empirically by sociologists. Various novels, plays, literary criticism, and works such as those by Goffman constitute some of the limited sources the sociologists can use for material relevant to these issues. All of the evidence, including that presented by Hyman *et al.,* underlines the problematic and variable character of the interview and everyday social exchanges.

To repeat, then, comparability is not possible in the sense of the classical experiment of exposing the same conditions to the same sample of subjects in identical fashion with complete controls. But with a theory of social process, by knowing what to expect and recording what actually happened we can at least control the situation more. What is needed is a more elaborate and precise theory, one which indicates the general social types to be found in society, the typical kinds of imputations made, and the kinds of interpretive "rules" employed for managing one's presence before others.

◆§ *Role Prescriptions and Interviewer Role Conceptions in Relation to Interviewer Effects*

The problems involved in meeting the role prescriptions set down by the study itself are not easy to solve. Hyman *et al.* indicate, for example, that many times it is not difficult to fall into some interview pattern almost automatically; too much stress often has been placed on ". . . the *'natural'* processes within the interviewer which presumably operate to cause bias." [16] The "natural" bias, of course, stems from the difficulty of avoiding the kinds of typical face-to-face encounters and relationships one experiences in everyday life. It is here that the problem becomes both interesting and susceptible to more analytical procedures. In Chapter II we distinguish between common-sense and scientific rationalities of action and how either ideal is impossible to maintain in everyday life, especially the use of scientific rationalities. The following comments by the authors are based upon excellent material on problems of role prescriptions and bias by showing the problems one of their experienced interviewers encountered while listening to an electrical transcription of a completed interview, and illustrates the problem of using scientific rationalities. He was asked to put himself in the role of the other interviewer and to record the answers on the questionnaire used. On the basis of this kind of material Hyman *et al.* note:

Yet the maintenance of the prescribed role is not always easy. The intensive interviews indicate that at times conflict is felt between the requirement as set down by the agency and what the interviewer feels is a legitimate deviation required to meet certain problems. Bias then occurs not out of ignorance, but because the interviewer decides he *has to* flout the rule. Thus, M, the very interviewer quoted above as accepting the prescribed role, remarks on a hidden crime while conducting an interview with a foreign person:

"I felt qualified to paraphrase with strictest faithfulness to the sense. I realize that this is indefensible so will make no attempt to defend it. Yet, I feel in doing as I did that I performed conscientiously as an interviewer in a public opinion survey." [17]

The next quotation then pinpoints the problem of how

scientific rationalities become entangled with the common-sense conceptions of the interviewer.

The case studies thus not only reveal the importance of the role *prescribed* for the interviewer by the agency in inhibiting natural biasing tendencies; they also reveal the importance of situational pressures in shattering the normal role with consequent bias. And what is suggested is that as such a role is shattered, the interviewer is forced into certain types of biasing behavior as a "task aid," as a means of coping with the problem.

Beyond this, they reveal the importance of *idiosyncratic* definitions of the role of the interviewer in producing bias. While the role is *prescribed by the agency* and usually maintained by various enforcement measures or by the interviewer's sheer acceptance of it on the basis of knowledge of the agency's demands, there may well be conflict with other definitions of the role proceeding from a variety of sources. For example, the interviewer may have views as to what other interviewers or his immediate field supervisor or particular respondents regard as proper interviewing behavior. While we have no evidence as to such direct *social* influences on the definition of the role, we do have considerable evidence that the definition may often proceed from certain *beliefs* the interviewer has as to the nature of attitudes, the nature of respondent behavior, or the quality of the survey procedures, although there is the possibility that they may also provide *gratification* for the various needs.[18]

The authors give additional material which documents the point neatly, showing in each case how much leeway there is for the interviewer, who, like the person in everyday life, tends to employ whatever undocumented conceptions and thoughts come to mind. The material is striking for the way it demonstrates the cogency of Schutz' theoretical propositions on the need to understand the structure of communication in everyday life. The material also shows that one could not possibly specify the literal moves, thoughts, utterances, and the like of the interviewer and respondent or any two actors. In addition to behavior not specified by formal roles and statuses, the situational determinants of a social world of ever changing meanings continually structure the problematic character of interaction. Canons of research demand that the interviewer operate somewhat like a computer with all the appearances of a fellow human being, but, so far as we know, persons in everyday life find it impossible either to present themselves as both or to receive presentations of others (regardless of the form it takes) which conform to the strict canons of scientific inquiry. To quote Hyman *et al.:*

What is clear is that the differing roles that interviewers define for themselves with respect to probing, rapport building, recording, etc., will account in part for differences in the results they obtain. It is also clear that there could be fruitful inquiry into the interviewer's *general* view of his job to determine the variability in the definitions given by interviewers. The interviewer has to engage in a *variety* of behaviors during an interview and while the role may be prescribed in certain respects, there may well even be aspects of his performance for which no definitions at all have been established by the agency, and other aspects where the prescription is ambiguous. Where there is no comprehensive standardized definition in the first place, it is only natural for interviewers to vary.[19]

The authors, however, then propose that better training or field instructions be developed to improve the interviewing and standardize definitions or to provide for more explicit definitions. Interviewers would then know more precisely the subtle details and variability which everyday interaction can take, in other words, to establish a knowledge of role-taking as social process.

But the authors' point of view should be extended. For example, interviewing can be one way in which social process is studied, especially in laboratory situations. Further, every field study should always include features which would allow basic theory on social process to be tested simultaneously with the conduct of the substantive research. It is doubtful if the interviewer can be trained to utilize literally the principles of social process in interviewing, for this would mean programing him like a computer. The program would ideally incorporate all of our knowledge about social process, and also anticipate all possible actions in every situational context where role prescriptions are not explicit. But in the final analysis, any attempt to do this would have to transform the interviewer into the living embodiment of a computer, in other words, it would necessitate a complete rationalization of the actor. But we want an interviewer who would be completely flexible with respect to mood, affect, appearance, etc., in his presentation of self as an interviewer; all of this while obtaining the standardized information required from a standardized schedule in a way which takes all idiosyncratic, situational, and problematic features into account. If the interviewer were like a robot with built-in speaking and tape-recording equipment, this would insure standardization and insure the researcher that standardized stimuli are being presented to the subject, but it would not allow any flexibility in the presentation of self.

It is obvious that more precise theoretical concepts and detailed knowledge about basic social process would enable us to understand how the interviewer alters the data collected in the interview and how he might cope with respondent effects. But the interviewer cannot suspend completely his own personal presentation of self, whatever other equipment enables him to manage his presence before others. The interviewer who is so versatile that he can gain "identical" rapport, maintain "identical" social distance and detachment, "identical" interest in the subject, and so on so as to satisfy the assumptions of standardization which will enable the researcher to employ measurement procedures literally can only be a constructed type, a model of the ideal interviewer.

The experienced interviewers described by Hyman *et al.* reflect this basic dilemma of the scientist interacting with his data at close range in a situational context. Hyman *et al.* continually recognize that "The interviewer as a member of society has some framework of role expectancies built into him." [20] The problem is having a theory that will enable the researcher to decide how much of what is "built-in" can be ruled out during an interview and how much of this "ruling out" affects the data obtained. The authors are aware that too much stress has been placed on asking questions and recording answers, and that the interviewer is overlooking ". . . the many judgments *he made* in the process." [21] But how do we avoid these biased judgments? Can they be transformed into scientific rationalities of action? The assumption is that better training and more detailed and standardized schedules can "correct" these biases. Thus, when Hyman *et al.* state that they seek a ". . . fruitful theory about the mechanisms underlying bias, the barriers to bias, and the correlates of bias . . ." they are seeking systematic ways of training interviewers who will not employ common-sense rationalities of action. The authors also worry about a lack of rapport, "noninvolvement," apathy, egocentrism, violent hostility, cynicism, or general detachment on the part of respondents from the interview even though detachment often leads to a reduction or absence of some form of bias and as such viewed as a "good thing." But, on the other hand, it is also viewed as "not a good thing" from the standpoint of "long-term public support of the *institutions* of interviewing, survey research, and democratic decision-making, or from the point of view of the seriousness of the sentiments expressed in surveys. It is not a good thing in terms of the value-systems of human beings." [22] Good personal relations are necessary for continued positive public relations and support and the maintenance of a viable democracy.

The implication is that persons in everyday life *should be* "rational," "responsible," "interested" citizens and, like our interviewer, they should not succumb to the vicissitudes of built-in common-sense ways (mechanisms underlying bias) of relating to each other. Thus, the routine features of everyday life are "problems" because they constitute obstacles to "good interviewing." This kind of formulation tends to demand that both interviewer and respondent avoid mechanisms which produce bias in everyday social exchanges. But if the respondent's and interviewer's "natural" or "normal" orientation to their environments is based upon such "mechanisms underlying bias," then the "ideal" interview would distort the responses elicited. I am assuming that scientific detachment in social science field situations is relative to the definition of the situation imposed by the actors. The study of such difficulties tells us something about both the structure of everyday life and the problems of scientific inquiry. The detachment that can be achieved resides in the ability to know what happens when field research is done. We may not be able to standardize every question and every set of responses, but we can know biases which do not interfere with the interview and are unavoidable, and employ biases which facilitate the flow of information and communication so long as we are aware of their use and effects and thereby have some control over them by knowing how to correct them later.

The following illustration from Hyman *et al.* reports material on the "cognitive bias" (notions about the nature of attitudes) on the part of interviewers.

Thus, among those interviewers who preferred precoded questions, 25 per cent gave as their reason, "respondents aren't articulate enough, don't make answers consistent, can't back up their opinions." Among those who preferred free-answer questions, 35 per cent claimed that "this comes closer to what people really think and it gets at people's real feelings" and an additional 18 per cent gave the clearly related reason, "The respondent feels freer and gets a better chance to express himself." [23]

The experienced interviewers are telling us that respondents' opinions have common-sense features. This is like saying that the interviewer seldom encounters a respondent who is always interested, explicit, and logical about the questionnaire and his responses and that questions which were not open-ended are not likely to reveal the subject's "real feelings." The interviewers described by Hyman *et al.* take a great deal for granted, they abandon scientific rules and substitute stereotypes, employ everyday role prescriptions and expectations, attempt to "educate" the informant, feel like staying and chatting with the respondent, and engage in a host of other common-sense activities. Their interest in subjects, their sympathy for them, their annoyance at the respondent's ignorance or lack of concern about issues, all demonstrate the relevance of common-sense rationalities for the way experienced interviewers conduct their work. Any disagreement with Hyman *et al.*, then, is not with their excellent data or many of their general interpretations of them, but with their remedies for "correcting" the situation. Such "corrections" presuppose a theory which specifies the actor's categories for interpreting his environment and the scientists' categories for evaluating the same social scene. When the interviewer is engaged in activity requiring the use of both common-sense and scientific rationalities, a basic incompatibility occurs which cannot be resolved without altering scientific rules of procedure. Hyman *et al.* lack a theory which acknowledges this basic discrepancy. If there is no theory which states that the actor's perception of the world has vague, ambiguous, retrospective-prospective, occasional features, then expressions by respondents and interviewers having these features will be treated as "error" or "inadequate." Hyman *et al.* document this time and time again when they refer to the respondent or interviewer as "undemocratic," "biased," "apathetic," and so on. The problem is never viewed as an unavoidable dilemma of field research.

✍§ *Another Approach to Interviewing*

Turning to Kahn and Cannell's *Dynamics of Interviewing,* we find an approach to interviewing different from that of Hyman *et al.* and a more explicit concern with basic theory. Their approach is rooted in cognitive theories of psychology, which, although similar to the "phenomenological" position claimed by Hyman *et al.,* tends to present a clinical view of the actor. Thus, while their position is compatible with that of Hyman *et al.,* their way of characterizing interviewing differs. They employ a useful dichotomy between rational and emotional forces for explaining the motivation of behavior. A brief vignette is provided to characterize a situation in which a hypothetical subject's behavior conforms to the rational model. In objecting to the use of a rational model to explain human behavior they state:

This inadequacy is inherent in the concept of the rational man, and is revealed most clearly in the attempts of users of this concept to explain "irrational" behavior, behavior which appears contradictory to the individual's manifest and stated goals. Such behavior was explained on the grounds that it stemmed from inadequate information, that the individual was occasionally under misapprehension about the actions which would contribute to his self-interest. The process by which a man decided whether to buy this or that was a simple sifting and weighing of economic alternatives on a rational basis, and if his choice was economically "incorrect," it was only because he had his facts wrong. In such an explanation, the complexity of motive patterns, the conflicts among a person's various goals, are largely ignored. Most important of all, perhaps, emotional factors, unrecognized needs and drives, and interpersonal influences are omitted from the conceptual scheme of the rational man.[24]

Kahn and Cannell do not employ the definition of the situation as consisting of common-sense rules of conduct to explain the motivated character of social action. Behavior, rather than being motivated by the culturally defined meanings attached to objects and events in the course of interaction, is a function of attitudes, motives, drives, needs, and the psychological perception of the environment. There is no clear statement about the role of sociocultural factors. The basic explanatory variables are located *within* the personality of the actor. The position I have taken differs in that the explanatory variables are located in the actor's social scene.

The difference in the approaches taken by Hyman *et al.,* Kahn and Cannell, and the position taken here, lies in the ways our respective actors are constructed. Neither Hyman *et al.* nor Kahn and Cannell makes the "rules" or "norms" of everyday life the critical feature. The present approach assigns "causal" status to such "rules." This means, operationally, that the researcher's manipulation of the environment would alter the actor's definition of the situation. Concepts like attitudes and emotional forces are assigned causal status by Hyman *et al.* and Kahn and Cannell, while "rules" and cultural meanings are treated as self-evident elements of social interaction.

The material presented by Hyman *et al.* is rich in the subtle details uncovered in the reinterviews with experienced interviewers. They have used a variant of the phenomenological method in a loose but effective way to extract the inner workings of the interview. They do not begin with a theoretical framework, but have employed a direct empirical procedure to infer the nature of social process. Kahn and Cannell, rather than seeking to discover the elements of a theory of interviewing, begin with a theory of behavior and seek to show how the interview is merely a special case covered by the theory.

The works by Hyman *et al.* and Kahn and Cannell are excellent examples of two complementary approaches to problems of interviewing and field research. We can build on their work by showing the relevance—more precisely, the necessary character —of common-sense rationalities of action for understanding basic social process and hence consider the interview as one variant of interaction in everyday life. This requires that we first clarify the implicit theory in Hyman *et al.* and the more explicit theoretical position of Kahn and Cannell. Our basic objectives continue to be: (1) to show the theoretical presuppositions inherent in research methods, and (2) to indicate how basic social theory is tested and enhanced by methodological interests.

✥§ *Interviewing as a Theory of Interaction*

The material presented by Hyman *et al.* is not organized in a form readily amenable to theoretical systematization or clarification. The quotations cited earlier, however, reveal the general nature of their theoretical position. They refer to supporting literature, primarily from social psychologists like Icheiser, Asch, Krech and Crutchfield, and Frenkel-Brunswik to show how general theoretical notions from social psychology can explain what they found of their experienced interviewers. For example, they shed light on how individuals tend to seek organized and meaningful perceptions of their environment and how they develop and use stereotypes and expectations which persist in spite of observable contradictions. The theoretical references are not offered as hypotheses to be tested but as explanations of problems discovered in the reinterviews of experienced interviewers about their work. Some of the propositions they cite from the literature are as follows:

1. Thus, Icheiser has stressed the frequency of the belief, the "tendency to overestimate the unity of personality," in accounting for misunderstandings between people. He also suggests that the operation of such a belief might well influence the behavior not only of the perceiver but also of the other person, in our case, the respondent. He suggests that there is a "tendency of other people, whether consciously or unconsciously, to anticipate and to adjust their behavior in some degree to the expectations and images we hold in our minds about their personalities."

2. Many psychologists have stressed the universal tendency of humans to organize and make meaningful their perceptions. For example, Bartlett talked of an "effort after meaning" and Asch showed experimentally how fundamental it is to develop an organized, unified impression of others from only discrete bits of information.

3. Psychologists might conceive of the role-expectational process as an illustration of the more fundamental law that perception of a part is determined by the properties of the whole in which it is contained. Thus Krech and Crutchfield in an application of this principle to the perception of individuals state, " . . . when an individual is apprehended as a member of a group, the perception of each of those characteristics of the individual which correspond to the characteristics of the group is affected by his group membership." Sociologists argue for a fundamental character to such expectations, in seeing regularities

of behavior corresponding to group memberships, and expectancies about the behavior of persons in given positions or groups, as part of social reality, almost as a precondition for society. The interviewer as a member of society has some framework of role expectancies built into him.[25]

The statements by Hyman *et al.* and the literature they cite on the nature of basic social process in the interview can be read as a set of propositions on how the interviewer and respondent are faced with the same features that confront all persons in social interaction. These propositions support the view that the interview will always contain variable meaning structures which influence all social interaction, even when one party (the interviewer) or the other party (the respondent) is trained (or has trained himself) to manage his presence before others carefully so as to avoid the kinds of bias and damaging effects which are so strikingly demonstrated by Hyman *et al.* Thus, no matter how much stress is placed on training and standardized schedules, the material Hyman *et al.* present is convincing in its demonstration of the presence of meaning structures anchored in idiosyncratic, situational, and differential cultural attachments and definitions. The routinization of such meaning structures would make interviewing procedures sterile and devoid of the very characteristics which make it part of, and a basic source of data on, social interaction and communication in everyday life.

Kahn and Cannell, using a different set of variables, come to a similar conclusion in the following:

1. Human behavior is directed toward goals.
2. As the need or desire of an individual is linked to a specific goal which he sees as a means of satisfying the need, there are generated in him specific forces to move toward that goal.
3. This combination·of need within the individual and perceived goal is what we shall call a *motive*.
4. Behavior takes place only after an individual sees a path leading to a goal that he is motivated to attain.
5. There is often more than one path apparent to the individual that represents some degree of goal attainment for him.
6. Several paths available to the individual may differ in the extent to which they will satisfy his goals.
7. Which one of the several possible paths an individual selects will depend on the amount or degree of goal attainment that each appears to offer (see principle 6 above), and also upon the

difficulties or barriers that the individual perceives in traversing a given path.

8. Perceptions are individual; that is, people see things differently, and what a person sees depends in part upon himself, his personality and his past experience.

9. Individual differences in perception can be understood largely in terms of the psychological field of the individual, and especially in terms of his needs and goals.

10. When we perceive an object or situation, we must somehow relate it to things already in our experience. Each new situation must be understood in terms of our past experience, even if in so doing we fail to apprehend the full complexity and meaning of a new situation. The process of perception involves the systematic modification and distortion of a situation, in ways which make it more understandable to us and more congruent with our experience and expectations.

11. Whenever a person's psychological field is such that motivating forces act on him in opposite directions, he experiences feelings of tension. Such feelings are unpleasant, and generate specific motivation to resolve the indecision and relieve the tension.[26]

The importance of the above 11 principles for interviewing is pinpointed in the following passage:

If the interview is a product of interaction, what becomes of the conveniently simple notion that the ideal interview is something that springs from the soul of the respondent to the notebook of the interviewer without encountering any contaminating influences en route? And what becomes of the corollary notion that any vestige of interviewer influence in the interview process constitutes bias and must be avoided at all costs? The answer to these questions is that they represent a concept of the interview and the respondent and interviewer roles that is rejected by the interactional analysis we have just made. That concept places primary emphasis on the interviewer's negative function, that of not influencing what the respondent says. What we propose to emphasize in the interviewer's role is the importance of controlling and directing the process of interaction between himself and his respondent in such a way that the basic objectives of the interview are met.[27]

While Hyman *et al.* provide us with evidence which strikingly demonstrates interviewing's basic dilemma between reliability and validity, Kahn and Cannell present material which acknowledges the inherent character of the discrepancy. Acknowledgment of this dilemma means seeking "successful" interviews in spite of known limitations and distortions. The theoretical

insights and practical recipes for establishing a "successful" relationship with a respondent, maintaining it so as to sustain communications and obtain particular kinds of information, and
finally leaving the scene intact so as to allow for the possibility
of return, underline the basic requirements for achieving an
understanding of the nature of stable social relationships and
thereby stable social order. Personnel departments in complex
organizations; professional persons such as lawyers, physicians,
social workers, psychologists; public agencies such as police, pro-
bation, child welfare; and finally research persons such as market
researchers, survey researchers, and university professors and
deans, all use the interview procedure, showing that it has become a routine procedure in everyday life. The study of interviewing *per se* by the social scientist provides another means of
understanding social order and social organization. The material
presented in Hyman *et al.* and Kahn and Cannell, especially the
verbatim interviews included in the latter volume, shows the differences between professional and nonprofessional interviewers
in seeking information from respondents. These differences underline how impossible it is for the interviewer to program his
questions, his self-role, and general relations with the respondent.
The "natural" or unavoidable problems summarized in the
following statements are basic to the interview and routine exchanges in everyday life:

1. The nature of responses generally depends on the trust
developed early in the relationship, status differences, differential
perception and interpretation placed on questions and responses,
the control exercised by the interviewer, and so forth. The validity of the schedule becomes a variable condition within and
between interviews.

2. Checking out responses for consistency and depth may
lead to uneasiness and avoidance patterns on the part of the
respondent. Provided that "checking out" or probing responses
is minimal or avoided when seen to be disrupting the interview,
the conversation can proceed through contradictory phases and
neither party may be aware of this or one party may be accom-
modating the other so as to maintain a "polite" relationship.

3. Both the respondent and the interviewer will invariably
hold meanings in reserve; much remains unstated even though
the interviewer may pursue a point explicitly. Direct confronta-

tions with issues on which material is withheld can be embarrassing to both respondent and interviewer even though the interviewer may have better control over the course of the interview.

4. The interview represents interaction in which meanings remain problematic even though it is intended, with full knowledge on both sides, to clarify meanings, intentions, and possible courses of action on the part of the respondent. The goals of the researcher are often subservient to the demands of polite discourse.

5. The basis for achieving meanings, knowledge, even when the basis or the kinds of meanings and knowledge are technical, relies continually on common-sense devices for making sense of the environment. The interviewer cannot possibly check out his own responses in detail and follow the testing of an hypothesis during the interview; he is forced to make snap judgments, extended inferences, reveal his views, overlook material, and the like, and may be able to show how they were made or even why they were made only after the fact. The interviewer cannot escape from the difficulties of everyday life interpretations and actions. The common-sense "rules" compromise literal hypothesis testing, but they are necessary conditions for eliciting the desired information.

ᘓᔓ *Interviewing and Measurement*

If the interview produces information which is lacking in reliability and validity, because the information is modified by common-sense rules of interpretation, in spite of efforts to train interviewers to behave "pleasantly" and to simulate "adequate" social relationships, then the measurement imposed will have to reflect the differential imputations that contribute to the nature of the data obtained. If we treat each interview as a sequence of acts which does not conform to scientific rules of conduct, then we can conceive of each interviewer as a generator of a set of common-sense events which has modified many rational features of detached scientific research. The interview, as a set of acts for testing specific hypotheses about substantive matters, strains conventional measurement devices because the measurement technique forces us to assume "identical" interviews with "identical" questions and responses. Every interview (regardless of whether it has standardized or unstructured questions) requires coding which assumes identicality or equivalence classes among widely differing acts, interpreted questions and responses. Each set of utterances is a time object and cannot be equated with another set of utterances in answer to the same question unless it can be shown or assumed that the same or similar conditions accompanied each event.

What are the conditions that would permit the construction of equivalence classes? Answering this question necessitates a discussion of "ideal" interviewing conditions as well as some theoretical knowledge to facilitate the use of conventional measurement devices.

Consider the requirements of the "ideal" interviewer necessary to meet the technical demands of the research. Extensive interviewing is hard work. The nature of the respondent, as an object of study, cannot be taken for granted. His every move and gesture can have some "meaning" in the interview situation, and the interviewer's every act has to be managed carefully. The attempt to minimize bias through training procedures assumes that our knowledge of basic social process is sufficiently detailed that the interview schedule can be programed precisely. But programing the interviewer with respect to the management of interpersonal transactions presupposes more knowledge than we now possess. It is impossible to anticipate all possible contingencies, much less expect the interviewer to contend with them adequately on each occasion. The best that can be hoped for is a schedule based on an extensive theory of social process such that the widest range of contingencies can be anticipated and known to the interviewer. The use of a tape recorder to tape interviews would facilitate the accumulation of a precise record of the exigencies which arise in them. Extensive training may produce competent interviewers, but it is impossible always to elicit the cooperation and trust of the respondent. The impression we must avoid is that all factors producing error can be eliminated. Bias in interviewing when translated into a set of variables provides data for testing a more general theory of social interaction. Consider the following suggestions:

1. Assume that the interview is being recorded electronically. The interviewer is provided with a pad for making notations

during the interview about his feelings toward the subject, whether he feels the response (each time) is "adequate" or "inadequate," is understood by the subject, and whether he feels impelled to "correct" or "help" the respondent.

2. Each question asked in the interview itself is presumably designed to test specific hypotheses. Expected responses are predicted for each type of respondent the researcher assumes will be encountered. The predicted responses should be sufficiently precise to permit a demonstration of exact correspondence with the respondent's answers as well as how the actual responses can vary and still be considered "acceptable."

3. The validity of each response assumes variable status depending upon the interferences recorded by the equipment and the interviewer and identified by the researcher. The respondent's perspective must be inferred from his responses but must also correspond to the researcher's theoretical expectations on how particular social types will respond to different questions.

4. To guard against overlooking differential perception and interpretation of questions by the respondent, the opening questions should be broad characterizations of the intended interest of the researcher. This allows for the respondent's definition of the situation to occur before committing him to specific meanings via fixed items of which he may not be aware. This insures that the subject is not making choices or decisions about questions or subjects he does not fully understand, merely to satisfy the interviewer and "successfully" end the interview.

5. Satisfied that the respondent "knows" what is being asked of him, the interviewer may proceed to ask him questions that both restrict the frame of possibilities and allow for the exact choice the subject is expected to make. The procedure of handing him the alternative possibilities one at a time so as not to reveal how many choices exist works well here and lessens the possibility of guesswork on the part of the respondent.

6. The electronic recording of the interview would free the interviewer for taking notes on all the extraneous features of the exchange. He can also be provided with a checklist on changes in role prescriptions and proscriptions, rapport, detachment, and so forth, which follows the schedule thereby permitting him to keep a "natural history" of the biases and errors that intrude throughout the interviews.

7. The "natural history" made possible by the use of electronic equipment approximates a sequential analysis of the material because the researcher can decide how both the extraneous influences and the inherent problems of theory and formulation interfered with the intent and outcome of the interview.

8. Each item, and the responses associated with it, should be linked directly with the set of variables that can undermine the identicality of the data to be tabulated for analysis. The temporal structure of meanings can be examined more precisely and the literal testing of hypotheses approximated.

The brief description above suggests that experimental designs could pinpoint more precisely the general problems of interviewing and facilitate the elimination of avoidable bias and error, while providing a framework to measure the influence of bias and error which are built-in features of the interview. For example, these procedures might be followed:

The interviewer and subject face each other separated by a two-way mirror, each having a desk microphone before him that feeds into separate tape recorders. The experimenter observes the interview and controls the exchange from a third room. Ceiling microphones in each room provide for general communication between subject and interviewer.

The interviewer and respondent are told that after each question and each answer the lights will be dimmed and some time given to "thought" about the question or response. During the "thought" period the experimenter can switch off one ceiling microphone and turn on the desk equipment. This permits him to ask independently both the interviewer and respondent their conceptions about the question or answer.

This experimental procedure breaks down each item of the schedule so that the experimenter can identify each step in the "natural history" of the interview. This permits him to estimate the initial "getting acquainted" period, its impact on the ways in which questions are asked by the interviewer and answered by the respondent. This amounts to an operational device for treating the interview as a time object subject to moment-by-moment interpretations and redefinition.

The experimental procedure would complement the field situation by enabling the researcher to anticipate bias and error more precisely. It would reveal which intrusions are avoidable and which are "necessary" for the exchange to continue. In short, it would indicate the way each participant stereotypes the other, and the bearing of this process upon the perception and interpretation of the questions and answers.

Separating the actor's stock of knowledge at hand from the meaning structures which emerge in the course of interaction enables the researcher to differentiate between the interviewer's research role and his private thoughts and feelings; between the subject's role in the interview and his unstated observations; between the researcher's use of common-sense categories to interpret the experimental scene and his use of an explicit theoretical framework for coding his observations. Although some of the elements operating in the interview can be adequately separated and studied experimentally, we will continue to rely upon common-sense knowledge and everyday language for negotiating our field studies.

I V

FIXED-CHOICE

QUESTIONNAIRES

SOME ADVOCATES OF THE INTERVIEW often point out that the questionnaire with fixed-choice response categories precludes the possibility of obtaining unanticipated definitions of the situation which reveal the subject's private thoughts and feelings. While fixed-choice alternatives may be adequate and necessary for obtaining factual data, seeking information on social process by this means may force the subject to provide precise responses to events and issues about which he may be ignorant or vague. Fixed-choice alternatives may preclude obtaining meaningful information on social process if the interactional context is restricted by questions asked. This chapter will discuss the following:

1. Do fixed-choice questions become "grids" through which our understanding of social process is distorted? The attaining of what kinds of information would be precluded by this method?

2. What would we have to know about language, cultural meanings, and the structure of social action to construct a successful questionnaire with fixed-choice answers?

3. What is the role of theory in coding and scaling fixed-choice responses? Our task will be to ask how the survey with fixed-choice questions achieves solutions to substantive research problems in spite of the lack of knowledge about basic theoretical issues which are presupposed in all field research.

⇜§   Social Process and Fixed-Choice Questionnaires

There are many sources in the literature which show considerable consensus on how one goes about conducting a survey
using fixed-choice questionnaires. The technical details do not
differ significantly, nor do the formal descriptions of what should
be done. Most likely to differ are the various unofficial ways in
which surveys are actually conducted. Information on day-to-day
problems in this kind of research is seldom available because the
unofficial practices are "buried" in the files of researchers, or in
unpublished reports because space did not permit publication of
such procedures. A list of variations from ideal procedures is im-
practical to compose and would probably dwarf the substantive
results and discussion. Yet a general account, omitting the details, of how a survey is conducted obscures the subtle inferences
and decisions required in each stage of the research. The evils of
data-reduction and the general problem of large-scale surveys
are reviewed cogently by Hyman:

Thus, it is the case that the survey analyst *marshals his associates to
act as informants* and to report to him on the subtle flavoring of the
data and to communicate unique concrete but strategic observations to
him. And this has led to the development of *interviewer report forms*
on which the human situation within which the data were collected
is described systematically for the analyst's benefit, to *interviewer's*
ratings of the respondent or to *"thumbnail sketches"* of the respondent
which are second hand but nevertheless evaluations of the respondent
based on someone's direct observation, to *coder "flagging"* or noting
of particular responses for the analyst's attention which convey
the character of a response subsumed under some more abstract
classification.

Thus it is the case that the analyst makes up for the inevitable
segmental character of the mass of processed data by *supplementary
classification and analytic procedures which convey the structural
or molar features of the phenomena.* The segmentalization is introduced in the course of the coding of total interviews, by *typological or
multidimensional classification* of respondents, and by *index-construc-
tion* or pooling of data from a series of related answers into a more
comprehensive description of the respondents.

There is the realization that the standardization of inquiry in
large-scale survey research, while making for efficiency and necessary to
insure comparability among field workers, at the same time may impose

some artificiality on the phenomenon studied, particularly when the analyst engages in a *series of prior planning procedures to insure that the standardized procedure will nevertheless be adapted to the natural frame of reference of most of the subjects under study*. This had led to such procedures as the *pilot or exploratory study*, prior to a major inquiry, the use of *pre-testing* of the questionnaire instrument, *community background inquiry and quasi-ethnological inquiry* in conjunction with a survey in order to formulate the inquiry in terms most meaningful to respondents.[1]

Hyman's remarks provide an explicit indication of the difficulties of conducting a large survey with a large staff and simultaneously incorporating divergent field settings that lead to variance in the data. The need for "thumbnail sketches," "flagging," etc., indicates how the survey has been confounded N times by unspecified assumptions, theoretical views, hunches and the like, of interviewers, supervisors, coders, observers, data analysts, and principal investigator. But can we assume that the interviewers, ethnological "scouts," coders, data analysts, and the director of social science research are all employing the same theoretical frame of reference and interpreting each event, respondent, etc., identically, that is, using the same meaning structures in different contexts with the same interpretive rules?

Hyman's account of the preliminary activities of a survey shows that a careful study builds on the advantages of participant observation, unstructured interviews with wide exploratory goals, pretesting via structured interviews, running accounts of interviewer-respondent interaction, and so forth. The field reports inform the researcher about the intrusions which can be expected to enter the final survey as well as provide an account of difficulties which influenced the actual collection of data. The preliminary material not only provides a basis for structuring the final schedule but also informs the tabulated results in much the same way that participant observation and open-ended interviews lead to after-the-fact interpretations and reinterpretations. There is an important difference here. In participant observation, and to a lesser degree in the unstructured interview situation, observers spend more time familiarizing themselves with the subjects under study. More time can be devoted to the subtleties of meaning used by the subjects. The survey researcher uses his field contacts as a basis for generating fixed-choice questions, but their meaning requires the background information gathered under less rigorous conditions. The rigor of the survey is diluted considerably by its reliance upon unstated "general knowledge" about the group studied, particularly about how the subjects perceive and interpret meanings in their daily activities. My answer to the question at the end of the last paragraph is "No" because I assume that the survey researcher views the various meaning structures as self-evident and merely to be taken as "given" and used instrumentally as background material when he engages in his preliminary forays. The actual analysis of tabulated data, therefore, is dependent upon implicit theoretical and substantive knowledge obtained under considerably less rigorous circumstances than that knowledge evident in the elegant tables presented. Background information provides the "sense" to survey data because contained therein are the common-sense meanings the researcher employed to construct the questions, the interviewers used to decide their adequacy during the interview, and which permitted the subjects to interpret their meaning, respectively. The meaning of questions with fixed-choice answers, like the punched holes on the IBM card, is dependent upon interpretive rules that make up a theory not subject to the same kind of programing. Accordingly, the survey researcher using fixed-choice questions cannot escape the same problems facing the participant observer and interviewer: he must develop a model which incorporates the language and cultural meanings inherent in (1) the actor's perspective in daily life, (2) the interviewer's perspective, and (3) the "rules" for translating these meanings into basic and substantive theory.

But how does this effect the objectives of the study, for example, the attempt to keep the "natural frame of reference of the subjects" intact? How is the problem of meaning handled? Standardized questions with fixed-choice answers provide a solution to the problem of meaning by simply avoiding it. A familiar solution takes cultural meanings to be self-evident in social research by relating the characteristics of different types of responses to "inner" attitudinal states of the actor. This provides an empirical solution to the problem of meaning; the empirical regularities are said to correspond to some set of hypothetical "inner" states, and this line of reasoning becomes a neat justification for using standardized questions with fixed-choices. If the responses are sufficiently clustered, if they "break," "split," etc., and there are few "no responses" or "don't knows," then some correspondence between "inner" states (read: attitude structures, personality types, drives, motives, anxiety states) and actual response patterns is claimed to have been established. Postulating inner states which are to correspond with "manifest" or observable responses permits a two-way stretch; if the predicted clusters do not "manifest" themselves, then one can start all over again by realigning the conceptual hypothetical inner states with the empirical clusters. Various statistical or methodological devices such as exhaustive cross-tabulation and collapsing of tables are helpful here.

It is sometimes difficult to know which came first, a theoretical framework that specified hypothetical inner states which have external patterns, or whether the empirical regularities of manifest data led to the notion of inner states. But regardless of the initial direction of this reasoning, it can be made defensible. Hyman, for example, defends the use of surveys to establish the motives for social action by indicating what the ideal survey should do and the kinds of rules that exist for telling the researcher and reader when he is "wrong" and when he is "right." The obvious procedure consists of establishing in advance both the conceptual structure of inner states and the manifest clusters which should then appear in the survey such that the correspondence is public and clear.

A strong argument can be made for eliminating much of interviewer bias by the introduction of fixed-choice questionnaires. Standardized questions with a finite number of choices that are self-administered give the appearance of objectivity and lend themselves to translation into numerical representations. But what are the ideal conditions? Consider the following:

1. Every subject's response pattern would have to be predictable on explicit theoretical grounds before the instrument could test hypotheses. Every question would have to be formulated according to specific theoretical interests, indicating what would be required to accept or reject the hypothesis associated with it.

2. Preliminary interviewing with open-ended questions and pretests would constitute trial runs which would help modify both theory and operational procedures because of the questions and answers obtained and their coding rules.

3. The elements of social process would have to be known in

sufficient detail to enable the researcher to use the questionnaire responses as "meter" readings of intricate social interaction and meaning structures which produced the responses.

4. The question and response would have to reflect the kinds of typicality that the actor uses to manage his daily world, be couched in the everyday language he is familiar with, and evoke replies which are not altered by the idiosyncracies of occasional expressions, particular relevance structures, a pretense of agreement, or the particular biographical circumstances of the respondent, unless such properties are variable conditions in the research design.

5. The various clock-time slices which make up the final distribution of respondents' answers must correspond with some set of identical intervals of the actors' experiences. More precisely, the various types of respondents (determined in advance by their response pattern in mock-up tables), conceived as equivalence classes (each type constitutes one class), would produce various responses to each question. Such a view presupposes identical ways of responding to the environments of objects projected by the questionnaire. The questionnaires presumably create a set of identical possible environments.

6. Each type of respondent would have to understand the meaning of the relevant questions identically, and somehow assign these meanings according to some existing common culture or "rules" shared by all but where the differential responses become indicative of different hypothetical inner states (and hence differential perception and interpretation of the same stimuli) which can exist in the same common culture. Stated another way, in these identical environments there are stimuli which communicate invariant meanings, for different equivalence classes of respondents, but in these identical environments the differential assignment of meanings is determined according to the actor's hypothetical inner states.

7. The observer's theory would have to include a subtheory of meaning structures, "rules" governing their use, and show how different types of actors (with different hypothetical inner states) are likely to interpret the questions. This assumes an invariant language structure which links the perception of the environment to inner states and corresponds precisely to meaning structures used by the actor for interpreting the symbolic forms which constitute the questionnaire. The content of the

message is invariant to the interpreter. The test of this assumption often consists of demonstrating to the reader that the respondents had no trouble filling out the questionnaire. To take this line of argument, the observer would have to show that the different types of respondents constitute equivalence classes with respect to their answers to the questions. This does not resolve the problem completely but does provide an operational test for the assumption that the content of each question is invariant to the respondent.

8. Fixed-choice questions supply the respondent with highly structured clues about their purpose and the answers expected. The "forced" character of the responses severely restricts the possibility that the actor's perception and interpretation of the items will be problematic.

9. A detailed and analytic knowledge of common-sense meanings as used in everyday life becomes fundamental for the construction of fixed-choice questionnaires, but this knowledge does not guarantee that the content of the questions is invariant to the interpreter. Textbooks on methods merely urge or state flatly that the wording of the questions must be "understandable" to the respondents and conform to their cultural or subcultural usage. But the textbooks and manuals say little about the structure of such everyday language and usage. The vocabulary used to tap the respondent's interpretations of different stimuli must be distinguished from the vocabulary employed by the social scientist for describing the actor's responses. Rules for translating the one into the other (and vice versa) are required. In order to predict the patterning in advance, some knowledge is required of how the hypothetical "inner states" of the respondent are linked to the way he decodes the meaning of the question (its content) and how he decides the appropriate fixed-choice response. But the actor's vocabulary, with its common-sense meaning structures, constitutes, in an important sense, a separate province of meaning from the hypothetical "inner states" of the actor. This would be the case if the content of the message were invariant to the interpreter.

Reference to hypothetical "inner states" obscures the relevance of differential socialization of subjects within a general common culture and how subjects' behavior is influenced by the unknown subcultural variability within the common culture. If in addition to subcultural variability we consider situational factors influencing the interpretation of events, then the variability is increased. But the content of the message is not invariant to the actor, to the variable meanings of the common culture and subcultures, and to variable definitions of situations unless there is one-to-one correspondence between meaning and proposition. These variations may be treated as "external" to the actor; at least they can be studied independently of conjectures about unobservable hypothetical "inner states" of individuals. Moreover, since in any case the "inner states" must be linked with external variations, why speak of them at all? Why refer to hypothetical constructs to account for something that can be described as beginning and ending in the observable world of everyday life? One answer often given is that the responses of fixed-choice questions can be linked to hypothetical "inner states" so that operationally the lack of a correspondence between meaning and proposition does not arise as a problem. Yet a key implicit assumption in the use of questionnaires is that the perceived content and meaning of the proposition presented is invariant to the respondent and can be ordered independently of hypothetical "inner states." Thus, variations in manifest content would be due not to semantic problems but to classes of "inner states." The researcher manipulates manifest responses by reference to a theory of attitudes (dispositions to act) to explain the regularities found in the manifest content. The net result is to ignore the relevance of social interaction in the researcher's model. Such a view forces us to reduce social behavior to hypothetical "internalized" norms and attitudes. A theory that allows the observer to decide the meaning of a proposition without reference to "inner states" avoids unnecessary reduction. Differential perception and interpretation could be a function of a set of variables located in the actor's environment of objects to be predicted and explained by changes in the social scene. Manipulation of the elements of the social scene produces corresponding changes in the actor's differential perception and interpretation. The actor brings to the situation his stock of knowledge and his evolving estimation of the appropriate "rules" called for over the course of a *changing scene*.[2] His hopes, fears, likes, dislikes, are not given prominent status in the explanation of general properties of social action but are viewed as significant for determining the substantive content of concrete acts. Stress is placed upon the invariant and variable conditions of the actor's definition and redefinition of an environment of objects during the course of social interaction. The correspondence between the hypothetical world inferred from questionnaire items and actual behavior of the actor remains an open empirical problem. Questionnaire items which seek to measure values, attitudes, norms, and the like tend to ignore the emergent, innovational and problematic character of everyday life by imposing a deterministic "grid" on it with its fixed-choice structure.

To recapitulate, the meaning of the set of propositions which constitutes a questionnaire assumes variable status for any sample of subjects unless the researcher adopts a theory of meaning and role-taking which corresponds to the mechanical or deterministic use of fixed-choice questionnaire items. I have argued that fixed-choice questionnaire items do not reflect *change* in the structure of social action in everyday life. The notion of underlying stable attitudes as determiners of social action avoids the use of concepts which indicate *change*. Instead, interpretive "rules" or norms, cultural meanings, and situational exigencies are viewed as stable or trivial by assigning them "self-evident" or residual status. Questionnaire items define social scenes in hypothetical terms which assume that both the meaning of the propositions and the differential responses are invariant to situational interpretations of "rules" and the actor's stock of knowledge at hand. In order for the researcher to understand how the fixed-choice questionnaire corresponds to the implicit theory of social action suggested in this book, the same procedures outlined at the conclusion of Chapter III for analyzing the interview would have to be devised. One would have to show the generally undisclosed variations which remain private to the respondent when he comes to interpret each item and actually makes his choices during the self-administration of the schedule. Otherwise the following theoretical position remains:

It is apparent . . . that the concept of attitude implies a consistency or predictability of responses. An attitude governs, or mediates, or predicts, or is evidenced by a variety of responses to some specified set of social objects or situations. Campbell (1950, p. 31) has summarized this view neatly in presenting an operational definition of attitude: *"An individual's social attitude is an [enduring] syndrome of response consistency with regard to [a set of] social objects."*

This definition does not divest attitudes of their affective and cognitive properties, which may be properties of, or correlates of, the responses that comprise the attitude. However, attention is focused on the characteristic of attitude that is basic to all attitude measurement: response covariation. In each measurement method, covariation among responses is related to the variation of an underlying variable. The latent attitude is defined by the correlations among responses.

The set of social objects that forms the reference class of an attitude distinguishes attitude from other psychological variables such as habit, temperament, drive, or intelligence. It is of secondary importance whether we call the variable an attitude, or a trait, or a habit. The operational definition will always be in terms of the referent class of stimuli.[3]

Thus, if the researcher is seeking a readily administered instrument which will insure him of quantifiable results, his model of the actor will be based upon the above theory of attitudes. The questionnaire items become "frozen" clock-time slices of hypothetically defined situations. The fixed-choice questionnaire provides standardized propositions (stimuli) , from the point of view of the researcher, but begs all of the relevant questions posed by language and meaning, treats the "rules" or norms as self-evident, and eliminates the problem of situational definitions by a static conception of role-taking. Questionnaire responses are like the punched holes of an IBM card; the meanings and rules for their creation and interpretation are not to be found in them *per se* or in aggregates of them, but rather in their differential perceptions and interpretations which produced the researcher's decision in composing them and the respondent's perception and interpretation of the action scene in answering them.

◄§ Comments by Critics and Users of Surveys

A look at some of the criticisms leveled against the survey should suggest something of its drawbacks. Hyman points to the innumerable sources of pressures, biases, and obstacles which can occur because of the organizational form of the survey, who sponsors it and supports it financially, and the problem of controversial subject matter.[4]

Hyman's book on survey design can be read as a set of intrusions which impinge upon survey researchers. He attempts to show that in spite of his agreement with many of the criticisms leveled against survey research, the method is useful and contributes significantly to our knowledge of human behavior. It could be argued that it is the researcher's faith in the method which insures its continual use rather than its demonstrated ability to predict and explain human behavior with the information it gathers. In fact, Hyman argues convincingly along these lines when he discusses the "cheater interviewer," the lack of communication, opposition from personnel, outside pressures to stress particular elements of the study, disagreement or total agreement among the research personnel, and the general organizational complex within which the research is organized,[5] implemented, and terminated, and his arguments and evidence to support them make it difficult to defend the use of large, costly surveys for testing hypotheses or exploring basic theory. Its most effective use might be in providing simple descriptive material of a non-threatening type from a large sample of individuals for some practical purpose.

Throughout the literature for and against survey and questionnaire methods, there are frequent references to the possibility that the data are the product of vague or loosely structured thinking on the part of respondents. Why not assume that the actor's thoughts about social objects are loosely structured but are perceived as concrete until we begin to probe them with specific questions that put him on the spot about matters which he takes for granted and to which he seldom gives much time? Survey research procedures do not assign variable status to ignorance, much less acknowledge it as a critical factor in the structure of social action.[6]

Krech criticizes surveys on the grounds that they are superficial and seldom ask theoretically meaningful questions and do not seek the "basic nature of the 'things' which all these interviewers, question-constructors and coders are presumably measuring, weighing, counting and reporting." [7] "The basic nature of 'things' is taken for granted by the survey researchers. This is often a function of the machinery necessary for conducting a survey, large or small. Choosing a problem motivates the selection of relevant questions that will "tap" the basic concepts. Some preliminary interviewing leads to a number of hunches and "feelings" about the nature of the "data" and the respondents. This material is then used, together with what is experienced and remembered by the researchers, as the basis for formulating questions of an open-ended or fixed-choice type. These questions are "pretested." Although changes are made on the basis of the results, they do not always lead to modifications in the original formulation of the problem. The questions are sharpened, and those which do not "split" adequately (according to the researcher's implicit criteria) are thrown out. The formulation of precoded questions requires theoretical precision, but the precision of a survey usually comes after the results are in and the researcher is faced with the task of deciding the significance of the cross-tabulations. The survey, then, is a progressively unfolding enterprise which assumes ever increasing precision after the determining assumptions have been incorporated into the initial formulation, that is, not until the coding is accomplished and the tables constructed.

By adopting concepts that represent factors "internal" to the actor, the survey provides a convenient device for obtaining material which supports the theory of attitudes as motivations to or as indicative of action by relying upon the empirical regularities whose procedures of assembly insure that the data will "behave" under appropriate manipulations. The actual procedures for framing questions remain unique to each survey, unless the strategies and coding rules are in correspondence with the properties of basic concepts.

◄§ *Theory, Coding, and Quantification*

Hyman notes the existence of standards, factors or principles of research, that are established by researchers and groups such as the Bureau of the Budget, the Standards Committee of the American Association for Public Opinion Research, and the like. The emphasis of such criteria, based on the collective experiences of survey researchers, is on the determination and avoidance of possible sources of error and the necessity of following particular procedures to insure comparability. The most difficult part of survey research, however, is omitted. I refer to the theoretical knowledge required even for making routine decisions, and to the theoretical commitments forced on the data by an arbitrary measurement system. The surveys reviewed by Hyman do not contain accounts of the moment-by-moment and day-by-day decisions which the analyst had to make in the course of conducting the survey. His is an important attempt to standardize the procedures involved in a survey, including the routine and often unnoticed errors and problems that can and do arise. A discussion of unstated conditions or rules governing social research omitted in Hyman's book is unavailable for the student interested in replication and literal hypothesis testing. The data and hypothetical situations Hyman discusses are already coded and abstracted from the actual rules and conditions on which they are based. Thus, some of the omitted crucial questions on the research process are: How does the observer decide to differentiate responses into various categories? How does he decide to assign numerals or numbers to some objects, while treating other responses as irrelevant? Chapters I and II revealed the critical importance of commonsense knowledge for making such decisions.

Hyman notes that the survey does not have any of the built-in features of controlled experiments or observations.

It is characterized by measurement conducted in a field setting at only *one point in time,* and does not routinely provide evidence on the time order of variables. Consequently, in particular instances, the inference as to causality from the empirical relationship must be safeguarded by special procedures.[8]

Hyman continues with the acute observation that the respondent ". . . symbolically creates or re-creates events thus locating the variables in the span of time rather than at the mere moment of measurement. As Vernon once put it: 'Words are actions in miniature' and thus the moment of measurement may compress within it a huge span of time." [9] This reference to the compression of time appears similar to the notion of experienced time described earlier. Hyman's usage, however, differs from my earlier comments. Hyman's solution to the temporal problem in relating variables is:

Merely on the basis of sheer *inspection,* the analyst can infer the time order. For example, there is no apparent difficulty in interpreting a survey-finding of a relationship between length of engagement and marital happiness. The first variable, *by definition,* preceded the second one in time. Even where the order is not absolutely clear by definition, the analyst, along with other reasonable men, can often make a safe guess. Consider the relationship between educational level and preference for different radio programs; it is almost sure that education precedes radio tastes. Consider the finding that persons on a low income level are less likely than those on a higher level to belong to formal organizations. Even though a few individuals may have lost their money after joining organizations by and large we can assume that present economic status is acquired prior to organizational affiliations. Similar assumptions can be made in studies which, for example, relate fairly permanent personality traits to performance in school or on the job.[10]

Hyman's statement suggests several points. One is that he has not clearly distinguishd between clock-time and time as constitutive of experience. The "huge span of time" quoted above apparently refers to clock-time not the actor's conception of time. Although the actor utilizes clock-time for orienting his actions, his experience with objects and events is not isomorphic with clock-time. Survey findings are invariably *after the fact* correlations or relationships, and the analyst must spend much of his time deciding what it all "means." He invokes some theory upon which he decides the time sequence of the variables and this, in turn, structures how relationships should be interpreted. The actor's experience of time is determined *after the fact* by the observer's procedures. According to the rule of observation the researcher should have a theoretical position which enables him to show how such correlations can be specified in advance of collecting and coding the data. If all events in daily life and the actor's orientation to them have their particular temporal structure, then quantitification of them includes unexplicated abstractions derived implicitly from a theory of social process, or established *ex post facto* by correlating attitudinal responses with a number of "face-sheet" characteristics included in the questionnaire. Theories in sociology assume that a person's "class" position, his "religion," "political" beliefs, and his "associational" activities influence his everyday behavior. But some question or set of questions which is intended to measure such concepts "operationally," and the persons' responses to the questions, are not always to be taken as literal representatives of the impact of these "variables" or conditions on the actors' everyday practiced and enforced conceptions about the world they live in, come to terms with, and alter. We have become accustomed to characterizing segments of life or properties of persons as if they were unidimensional variables that can be translated into continua which can be expanded or contracted (for measurement purposes), depending upon how well the responses "split" on a questionnaire. But the question is whether and to what degree these "structural" variables (e.g., occupation, income, education) influence the actor's everyday behavior. In other words, do such arbitrary or "natural" organizational (e.g., elementary school, high school, college) temporal breakdowns correlate significantly with attitudinal or other variables? Bennett Berger [11] shows concern with this question when he recommends that age be defined as a cultural variable not a structural one. This would alter the purely quantitative determination of age so that the structure of its properties is seen as problematic, requiring more explicit conceptualization and empirical study.

These structural data are usually assembled and described with the use of common-sense meanings. By assuming that structural or attitudinal variables are automatically quantifiable, we have forced concepts to take on the appearance of precision so they can be sliced into dichotomies, trichotomies, ordinal ranks, intervals, and metric distances. But the concept is not *per se* quantitative; it becomes so only when placed in some theoretical framework which explicitly generates meaningful dichotomies, trichotomies, ordinal relationships, intervals which are assumed to be equal, and distances which have metricized features. The notion "variable" can mean a nonadditive collection of elements which characterize some feature of the actor's culturally defined world. The "variable" would not constitute a unitary, differentiable continuum or even a dichotomy, necessarily, unless specifically called for and justified by the theory. Any understanding of coding operations, as they relate to the structuring of questionnaires and interview schedules, must take into account what is supplied by the common-sense knowledge of the world we share with the respondent, our sociological theory, and what is imposed by the measurement devices.

The two- or multivalued (dichotomy, trichotomy, etc.) system assumes that the elements which differentiate categories and the decisions which lead to placement of coded responses into one cell or type as opposed to another cell or type are identifiable, unambiguous, and discrete.

Coding under two- or multivalued logic or one of its logical derivatives, (e.g., set theory, real number system) automatically assumes an axiomatic base for the structure of social process. Yet we usually begin our surveys by initially imposing a form of arbitrary modality such as "very great," "fairly great," and "slightly great," or five-point breakdowns of "strongly agree," "moderately agree," "neutral," "moderately disagree," "strongly disagree." If the actor's experience of his world corresponds with general modal breakdowns, while the researcher has imposed a measurement framework which assumes an axiomatic base but avoids the logical structure of such modal experiences, then we cannot test hypotheses literally. The solution adopted can be recommended only by fiat.

Sociologists who place quantification of findings ahead of literal hypothesis testing recommend fixed-choice questionnaires because this method insures quantified results. Arbitrary coding rules and scaling devices transform the structure of social action into quantifiable elements because such procedures arbitrarily fuse common-sense knowledge and modal judgments with logical or statistical operations. Once imposed such coding rules and scaling devices act as a filter to obscure how the researcher's implicit common-sense knowledge enters the decision-making process identified as "scientific rules of procedure," while simultaneously transforming the actor's responses.

If some form of fixed-choice questionnaire items are ever to serve as useful operational definitions of sociological concepts, they will have to be constructed in such a way that the structure of everyday life experience and conduct is reflected in them. We must be able to demonstrate a correspondence between the structure of social action (cultural meanings, their assignment in situational contexts, the role-taking process) and the items intended as operational definitions thereof. Unless this correspondence is achieved, our findings will reflect our inadequate methods and not generate theoretically defensible propositions.

V

THE DEMOGRAPHIC

METHOD

DESCRIPTIVE ACCOUNTS of the number of births, deaths, movements of persons from one geographical location to another, by age, sex, etc., have been useful to sociologists for studying social organization and the comparative structure of societies. Such data are usually viewed as basic social facts which stand by themselves. This chapter comments on the logical and theoretical status of primary population processes (for example, the descriptive counts of births, deaths, geographical movements by age and sex, etc.) particularly when they are linked to social processes which produce or account for differential fertility, migration, mobility, illegitimacy, and the like. Distributions of these vital processes and movements, by age and sex (and other categories), can be viewed as ways of describing properties of such social structures as dyads (e.g., parents in a nuclear family), collectivities (e.g., smokers versus nonsmokers, users of contraceptives versus nonusers, high-income versus low-income families), organizations (families considered as units, hospitals), communities, regions, states or provinces, nations, etc. The demographer may direct his attention to some distribution or set of distributions of counts to make inferences about the biological and social forces which could have produced them. Predictions are attempted by projecting conclusions from some given set of data. There are a few demographers who ask for increased theoretical knowledge [1] as a means of bettering our demographic predictions, and those who do advocate such improvements are most likely to be sociologists interested in using demographic data for testing sociological theories. Two common notions often implied in the study of population are that demography is a separate discipline and that the available factual data are inherently meaningful. These notions suggest the phrase "the demographic method." Many demographers and ecologists would probably deny the relevance and validity of social process for the understanding of social structure. Such researchers usually avoid the study of social process by simply denying its relevance. They may be characterized as "archeologists by choice" of contemporary society because they deny the relevance of cultural decisions which contribute to the ecological structure of social organization. Archeologists, on the other hand, are anxious to obtain data on cultural decisions. One statement of this noncultural view is contained in a recent paper by O. D. Duncan and L. Schnore.[2] They argue that the ecological perspective (which for them would include population analysis) is best suited for the study of social organization as they conceive of it. The basic difference between Duncan and Schnore's perspective of social organization and that of "behavioral" and "cultural" sociologists lies in their denial of the relevance of culturally defined and group shared ideologies, values, and norms. Thus, in stating that "communities with differing economic bases are expected to evidence differing rates of growth and hence differential opportunities for social mobility," the authors would deny the relevance of policy decisions made by individuals in a group context, the importance of individual and group shared ideological and value commitments, political exigencies, and the like. Duncan and Schnore believe that behavioral and cultural perspectives are corrupted by what they deem to be a blanket "commitment" to "subjective elements," individual motivations, and "cultural traits." They erroneously assume that all "behavioral" and "cultural" sociologists are committed to Homans'[3] psychological reductionism, and that only the ecologist is interested in understanding the behavior of aggregates. Finally, Duncan and Schnore accept the fact that the "ecological" approach "borrows presuppositions about cultural continuity and the diffusibility of culture patterns," but they would deny the relevance of cultural meanings—

including those the actor has about his environment and how such meanings influence his actions particularly in determining where he builds cities, how he builds them, and so on—although such meanings are differentially distributed and continually defined, redefined over time in different cultures and within different sectors of pluralistic societies. The necessity of various forms and contents of human communication for the emergence, maintenance, and alteration of social structures is irrelevant for the demographer-ecologist. This chapter will neither make further comments about nor cite references to demographers and ecologists like Duncan and Schnore. Critical remarks about the sociological demographers given below assume agreement with their interest in acknowledging and integrating behavioral and cultural variables with demographic and ecological ones; my intention is to seek more explicit consideration and discussion of social process in demographic studies of social structure which presuppose notions of social action.

The thesis that sociological theories about social process are presupposed in explaining differential descriptive counts contained in demographic data is shown with clarity in a recent text by William Petersen.[4] The following quotations are intended to indicate the relevance of theory for a sociologist who uses demographic data. Subsequent comments are intended to underline and extend the relevance of such theoretical propositions. Propositions about population linked to the basic social processes as conceived of in earlier chapters should lead to more precise tests and expand our knowledge of social and cultural forces that produce and influence population distributions. The following example illustrates the connection between family size and cultural conceptions:

The "new look" in family size, like any other change in style, has spread in part simply by contagion. But it has also been motivated by the deepest aspirations of the American middle class. With a certain exaggeration, the United States can be termed the country of upward mobility. The behavior patterns of the typical American, to the extent that such a person exists, can probably be best defined in terms of the hopes and expectations excited by the "American promise" of a happier life. In the past middle-class parents regarded it as their duty to offer the maximum advantages to a very small number of children; and this value was certainly an important reason for the spread of the small-family system. Today, however, the psychologists' dictum that the single child is more likely to be neurotic has been spread through women's magazines to become a commonplace of middle-class lore. Whether it is true or not is beside the point; the theory, even if spurious, has been widely enough accepted to affect present attitudes and behavior, as the Indianapolis study indicated. If one has children at all, one must—for their sake—have at least two, and preferably three. The fact that the new trend in family size has been based on a re-interpretation of the parents' duty, rather than on an attempt to reject it, indicates a greater likelihood of permanence.[5]

Petersen has stressed a number of factors, some of which imply rather complex social processes that research has not as yet documented but appear quite plausible. The general implication is that there exist culturally defined conceptions which orient people's social action. If the new trend in family size has a like-lihood of permanence, then the statistical manipulations possible with new demographic data are of limited usefulness in testing Petersen's hypotheses unless we have independent data for particular families on the nature of cultural definitions of the "happy life," "deepest aspirations," optimum number of children, and the like. To obtain such knowledge requires that we understand the temporal structure of these cultural conceptions, the conditions motivating prescribed modes of conduct, and the variations likely to take place. In short, this kind of information is needed to explore the extent to which the notions mentioned by Petersen can be useful for basic empirical research and predictions on a short-run or long-run basis. But there is implied in Petersen's view, and particularly in the implicit broader theoretical assumptions of many demographers, that family size is the product of the rationalization of society in Weber's sense, that is, "the transformation of an uncontrollable and unintelligible world into an organization which we can understand and therefore master, and in the framework of which prediction becomes possible."[6] This assumption of rationality requires theoretical and empirical clarification. Its present status in population studies is not always clear. I shall elaborate this point throughout the remainder of this chapter and make it the central notion around which I discuss theoretical presuppositions of demography.

Knowledge about the common-sense properties presupposed in the sociological concepts employed by Petersen would extend the observer's analytic precision about family life and size and about the actor's conception of them. The following quotation indicates further theoretical arguments on the notion of family size.

The small family of the recent past was, one might say, built into the small apartment, which made an additional child an expensive and bothersome undertaking. During the postwar period, it will be recalled, many middle-class families have moved to the suburbs, which combine urban amenities with a style of life that invites, almost demands, children. Hardly anyone rents a house in the suburbs; and home ownership, which increased by half between 1940 and 1950, has always been associated with large or middle-sized families. It may be less meaningful than it once was to speak of the family's loss of function, for in the suburban setting the home is apparently becoming the focus of a significant family life. If the wife works, as she often does, it is not as a rule in order to establish a career independent of her role as wife and mother, but in order to supplement her husband's salary or wage. If the man is usually away at work during the day, he spends evening and weekends with his family; the do-it-yourself craze that has spread through American suburbia is a way of bringing the continuous extension and decoration of homes under the heading of "fun." Parents no longer educate their children directly, but they are enormously concerned with finding a "good school" or trying to establish one through a Parent-Teacher Association. When details of this kind are added up, the sum is a milieu in which a childless couple feels out of place.[7]

Although some sociologists may question some of the specific points made by Petersen, few would question the general importance of the *kind* of sociological variables he has underlined. The form of everything he has said is in line with current research and theory in sociology. How these factors actually influence family size, however, judging from Petersen's coverage of the literature, has not been studied extensively by demographers or sociologists interested in population problems. Petersen's remarks, in contrast to many demographers, suggest the importance of studying the social bases of fertility and family size and the culturally patterned factors in other demographic and population distributions. The following quotation pinpoints this emphasis and serves as a basis for a consideration of Weber's notion of the rationalization of society:

The institutional setting that the three-child family now has suggests that—if the general social and economic conditions remain more or less the same—a relatively high fertility is likely to be a fairly stable element of American Life. This does not mean, of course, that it will be. It means that potential parents' decisions on whether to have children are determined not only by their "selfish" desire for "comfort" but also by "pride in progeny." Now that birth control is all but universal, it is the relation between these that principally determines the size of the family—and the accuracy of population projections.[8]

The comments by Petersen suggest that the cultural factors of "selfish" desire for "comfort" and "pride in progeny" are, "if the general social and economic conditions remain more or less the same," the basic sociological variables requiring study. One possible interpretation of Petersen's remarks is to view family size as the consequence of a set of problematic decisions to have children, decisions arrived at by common-sense rationalities. The very ways in which such decisions *are made* are vague, highly situational, and sub-culturally variable. But the demographer often refers to the abstract process of the rationalization of society, implying that the actor possesses a perspective oriented to making decisions governed by ever increasing rationality. From the actor's point of view, his world is intelligible and controllable and knowledge of this point of view provides the social scientist with a basis for predicting the future course of the actor's conduct with respect to family size and fertility. Petersen, however, does not view desire for "comfort" and "pride in progeny" as rational decisions, even though he explicitly refers to the rationalization of society.

The upshot of this discussion is to point out the attribution of rationality to the actor which the concept of the rationalization of society implies. The implication is that the progressive rationalization of society, manifested by increasingly bureaucratized institutions and patterns of thought, influences the actor in everyday life in much the same way as a scientist is influenced by following scientific rules of procedure. The argument makes good sense up to a point. But how do we know when rational features or common-sense rules of conduct apply to family planning? This may be a subtle distinction to most demographers but one which is crucial for their argument. Even granting the implicit assumption that all families, at least in the United States and the westernized portions of the world, in general, will become similar and will employ identifiable strategies for planning their family, the theory as outlined above does not provide for the difference between "rational" procedures on the one hand, and "common sense" or "traditional" procedures on the other. Hence the "accidental" cases of births reported in the recent study by Freedman, Whelpton, and Campbell [9] might easily be treated as trivial unless theory is clarified. These accidental cases amounted to about 25 per cent of those families using contraceptives.[10] The same table reveals 24 per cent "other unplanned" pregnancies after use of contraceptives began. These are large numbers by any standards. Yet they are not treated as important. The accidental cases are not treated as an integral feature of planning families. The authors stress the higher number of "planned" pregnancies among the college educated women. The stress on "rationality" in family planning among the educated obscures the fact that half of their sample had *unplanned* children *after* use of contraceptives began. By not questioning the "rationality" of the actor's attitudes and background characteristics, the authors overlook the influence of "un-rational" features of their data for all levels of educated women. But the problem cannot be avoided, for without an explicit notion of rationality the data remain obscure. For as matters now stand, we must honor an ambiguous notion of rationality. Petersen, for example, notes:

It is necessary to look for causes, thus, not so much in the living conditions in cities as in the ideas and aspirations associated with the urban population. The greater rationality (in Max Weber's sense of the word) of town life presumably induced a larger and larger proportion of the population to weigh the advantages and disadvantages to be derived from each child and to adjust the size of the family accordingly. In the 1930's almost every demographer thought in terms of such a stylized picture of Rational Man and believed that the downward trend in fertility would continue. Once it became general to adjust family size according to the loss in money and convenience incurred from having children, many couples, perhaps eventually most, would have none at all.

In the post war decade, however, there has been a wholly unexpected revival of births. In general, this has been most marked among the social classes that previously had shown the greatest decline.

Much of the baby boom was the reflection of the new family-building habits of young women. In 1950 their median age at marriage was 20 years—or a year and a half younger than in 1940.[11]

The material quoted above alludes to several forms of rationality. "Selfish" desire for "comfort" versus "pride in progeny" are conceived as alternatives arrived at by deliberate choices, but strict rationality in the choosing process is not implied. This suggests that the rationality of the decision is relative to the end it is intended to achieve. For example, the "good of society," the prospective child, the present "comforts" of the couple, future aspirations, etc. Petersen's remarks can be extended to relate specifically the theoretical propositions about common-sense ways of making decisions, to the actor's conceptions of "comfort" and "pride" with respect to living standards and children.

According to the argument of this book the demographer's or sociology student's conceptions of population should include the notion that conscious, deliberate, "rational" thought about family size is limited by many common-sense features of everyday life which include such things pointed out by Petersen as, for example, community conditions in which a childless couple feels "out of place," or a "feeling" on the part of the wife that four children "would be nice." The notion of "rational" arguing by a "well-educated" husband with a "well-educated" wife as a major determinant of family size remains unclear. The rationality of available techniques for limiting family size does not mean that even the most highly educated and most economically well-off families i.e., the families which *other things being equal* might be most "rational," will behave in accordance with the rationality inherent in the use of contraceptive techniques. Compare this with the account given by Notestein:

1. The high level of births of the 'forties has definitely postponed the date at which maximum populations could be anticipated in any realistic terms. It is much less clear that the birth boom will have added very much to the population that otherwise might have been expected by the end of the century. . . .

2. In this type of population (the United States, western Europe), in which there is a large measure of rational control of fertility, the annual increments to the population are likely to be irregularly distributed through time because childbearing is sensitive to the swings of the political, social, and economic climates. Such swings produce

irregularities in the age distribution that bring complicated problems of social-economic adjustment.[12]

Notestein appears to attribute rational control to fertility but then states that "childbearing is sensitive to the swings of the political, social, and economic climates." Presumably it is individual families, or, more precisely, individual actors, who are sensitive to political, social, and economic situations. The demographer, even if sociologically inclined, likes to point out that he is interested in the behavior of aggregates. Yet the explanations contained in Petersen's and Notestein's remarks mean that distributions of births, deaths, migrations and the like require explicit and implicit references to social forces and the decisions of actors which are not easily measured. Simple classification requires theoretical justification. Notestein for example, alludes to social forces and the decisions of actors when he describes "Regions of Transitional Growth" or "Regions of High Growth Potential." [13] For the former he refers to how the "processes of modernization have already begun to reduce fertility and mortality," and how the "agrarian family, and the attitudes toward childbearing that accompany it, are still important, but are being modified by the encroachment of an increasingly urban and secularly minded community." [14] For the latter notion of high growth potential, he notes "the birth rates are very high and sufficiently resistant to change to guarantee rapid and sustained population growth any time it becomes possible to achieve something less than extremely high mortality" [15] Further, "If large amounts of capital were available and would be used for development, the regions could carry much larger populations than they do at present, and provide much higher levels of living than exist today. . . . Moreover, development would cut the death rate long before the slower processes of social reorientation would begin to put pressures on the birth rate." [16]

The kinds of statements given by Notestein and other demographers assume many complex variables requiring theoretical clarification before literal measurement can be achieved. Distributions of births, deaths, and number of migrants can be cross-tabulated by age, sex, occupation, nationality, race, marital status, income, and so on, but the difficult to measure and often slighted complex social processes, either implied or explicitly referred to by the demographer, are nevertheless invoked as the explanatory variables. The generalizations generated presuppose more basic social processes about which we know very little. For example, Notestein remarks:

> The most difficult problems are those in the fields of social science and social engineering. They are the inter-related processes of social, economic, and political change which come to a focus in the problems of population growth. These problems of change should lie at the heart of the social disciplines. Unfortunately, the social sciences, including demography, have little to contribute. We know very little of the processes of change, and are not trying very hard to learn. Yet, it is on the more adequate knowledge of the processes of change in demographic, social, economic, and political fields that the chances for sustained advances in health and material welfare of half the human race may well depend.[17]

Demographers do not seriously consult theories of basic social process: how persons perceive and interpret their environments so that cultural definitions continually alter the meanings placed upon even the most clear-cut and unambiguous matters. There is change in meaning derived even from "sound" medical and scientific knowledge, or from the most "obvious" social, economic, and political conditions which should convince people to have or not to have more children; to eat or not to eat certain foods and live longer; to learn to recognize certain "signs" and seek medical care earlier; to realize political situations and act accordingly; to reorganize economic conditions and avoid migration to a new area; to acquire knowledge about occupations which need more personnel and then make the necessary switch; and so on. In seeking a rational set of conditions in his data, the demographer, even when recognizing that cultural patterns shape the progressive rationalization of society, continually imputes rationality to his actor even while simultaneously stating the importance of highly problematic social, economic, and political factors. Obviously a clarification is required which would show the extent to which the rationalization of society, urbanization, and secular ways of thinking are transformations of strict rationality in the scientific sense. This entails showing how cultural definitions and action patterns based on common-sense conceptions of kinship, primary relations, religious beliefs, health, the "good life," and so on, alter strict rationality. By continually referring to such complex cultural factors the demographer apparently thinks he has gone as far as he should go and that no further consideration of them is necessary. This is because cultural variables are not subject to the same quantification as births, deaths and migration events. The demographer avoids the further study of variables he cites as cultural because they are difficult to study and compromise his concern for "hard" data. There is also a tendency to confuse policy and "good" planning with an enforced and practiced social order. This is evident in the demographer's interest in optimum population and "population problems." Demographic "facts" are seen as more objective because their empirical representations are more readily available than data at the level of everyday social process. This is not to deny the influence of biological and physical factors, but to recognize that cultural conceptions whose measurement properties remain unknown are a necessary feature of the distributions demographers seek to explain and predict. The assumption, often denied, is that such cultural definitions and rules of conduct at the level of social interaction can be understood with rational procedures and definitions which will show how they correspond to demographic distributions. Sociologists are interested in studying how the rationalization of society destroys or alters traditional structures of everyday life. Demographers assume that the effects of rationalization are known and that "optimal" population balance can be achieved rationally. Both the sociologist and the demographer presuppose that notions like rationality and rationalization are conceptually clear and measureable.

The notion that family size is a function of the rationalization of everyday life has led demographers like Notestein to imply that something like a "rational" man will gradually stabilize his own behavior and thereby stabilize the population distribution in western and westernized lands. Petersen has stressed the influence of more common-sense notions like "comfort" and "pride in progeny"; both of these notions are intended as cultural variables. A theory which considers anything, whatever it may be, as "rational" about family planning, however, must give variable status to the notion of rationality. This does not mean that rational choice does not exist in everyday life. Schutz explicitly states that "rationality" in everyday life clearly exists and consists primarily of a concern for "clearness and distinctness" when they are consistent with the actor's practical interest and circumstances.

> This does not mean that rational choice does not exist within the sphere of everyday life. Indeed it would be sufficient to interpret the terms clearness and distinctness in a modified and restricted meaning, namely, as clearness and distinctness adequate to the requirements of the actor's practical interest. . . . What I wish to emphasize is that the ideal of rationality is not and cannot be a peculiar feature of everyday thought nor can it therefore be a methodological principle of the interpretation of human sets in daily life.[18]

Garfinkel, in an article based on Schutz' work, notes that the researcher cannot treat scientific rationalities as corresponding to the actor's rules for interpreting events in everyday life but only as ideals for governing his own activities as a social scientist.[19] Garfinkel inventories the various rational properties of conduct and the conditions under which rational behavior of different types occurs in social systems. The following summary of his more elaborate remarks briefly indicates some of the various circumstances under which the actor might be said to be acting "rationally." (a) The actor's categorization and comparison of experiences and objects. (b) The actor's use of means that worked in previous situations for achieving solutions to present ones. (c) The actor's analysis of various alternatives and the consequences that might follow different courses of action. (d) The actor's concern with the expectations that should follow his or others' scheduling of events. (e) The actor's attempt to establish some rules that will enable him to predict future situations and reduce the element of surprise. (f) The fact that the actor allows himself some possibility of choice and entertains various grounds upon which some choice is made.[20]

The import of Garfinkel's comments is that the sociologist must establish a model of the actor which permits him to decide both the theoretical *and* the empirical properties of the rationalities of action. He argues that the strictly scientific rationalities cannot be followed in everyday life because they would create anomic or senseless conditions in the actor's interaction with others.[21] The problem in the study of demographic data, as in sociology in general, is to construct a model which will distinguish the researcher's rationalities as a scientific observer, the common-sense meanings used by organizations and agency personnel for interpreting and classifying events into categories, and the actor's interpretive rules for making sense of his environment. The problem of rationality in population analysis is considered further in the following discussion of urbanism and urbanization.

Petersen notes the difficulties of distinguishing between urbanism and urbanization. He suggests that ". . . *urbanism,* the culture of cities, is the way of life of city dwellers; *urbanization* is the process of city formation, or the state of being a city. The correlation between the two, which once could be assumed, must now be a subject of empirical investigation." [22] Urbanism is contrasted with some opposite ideal type like "folk society," following Redfield. Redfield, among others, Petersen notes, has characterized the folk society as small, traditional, spontaneous, personal, and kinship oriented, to mention a few characteristics, while Wirth (who relies on Simmel) refers to urbanism as impersonal, competitive, formally controlled, superficial, transitory, and characterized by secondary relationships, to mention the general features. To quote Petersen again:

In a population analysis the most interesting element of the polarity is perhaps that discussed in detail by Weber in his contrast between traditionalist and rational. In his words, *Traditionalism* is "the belief in the everyday routine as an inviolable norm of conduct." "Domination that rests upon this basis, that is, upon piety for what actually, allegedly, or presumably has always existed," he termed "traditionalist authority." A *rational* pattern, on the other hand, denotes "the methodical attainment of a definitely given and practical end by means of an increasingly precise calculation of adequate means," or, on an abstract level, the "increasing theoretical mastery of reality by means of increasingly precise and abstract concepts." The rational sector of culture, in short, includes any area of social life in which a realizable end is consciously sought by nonmystical means. In Tylor's classical definition of culture, belief, art, morals, custom, and habits are mainly nonrational in Weber's sense. These have functions but not purposes; they are not adaptations consciously contrived in order to meet definite needs. Even "knowledge" and "capabilities," which can be taken as the rational elements in this definition of culture, are often also in part non-rational.[23]

Petersen correctly points to the "nonrational" features of culture as defined by Tylor. But a confusion is possible here, stemming from Petersen's characterization of rational sectors of culture as "any area of social life in which a realizable end is consciously sought by nonmystical means." The remarks by Schutz and Garfinkel on the properties of rationality are more precise and imply that much remains unspecified in the work of Weber. Petersen, of course, cannot be expected to present a lengthy analysis of rationality in a book on population. Viewing rational and "nonrational" or traditional action as a simple dichotomy is not adequate because some of the phenomena that would be included in the two alternatives are not sufficiently covered by either one of them. This is evident in Petersen's reference to "knowledge" and "capabilities" as "in part nonrational." The difficulty of using Weber's ideal types is best seen where Petersen notes that "the development of advanced civilizations from primitive societies has in large measure consisted in the extension of the area of rational action." [24]

I am arguing not that "advanced" civilizations do not or cannot be conceived as incorporating more rational action but that the lack of any clear-cut conceptual and empirical specification of what is meant precisely by rationality and traditionalism at different levels of analysis and sectors of society makes it difficult to show how "advanced" civilizations differ from or are in some respect the same as "primitive" societies. The following from Petersen assigns critical importance to a conception of rationality which appears to give it invariant content and structure: "In the modern West in particular, the calculated choice between alternative acts on the basis of their probable consequences is a usual behavior pattern. In technology and commerce, two broad areas of life whose rational element is strong in many cultures, Western man has reached the ultimate point—scientific method and bookkeeping. And, what is more important in this context, this view has spread from these institutions to others, such as childbearing, which in other cultures are typically regulated according to traditionalist norms." [25]

To define as "rational" a culture in which scientific technology is present raises the question of why persons of all levels of education who know the efficacy and availability of the technology do not automatically avail themselves of it and act "rationally." More important, the preceding illustrative material from sociological demographers is not explicit on how the rational view built into scientific method and bookkeeping "spreads from these institutions to others, such as childbearing, . . ." and influences parents to be "rational" in their use of contraceptives, in their analysis of how many children they should have, their future potential, and so on. The present critique somewhat exaggerates the emphasis on an undefined "rationality" if one recalls the above quotation from Petersen saying there exists a desire for "comfort" and "pride in progeny" or Notestein's statement on the importance of social, economic, and political "climates" on family size. I am not saying that a contradiction exists or that Petersen and Notestein are incorrect, but that their important comments reflect an unclarified set of theoretical presuppositions which should be specified. What we want to know —as surely Petersen and Notestein do—are the obstacles to and the influence of increased rationality on the traditional or common-sense thinking and actions in everyday life. A desire for "comfort" and "pride in progeny" as well as "social, economic, and political climates" as contingencies of everyday life, however, are not conditions which the actor meets with scientific rationalities. But Petersen and Notestein belong to a small group of social scientists using demographic data who acknowledge the relevance of the actor's rationalities and cultural variables.

Most demographic views about man have stressed his increasingly rational technology. And although rationality is linked to increasing urbanism, industrialization, rational bookkeeping, bureaucratized management of organizations, and a technology governed by scientific method, few demographers would acknowledge the relevance of studies of complex organizations which reveal the "informal" or unofficial structure and ideologies as most critical for understanding how decisions are made. Demographers and ecologists are seldom interested in showing empirically how different ideologically folk or rural life is from urban life and the influence of ideologies on the actor's everyday decisions.

Sociologists point to the importance of family, primary groups, and the mass media in everyday decisions. Studies contrasting "primitive" and urban decision-making in everyday life, however, are unavailable, and existing case studies are seldom comparable. Few studies have gone beyond a polarized ideal-type analysis. The assumptions that there is an overlap of traditional and scientific rationalities of action and that situational contingencies by type of actor are important require empirical study. Even though there is a lack of a concern for explicit theory in demography, the availability of demographic data, regardless of its drawbacks, has been an important influence in sociological studies. The problem has been compounded because both general sociologists and demography oriented sociologists have made little effort to extend and operationalize Weber's truncated discussion of traditional authority and to formulate a more detailed specification of rationality. These concepts have retained their ideal-type status and have been limited in their application to abstract formulations about industrialization, urbanism, migration, family size, and the like. The availability of demographic data has served only to impede conceptual clarification. The use of polarized ideal types and ecological correlations [26] obscures analysis of the elements subsumed under them and limits the possible range of combination of these elements, thereby impeding the specification of the properties of these types so as to show their interaction and combination. Without a theory to tell us or guide us, the polar opposites e.g., rational-irrational, folk-urban, stand by fiat and the possibility of "mixtures" in set theory terms does not arise. The large number of accidental births shown in studies of family size can be read as revealing the persistent intrusion or "survival" of traditional cultural definitions about planning families. The data reveal differences in the availability of better medical facilities, welfare programs, and knowledge about when to obtain medical care. Studies of the "attitudes" of parents on family size often assume that "rationality" prevails and this structures the kinds of questions asked. Such studies do not measure the social processes within which "rational" or common-sense decisions are made. Rather than cross-tabulate family size with income, education, occupation, religion, and the like, it might be more meaningful to ask how families exposed to scientific training and procedures, as opposed to families not so exposed, conceive of family life in general? And specifically, do they give careful consideration to the desired number or spacing of children? Do they make estimates of their future income and how carefully? How careful are they in using contraceptive methods and devices? In short, what kinds of rationalities are employed in decisions about family size, migration, occupational changes?

⇜§   *The Life Table as a Model of Social Order*

·In this final section I wish to show the usefulness of demographic techniques by describing one in particular, the life table, and attempting to indicate how the theoretical suppositions assumed in its use can be clarified so that it may be better applied in sociological research. Let us begin with George W. Barclay's description of the life table:

The life table is a life history of a hypothetical group, or *cohort,* of people, as it is diminished gradually by deaths. The record begins at the birth of each member, and continues until all have died. The cohort loses a predetermined proportion at each age, and thus represents a situation that is artificially contrived. This is done by means of a few simplifying assumptions, which may be described as follows:

a. The cohort is "closed" against migration in or out. Hence there are no changes in membership except the losses due to death.

b. People die at each age according to a schedule that is fixed in advance and does not change.

c. The cohort orginates from some standard number of births (always set in a round figure like 1,000, 10,000, or 100,000) called the "radix" of the life table. This standardized aspect facilitates comparison between different life tables. Also the proportion surviving from birth to any given age is apparent from a glance at the table itself—for example, if 5420 members of a starting cohort of 10,000 survived at age 35, it means that exactly 54.2 per cent reached that age.

d. At each age (excepting the first few years of life), deaths are evenly distributed between one birthday and the next. That is to say, half the deaths expected between age 9 and age 10 occur by the time everyone reached age 9½. (The significance of this assumption will be seen somewhat later.)

The cohort normally contains members of only one sex. It is possible to construct a life table for both sexes together, but the differences between male and female mortality at most ages are sufficient to justify treating them separately.[27]

It will be seen that the life table can be conceived as a model for characterizing elements of social order. The rules governing conduct in this order can be stated fairly precisely. The model or ideal population can be used so as to derive probabilistic estimates of future time periods given certain specifiable conditions. This model has been applied to a variety of problems.[28] The life table is intended to show an ideal set of conditions whereby a given distribution is produced. The pivotal feature of the model revolves around the assumptions of how persons manage to "survive" each successive stage in some organization, marriage, chronological age, and the like. Like all models, it exaggerates certain conditions in the sense of an ideal experiment. The control comes from showing first how a given distribution is achieved step-wise over time if particular conditions are assumed. This permits predictions of future states according to specifiable assumptions and enables the researcher to compare his "programed" distribution with that achieved "naturally." By showing what *would* happen as opposed to what *will* happen if certain conditions hold, it is possible to identify some of the sources which contribute to variations, say, in mortality. But if we are to use the life table as a model for more precise predictions, more specific theoretical information is required. We must generate new distributions which would restrict the frame of possibilities such that actual cases could be examined to test the validity of the ideal model. The artificially contrived conditions producing the programed distribution could then be made to correspond to basic and substantive theory more precisely.

Demographers prefer to work with data they often know have drawbacks but with which they feel "at home." This is often the result of having easy access to information assembled by local, state, national, and international agencies which is already "packaged" in quantitative or quantifiable form. The data come from sources over which the demographers seldom have any control and their packaged character precludes breakdowns and assimilation of new information which would permit more theoretical alternatives. Careful study of the conditions which surround the construction of a given distribution is necessary if the data's value is to be estimated effectively. The drawbacks to such studies are due to distortions of records by common-sense conceptions of personnel who must record the raw data according to some set of rules. Each successive alteration further influences the final distribution. Without studies of such influences, the demographer must attempt secondhand determinations of the sources of error and attach some qualifications to the analysis and presentation of his data.

The rather sketchy remarks on the life table are intended to stress the importance of explicitly specifying theoretical assumptions in advance of using demographic data. The data suffer from organizational limitations; this has led to theorizing which is very abstract and only fits available data after the fact. But the theory is difficult to translate operationally except for obtaining gross measures which allow a variety of interpretations. These interpretations usually presuppose basic social processes. Unless the demographer seeks more elaborate theoretical frameworks which would explicitly indicate assumptions about social process, he can seldom know if other data are even available for confirming or discrediting his hypotheses.

The lack of theoretical specificity of most demographic explanations of descriptive counts has led to a lack of concern with —even deprecation of—social process. The discussions by demographers of an entire economy or society, of metropolitan areas, geographic regions, rural-urban populations, and so on, imply that such gross characterizations not only are the most "important" ones but are somehow independent of the social processes which may have contributed to their production. The tendency is to reify social structure. The implication is that vital statistics, census material, and data on migration are or can be treated as independent of basic social processes. But at least a few demographers explicitly refer to differences in "attitudes" toward fertility, the influence of social, economic, and political "climates," the so-called "push-pull" factors in migration, the influence of "occupational strain" on mortality, and the resistance of "cultural factors" to technological innovations. These latter are demographically oriented sociologists, and they are in the minority among demographers. Demographers often assume cultural influences but these cultural variables are not explicitly linked to nor considered relevant for demographic "facts"; the implication remains that it is the "hard facts" which are more important. The understanding of why and how persons go about their daily life, which produces what are recorded as "demographic facts," requires an appreciation of how everyday common-sense meanings are normatively governed. Analysis of demographic data requires knowledge of how these meanings are fused with recording procedures to produce the regularities we label the "social structures." An extreme example of my point which does not deny many important uses of vital statistics would be to view age and sex as "achieved" statuses that require the specification of those conditions under which persons are treated as "male" or "young" or "homosexual" by the imputations of others, how they conceive of themselves and manage their presence before each other. The demographer may rightfully take age and sex (and color as identified by registration offices, hospitals, censuses) as givens, but there may be occasions when the sociologist may wish to know the conditions under which persons feel they or others are "too old" to migrate, enter a particular occupation, become a "mother" again, and so on. My point is that measures of such characteristics for sociological purposes may not take the form supplied by vital statistics information or census bureau material. The quantitative representations supplied by the agencies who produce such distributions do not correspond necessarily to the sociologist's criteria for achieving literal measurement.

The demographic method consists of techniques for translating precoded information into findings which have the appearance of rigor, quantification, and literal hypothesis testing. Even if distributions of births, deaths, marriages, migrations, and the like were almost perfect representations of actual events, the sociological use of demographic data should remain limited to interpreting them via its own theories of process and structure, and restricting the frame of possibilities such that more elaborate and theoretically derived hypotheses could be tested with independent data collected by the researcher's methods. The distributions themselves assume relevance within the context of the everyday and organizational terms under which they were assembled, and the sociologist must often be prepared to study these everyday and organizational conditions. The sociological use of such data may depend upon independent theoretical derivations and additional data based upon a more complete examination of the decisions which entered into the initial construction of the official information. Independent data, based upon sociologically relevant concepts, would seek elements of social process presupposed in the differential distribution of births, deaths, marriages, divorces, migrations, and so forth. Techniques such as the life table are valuable aids in forcing the researcher to make his assumptions explicit and to push beyond the limitations of precoded demographic data.

V I

HISTORICAL

MATERIALS AND

CONTENT ANALYSIS

HISTORICAL MATERIALS and content analysis are not field methods as is the gathering of data by actual participation, interviewing, questionnaires, censuses, and so forth. These methods usually refer to materials produced in the past and which are in many ways unique records and expressions of behavior that the sociologist seeks to reconstruct and/or analyze by means of some set of interpretive categories. The set of interpretive categories would presumably be based on a theory purporting to explain and reconstruct the material.[1] In placing the use of both historical materials and content analysis in the same chapter, I wish to stress the fact that the materials subject to content or historical analysis must be ordered by some sociological theory even in cases where the researcher is presumably reconstructing someone else's theory of society.

Historical materials and content analysis are useful to the sociologist for suggesting hypotheses, testing them after the fact under various limitations, and helping to establish a general perspective in which to place contemporary sources of data. Literal hypothesis testing would be difficult, if not impossible, at the present time because both our concepts and sources of data are too composite. Refinements in theory lead to more precise techniques on how such materials could be broken down into more precise units of analysis. Historical and contemporary non-scientific materials contain built-in biases and the researcher generally has no access to the setting in which they were produced; the meanings intended by the producer of a document and the cultural circumstances surrounding its assembly are not always subject to manipulation and control. It is difficult to separate re-construction or re-creation from imputations and innovations supplied by the researcher's own perspective. The following statement by Gottschalk is worth quoting here: "He [the historian] must be sure that his records really do come from the past and that his imagination is directed toward *re-creation* and not *creation*." [2] He pursues this point as follows:

It is a platitude that the historian who knows contemporary life best will understand past life best, since present generations can understand past generations only in terms (like or unlike) of their own experience. . . . As a general rule, those historians can make the best analogies and contrasts who have the most analogies and contrasts to choose from— that is, the widest range of experience, wisdom and knowledge. No platitude tells how to acquire a wide range of experience, wisdom and knowledge and how to transfer those qualities to an understanding of the past.[3]

It is the historian's imaginative ability to engage in such comparative conceptual play, backed by logical argument and careful use of documents, which meaningfully explains the past. The extent to which the past can be explained may vary with the materials available, supplementary information, for example, a particular vernacular and syntax which contains unstated meaning structures requiring an understanding of the everyday life of particular persons and eras.

According to Gottschalk, there exists a series of general rules developed and used by historians for deciding the genuineness and the type or source of the data. The historian often focuses upon a particular period of interest to him and attempts to abstract the specific and general features of that temporal span, while focusing upon the substantive elements of a society, groups or persons within it.

The problem for the content analyst is to employ a theory

which is sufficiently precise to enable the researcher to specify in advance what he should look for in some set of materials, how he is to identify and extract the material, how he must code it, and, finally, how its significance is to be decided. Measurement in content analysis as in the analysis of historical documents requires that the researcher (and/or coder) use some *a priori* scheme in a standardized manner. The observer assumes, as he has in field situations, the role of a measuring instrument. He imputes significance to material in such a way that equivalent content is detected and properly counted. The remainder of this chapter will explore the consequences of these procedures for the value of historical documents and content analysis.

✎§ *Historical Documents*

Gottschalk refers to the temporal problem of reliability in the expression of opinions, editorials, essays, speeches, pamphlets, and letters to the editor. He notes:

In fact there is a school of historians who contend that values and ideas change with periods of history, that what is a justifiable principle of esthetics, morality and politics at one time may be less so at another, that thought patterns are relative to contemporary conditions arising out of the cultural and historical climate of a given area and time. That belief, which would deny the validity of absolute principles in history, is sometimes called *historical relationism* or *historicism*. It insists upon the relation of ideas to historical circumstances (including other ideas); it maintains that ideas are only "reflex functions of the sociological condition under which they arose." This kind of *historical relationism* is closely akin to the sociology of knowledge *(Sociologie des Wissens)*. It stems from Hegel and Marx through Weber and Troeltsch to Meinecke and Mannheim.[4]

In a footnote to the passage just quoted, the author notes that Troeltsch and Mannheim insist that ". . . their brand of historicism does not include historical *relativism,* which they distinguish from *relationism* and repudiate as denying all concept of carry-over and totality. They advocate the search for absolutes. . . ." Gottschalk argues against the notion that historical knowledge is always relative to the conditions of the time and place in which

events occurred, yet he would agree that if we are to understand
the literary products of previous eras, we must understand the
era sufficiently well to determine whether or not a significant
relation between the work and its time exists. Thus,

while it undoubtedly is true that they largely reflect the cultural atmosphere of their times (*Zeitgeist,* "climate of opinion," milieu), the
historian who does not already know those particular times well can
not tell to what extent the documents are influenced by, conflict with,
or exert an influence upon that cultural atmosphere. The *Zeitgeist* must
therefore be studied in order fully to understand any personal document; and yet it is also true that the documents of a period will enable
the historian better to appreciate its cultural atmosphere.[5]

Presumably, then, the researcher needs a theory which will
seek to establish what invariant relationships exist over time as
well as the particular and variable features of given eras. The
problem of meaning is a central issue again. Gottschalk is clearly
aware of this problem and recognizes the necessity of determining
the denotative and connotative meanings in force at the time a
document was produced, "for the meanings of words often change
from generation to generation." Thus, "The historian's task is to
understand not only what the document's words formally mean
but also what his witness *intended to say.*"[6] The historian and
the sociologist using content analysis are confronted with the
same problem of meaning. Decisions about the relevance of given
material for analysis must be recommended by some existing
criteria. Gottschalk stresses this point and indicates how difficult it is to secure agreement on the *"underlying causes"* of an
historical event.[7] The same can be said of content analysis in
that the number of independent variables is virtually infinite
depending on the categories employed and the "regularities"
which result.

The researcher's theory must seek invariants while simultaneously acknowledging and studying the temporal conditions
which influence social process and social structure.

Gottschalk acknowledges the sociology of knowledge problem
in the following discussion:

To recapitulate, there are at least three ways in which the present
determines how the historian will interpret the past. The first of these

is derived from the inescapable tendency to understand others' behavior in the light of one's own behavior patterns; this results in *psychological analogies* between the historian's mental processes and those of the historical personalities whom he studies. The second is due to the fact that the contemporary intellectual atmosphere is a deciding factor in the historian's *choice of subjects* for investigation—not to mention the selection and the arrangement of his data. The third comes from the historian's exploitation of current events in lieu of a laboratory; from the episodes and developments of his own day he draws *historical analogies* to the episodes and developments of the past. Thus history becomes "the living past," the memory of living man, meaningful but having little objective reality except in so far as it is confirmable by a critical analysis of surviving testimony.[8]

In his use of historical documents or contemporary materials from which he wishes to extract information or which he treats as data, the researcher relies upon his everyday common-sense knowledge of life around him as well as upon his general knowledge of various subjects related to that under study. Theory to an historian is sometimes a set of generalizations about some period of time, while to the sociological content analyst it presumably includes an analytic framework with invariant properties that correspond to empirical events. The researcher must relate the categories to some theory about social process and structure, and show how he came to develop the categories and the rules whereby material was coded into the categories.

✑§ *The Analysis of Qualitative Materials*

Much of sociological research requires the analysis of qualitative materials. The notion of "communication content" (the phrase used by Berelson) [9] obviously can refer to any set of symbolic structures which can be assigned meaning according to some set of rules. Thus, when the sociologist uses the official records of, for example, a mental hospital, prison, or court system, some form of communication content analysis occurs. Any researcher who has worked with official records has experienced the problems of making sense of often abstract and highly condensed incomplete records of complex events. Invariably, organizations develop various ways of communicating official and unofficial material which is not recorded but nevertheless treated as basic information when writing and reading actual records. Official records are often written for an audience which is expected to see the organization at its best. Therefore, the propaganda slogans employed by the Russians, the "themes" of some plays or novels, the writer's "personality structure" as revealed in certain passages of a book, the official records of clients or employees in complex organizations, all reflect something "understandable," but one must remember that the public and private character of the meaning structures communicated can vary with the ways in which the materials are assembled, the projected audience envisioned by the writer, the various audiences who might be exposed to the materials under consideration, the language used, and the cultural and subcultural definitions employed.

Content analysis is valuable for suggesting hypotheses and developing a broader understanding of the subtleties and nuances of symbolic expression. What are its procedures? Berelson notes that

content analysis is ordinarily limited to the manifest content of the communication and is not normally done directly in terms of the latent intentions which the content may express nor the latent responses which it may elicit. Strictly speaking, content analysis proceeds in terms of what-is-said, and not in terms of why-the-content-is-like-that (e.g., "motives") or how-people-react (e.g., "appeals" or "responses").[10]

Berelson's definition stresses the interpretation of communication content which is independent of the writer's motives or reasons for writing, his intended audience, the desired effects, or the actual interpretations of some set of audiences. Berelson states three reasons for this:

(1) the low validity of the analysis, since there can be little or no assurance that the assigned intentions and responses actually occurred, in the absence of direct data on them; (2) the low reliability of such analysis, since different coders are unlikely to assign material to the same categories of intention and response with sufficient agreement; and (3) the possible circularity involved in establishing relationships between intent and effect on the one hand, and content on the other, when the latter is analyzed in terms referring to the former.[11]

Cartwright objects to Berelson's limitation of content analysis

to "communication" and "manifest" content, preferring to substitute the term "linguistic" for communication and to remove
the restriction to manifest content.[12] Except for these objections,
he agrees with Berelson.

Another requirement which Berelson makes of content
analysis is that the analytic categories be sufficiently precise to
enable different coders to arrive at the same results when the
same body of material is examined. This means that the categories must be specifiable by a body of theory and by a set of
coding rules which are invariant to the user's interpretation
of them.

Berelson then refers to the necessity for "systematic" analysis
which would analyze *"all* of the relevant content . . . in terms of
all the relevant categories, for the problem at hand." [13] Yet he
then notes that a second meaning of "systematic" refers to the concern for securing all material relevant for the testing of an hypothesis. But only certain relevant content will be important for
certain relevant categories for the test of an hypothesis. The
second meaning of "systematic" is intended, states Berelson, "to
eliminate partial or biased analysis in which only those elements
in the content are selected which fit the analyst's thesis." [14] If
the theory states explicitly which elements are relevant, then
material which would refute the researcher's hypothesis should be
specifiable.

Finally, Berelson points out that some analytic categories
should appear in the content analysis in such a way as to permit
statements of relative emphasis such as degree of presence or
absence of an item. This requirement establishes the concern for
some form of quantitative analysis, even if it means only
noting frequency by "more" or "often." [15]

Berelson then lists several assumptions of content analysis.
The first covers the assumed correspondence between the intent
of the message (independent of the latent intent of its creator[s])
and the content, and between the content of the material and its
effect on some audience. The nature of the originator's intentions
is viewed only in terms of the manifest content of the message.
The presumed effects of the content on some audience also are
taken from the manifest content. The danger here, to paraphrase
Coombs, is that the categories may be devised to ensure that

"supportive" material will be forthcoming from the content analysis.[16] It is difficult to demonstrate that the method of analysis did not ensure the results by imposing substantive categories with no justification—theoretical or empirical—other than the methodological. It is clear that a precise theory with independent measures of its basic concepts is required if this danger is to be avoided. Berelson's implicit assumption, not entirely specified, is that the content of the message somehow communicates meanings which can be imputed to both originator and receiver quite independently of information about the encoding and decoding activities of these actors. We are not surprised by Berelson's next assumption that "study of the manifest content is meaningful." He continues, "this assumption requires that the content be accepted as a 'common meeting-ground' for the communicator, the audience, and the analyst. That is, the content analyst assumes that the 'meanings' which he ascribes to the content, by assigning it to certain categories, correspond to the 'meanings' intended by the communicator and/or understood by the audience. In other words, the assumption is that there is a common universe of discourse among the relevant parties, so that the manifest content can be taken as a valid unit of study." [17] Berelson acknowledges the view that different "psychological predispositions of the reader" can confound the meaning of a message, but he argues that different "levels" of communication can be conceived such that a continuum serves as the model. Some communications are clearly understandable to everyone and other communications are open to as many interpretations as there are audiences.[18] He argues for the use of "relatively denotative communication materials and [that we should] not deal with relatively connotive materials." [19]

   This is a curious assumption. It presupposes a common culture unequivocably translatable into written symbolic forms. The meanings of these forms are assumed to be in one-to-one correspondence with the intentions and understandings of writer and audiences. We are not disputing the existence of a common culture between communicator, audience, and analyst. But what are the properties of the concept common culture upon which content analysis rests? What kinds of discrepancies are seen to exist among the intentions of communicators and their expressions, audiences' expectations and perceptions, and finally analysts' expectations and their perceptions? This is not a problem unique to the content analyst. Any field researcher is confronted with the task of deciding how meanings are assigned to events. But in content analysis the project cannot get off the ground without some preliminary specification of the linguistic problems involved and of the cultural definitions presupposed in each analysis. Since the content analyst is dealing exclusively in meanings of verbal communications, the categories used obviously presuppose rules which define the provinces of meanings under which elements in communication are to be assumed. The assumption that a quantitative description of communication content in terms of the frequency of occurrence of some defined characteristics is possible requires that the categories employed stand in some specifiable correspondence with the characteristics, and that equivalence classes exist among the characteristics thereby permitting counting to take place. But Berelson does not explicate the theoretical assumptions and methodological procedures for generating equivalence classes. The fact that a researcher finds certain newspapers, magazines and novels to contain "bias" which can be "counted" does not mean that the producers or audiences of such "bias" perceive and interpret it as such. If analysis of manifest content did reveal the intent and perception of communicator and audience, then the content analyst would assume the function of "informing" social scientists and laymen about the "real meanings" of such media.

Cartwright's paper presents a more critical view of content analysis, although he attempts to show its usefulness if it can meet some of the following required explicit procedures:

There are two basic kinds of questions that are raised in most descriptive studies: (1) How do symbolic materials vary over time? and (2) How do materials produced by different sources differ from one another? . . . In establishing trends over time and in comparing different kinds of materials, it is essential that the same system of categories, the same operational definitions of the categories, and the same units of recording and of enumeration be used in quantifying the materials being compared.[20]

Cartwright recognizes that many content analyses are of little significance because they are preoccupied with "counting" and presenting numerical findings which are "objective." But the question of how the *cultural meaning* of symbolic materials can vary over time by writer, reader, and analyst is not given problematic status by Cartwright.

What is missing, then, from the Berelson and Cartwright material is any explicit reference to the normative rules governing communicator, audience, and analyst interpretations of the meanings of one another's communications. It is difficult to formulate what the rules governing interaction in face-to-face communication are, even when the researcher is prepared to indicate the rationalities of action presupposed in his theory, together with independent measures of meaning. Each verbal expression is subject to differential interpretation by some specifiable audience (including the researcher) and, therefore, cannot be understood apart from the rules governing the analysis of the material and the rules imputed to the audience for whom it was intended.

The recent work conference on content analysis sponsored by the Social Science Research Council's Committee on Linguistics and Psychology [21] provides some excellent ideas and data on the relevance of language and meaning for the analysis of qualitative material and goes a long way toward correcting some of the problems mentioned above. Specifically discussed are the difficulties of quantitative content analysis, the problem of whether the intended meanings of the speaker or writer differ from the ordinary use of such words and their interpretation by the analyst, especially when coding, as well as the situational and behavioral contexts of the communication.[22]

There is a critical discussion by Mahl of the "representational model" (as used by many sociologists, psychologists, and political scientists, and typically found in works like Berelson, where the face validity of manifest content is taken for granted) and a presentation of the "instrumental model":

The term "representational model" was used by the author [Mahl] to describe the approach which assumes that behavioral states in a speaker are necessarily directly represented in the symbolic content of messages he emits: to cite the example used by Osgood in the preceding chapter, when a person says he is frightened or talks of frightening things that is taken to show that he *is* frightened. In practice the converse is also assumed: that when he is frightened, the words of any message he utters will *necessarily* refer to "fear," "frightening things," or "frightening experiences." Thus, this viewpoint assumes the face validity of the manifest lexical content of a message. Beyond this simple matter of face validity, however, there is a more fundamental and pervasive implication of the representational viewpoint: the implicit assumption that there is an isomorphic relation between behavioral states and quantitative properties of lexical content. This is illustrated in the frequency approaches to manifest content which assume, for example, that the more units of content there are in a language sample about an emotion, the greater the intensity of that emotion in the speaker at the time he uttered the content. The assumption of isomorphism also underlies those interpretations of contingency analysis which conclude that contingencies in messages directly reflect behavioral associations.[23]

Adherents to the representational viewpoint assume that the relationship of behavioral states and messages can be determined by analysis of the semantics of written or oral utterances. "Therefore they restrict their analysis to the contents of messages, with conventional semantics defining the contents." In this respect they differ from the adherents to the instrumental viewpoint who ". . . assume that the pragmatics of language can be determined only on the basis of an investigation of pragmatics themselves, by including the situational and/or the nonlexical contexts of messages in the analysis." [24]

The crucial point of Mahl's remarks is to be found in the distinction between "conventional semantics" and the "nonlexical contexts of messages." Saporta and Sebeok raise a similar issue when they speak of words having the same "distribution" but different meanings.

The distribution of a linguistic form means the sum of all its environments. . . . Thus, "if A and B have almost identical environments except chiefly for sentences which contain both, we say they are synonyms: *oculist* and *eye doctor*. . . ." In short, how do we know that *sit* and *chair* are more similar in meaning than *sit* and *door?* One epistemological problem which eventually must be explored is whether some nondistributional method of arriving at the difference in meaning is possible; if not, the argument becomes circular, since the only evidence for difference in meaning turns out to be the distributional difference. An independent method for determining meaning differences must be feasible before any statement about distributional correlates becomes testable.[25]

The "epistemological problem" or the problem of nondistributional methods of arriving at meaning receives further attention in Pool's summing up of the conference when he states that: "Most content analysis procedures use the coder as a judge of what lexical forms convey what meanings of interest. They have relied on the common sense of a coder who was, of course, a user of the language in which the analysis was being done. His common sense enables him to recognize, for example, that the phrases 'a man of courage,' 'a brave man,' and 'a guy with guts' all mean the same thing." [26] The problem of equivalent meanings cannot be resolved by linguistic analysis *per se,* or by dictionary definitions of the manifest semantic properties of the utterances under review. And if we must rely on human judges, then we should know as much as possible, to paraphrase Pool, about how the "human computer" goes about encoding and decoding messages. But acknowledgment—explicitly by Pool and implicit throughout all books on content analysis—of the importance of the common-sense meanings does not mean recognition of or insistence on the study of how persons impute meanings to their environments and establish equivalence classes based on dictionary definitions and on the use of everyday language, gestures, appearances, intonational qualities of the voice, and the like. Instead it is often assumed that such meanings are self-evident, that native speakers of a language are more or less interchangeable, that the manifest content is sufficient for study, or that judges are interchangeable. The structure of common-sense knowledge remains a barely recognizable problem for sociological investigation.

✑ Conclusion

Our brief discussion of the sociological use of historical materials and content analysis has attempted to show the importance of unstated meaning structures for understanding such documents as diaries, newspapers, interviews, official records, and novels. Current methods tend to impose meaning on the materials in the process of selecting and extracting what seems relevant. This is like saying that meaning is assigned to the content by the mechanics of the method which presumably is intended to "discover" the meaning of that content. The following remarks summarize this chapter.

1. The researcher cannot appraise the conditions that led to the production of the document without some theory which accounts for the common-sense meanings used by the actor and by the social structure within which the material was produced.

2. Content analysis of material assumes that certain "themes" are invariant to the connotative content of the communication. Such "themes" are part of the researcher's theory that is independent of the actor's perspective.

3. It is difficult to establish the sampling distribution of the different possible types of utterances contained in documents. The researcher is forced to assume that the sample he uses is a representative one. The situational context may be completely absent, as in the case of public documents, or it may be described from the standpoint of only one participant or observer.

4. The interpretation of any document, novel, or newspaper account is continually subject to the possibility of reinterpretation in light of "second thoughts" or additional information. Conditions that restrict the range of possibilities for reinterpretation and test hypotheses by demanding that the data contain particular features dictated by theory are difficult to meet because unknown factors operate in data selection and the nature of the informational content is decided after the fact.

5. The materials may contain idiomatic expressions, group-specific jargon or connotations which the researcher often must try to determine without prior knowledge of the writer's objectives or way of interpreting the world.

6. The researcher is often faced with documents to which standardized meanings have already been imputed and which he can seldom investigate independently. Such meanings require a model of the actor that takes into account the ways in which cultural meanings are given expression via written symbols.

7. The coder of documents and mass media material must be, according to writers on the subject, a "sensitive person" who can detect nuances in symbolic material. But ideally, the coder should also function as an automaton coding various responses, sentences, phrases, and comments according to a prearranged set

of rules that provides for a precise correspondence between some expressed form and the object to which it refers.

8. A theory of signs is required for the content analyst or historian. For the historian who must decode ancient and medieval symbolization this is a well-recognized fact. For the sociologist this is seldom a source of concern because he too often assumes that the language of the materials he submits to content analysis contains "obvious" meaning structures which simply require "counting" under some set of *a priori* or *ex post facto* categories.

9. The social scientist cannot afford to rely upon his own common-sense understanding for his content analysis of communications. To do so would make it impossible for him to differentiate between what he can understand because of his theoretical framework and what he can understand as a member of the same society (or even the same audience) in which the communication was presented.

10. A newspaper article, public document, radio news story, or television commercial may be written under the editorial guidance of many persons with a variety of differing intentions. The ways in which such communications are perceived and interpreted by an audience can vary with the audience and communicator's normative conceptions about their environment at the time of communication; with different social types of actors who may be in different structural and locational arrangements in society and oriented to the communcation according to their social identity and official and unofficial statuses and roles.

11. The intentions according to which the communication is produced can be independent of the social scientist's interpretation of it, and independent of the actors who are exposed to it (and who may ignore, misunderstand, distort, etc.) .

12. Categories for subsuming "counts" or elements of communication, presumably derived from the social scientist's theory, must be consistent not only with that theoretical conception of the content but also with the actor's perception of it. The content analyst, however, may or may not choose to study those who produced the communication. The originator's goals may or may not be relevant to the study, depending upon its focus.

13. The fact that content analyses are conducted and have

been conducted implies the frequent expectation that meaningful regularities or patterns may exist in communication, but we cannot assume the significance of a content analysis only by virtue of its categorization and careful counting of items subsumed under these categories unless we know how the researcher decides what his categories are, how they are to be used, by reference to the theoretical presuppositions inherent in the method of analysis.

V I I

EXPERIMENTAL

DESIGNS

IN SOCIOLOGY

IN THIS CHAPTER I consider the relevance of experimental designs to be carried out in laboratory settings for the testing of sociological theory.[1] The purpose of this chapter is to recommend experimental research on the problem of cultural meaning as a necessary condition for an experimental sociology that can explore theories of role-taking and social organization.

A frequent criticism leveled against experiments in social psychology and sociology is that they are too "artificial." Critics do not honor creation of an experimental situation in which some attempt is made to manipulate conditions under which some specifiable outcome or set of outcomes can be predicted. A confusion frequently arises here when the experiment is viewed as an attempt to duplicate "real-life" situations.[2]

Claims that laboratory experiments are not possible in sociology follow from the view that our variables are obscure and that we are unable to specify how they can be manipulated (except in theoretical and empirical exercises which do not commit us to precise operational procedures). The lack of solutions to the problem of meaning in sociology and social psychology precludes our moving from the abstract propositions we call theory to the operational procedures that permit controlled manipulation of important variables. Field research seldom renders theory more precise because the research techniques are invariably based upon difficult-to-measure composite observations or "packaged" data presupposing meanings that are never conceptualized and studied independently of the substantive objectives for which they were originally assembled. The language, gestures, and meanings used to frame the questions and interpret answers inform the researcher implicitly about the correspondences among concept, operational procedures, and observations. The observations reported are often abstract constructs based on implicit common-sense constructs used to decide the meaning and relevance of the researcher's perceptions.[3] The researcher's experience of an event (object or question) and the circumstances surrounding the experience are not necessarily identical with the subject's or with another researcher's experience of the same social object. The same object may emit one set of properties, identical on all occasions, but they may be differentially experienced by researcher and subject. This puts into question the meaning of the object as an identical stimulus to different subjects, especially if the researcher assumes the object is perceived identically by himself and his subjects.

Two experiments by social psychologists have revealed the influence of normative rules of conduct, under experimental conditions, on the perception and interpretation of physical objects. Asch's experiment used seven confederates for each experimental subject to show how announced perceptions of group members influence the experimental subject significantly.[4] Sherif's work with the autokinetic effect showed how experimental subjects' judgments could be influenced by the judgments of paid participants.[5] These are but two of many experiments designed to show how the normative features of social structures influence and control the perceptions, interpretations, and behavior of subjects. These experiments, by social psychologists, are among the most important data supporting sociological conceptions of normative structures as independent of the psychological make-up of the individual actors.

If the meaning of physical objects can be drastically altered by normative rules governing social action, then social objects (for example, goals, authority, laughs, frowns) present the additional problem that in simulating them experimentally (or in studying them in field settings) the researcher must distinguish between his own perceptions and interpretations and those of his subjects toward the same social objects. Establishing consensus among researcher and subjects on the properties of a single social object is a necessary condition in the development of equivalence classes for measurement. The researcher's presentation of social objects (e.g., questionnaire items, authority relationships under experimental conditions) to subjects requires that he assume they are referring to the same sensory observations, visual field, and experience of the social event. Another assumption is that one researcher's description of observed behavior would be identical or "obvious" to any other observer. Further, it is assumed that the subjects invariably experience the same states imputed by the researcher's descriptions. The relation between sign and social object is not one-to-one. Verbal instructions may appear standardized (especially if presented by electronic recordings), but their "obvious" character and meaning cannot be taken for granted. The observer's and subjects' constructs for making sense of the "same" environment of objects require further conceptual and empirical clarification if sociological theories are to be tested in laboratory settings.

❧ *Experimental "Variables" and Their Measurement*

It does not follow from the ambiguities inherent in the actor's management of his daily affairs in everyday life that the sociologist's measurement of the actor's ways of attending the world also has to be ambiguous and unstructured.

Studies such as those cited by Asch and Sherif are clearcut as to what was being manipulated in the experiment, and the responses are immediately understandable without elaborate measurement devices. The purpose of Asch's experiment was clear and did not require the introduction of meaning structures specifically derived from a theoretical framework or the creation of artificial social processes and social structures that are not easily communicated. Sherif's study attempted to provide an ambiguous stimulus and thereby allows for the possibility of one subject's influencing the judgments of another. But the experimenter's task becomes confounded when it comes to creating a feeling of "rejection" among subjects, of perception of "acceptance" or "friendliness," of "privileged" and "underprivileged" groups, of "status hierarchies," and the like. Perception of social objects presupposes meaning structures more ambiguous than the perception of physical objects.[6] Researchers usually rely upon their common-sense knowledge of the dimensions of social perception. But if a notion of this kind, for example, "friendliness," is conceived as some sort of continuum, with high and low degrees of expression measured on a scale of some sort, either built into the study or imposed later on a set of responses, the measurement system transforms common-sense conceptions of that notion into the desired measurable product. This discussion is not simply a case of obtaining operational measures; nor is it intended to deny the importance or relevance of experiments by Asch, Sherif, Festinger, Kelley, Thibaut, and others. Such "variables" as "cohesiveness," "rejection," or "friendliness" are not automatically significant and meaningful because they are made operationally measurable by some set of questions or sociometric choices. The operational measures of such concepts do not make explicit provision for the unstated common-sense meanings which are built into the concept's use. The most obvious kind of measurement in social experiments is the observer's literal account in simple descriptive terms of predicted differences. To label as "findings" the "outcomes" of a series of general descriptions that are built into coding procedures and the instructions of an experiment makes for neither a rigorous study nor even an elegant experiment.

Each sociological variable is located within a particular time perspective. Structural or locational variables such as occupation, age, sex contain unspecified compressions of relevant cultural meanings. The variables determining social perception include ambiguous cultural "rules" of interpretation and cannot be treated as self-evident.

If we lack sufficient theoretical precision to know how to invent and communicate the simple instructions to experimental subjects that would create social structures, then our knowledge of basic social processes is too limited to program subjects' actions so as to produce a clearly noticeable difference in some type of social meaning. An experiment which attempts to create differences in "cohesiveness" or "hierarchies of social status" presupposes that the interactional ingredients which produce, maintain, alter, or destroy "cohesiveness" and "social status" are known to us. The ways in which "cohesiveness" and "status hierarchy" are conceived should provide the operational clues for their experimental creation and alteration. Concepts like "cohesiveness" and "social status" presuppose a set of definitions which can be operationally translated into and produced by specific instructions that would convey meaning structures that subjects could readily understand. The variables are clearly not structural or locational *per se,* and the researcher cannot rely upon assumptions which assume these are so and, therefore of self-evident meaning.[7] The social psychologists have performed laboratory experiments with cultural variables (conceived in psychological terms), while most sociologists and anthropologists have tended to prefer field research. Moreover, the social psychologists have addressed precisely those problems that are fundamental to the sociologist: the problems of how a stable system of social action is achieved, maintained, and altered. Sociologists and anthropologists are seldom enthusiastic about the experimental manipulation of "cohesiveness," "hierarchies of social status," "group goals," and the like. The sociologist prefers to speculate about social process while seeking documentation; for example, in the amount of crime and suicide in a community, in variations in residential location by income, education, occupation, and so forth. The cogency of such variables often appears to be decided according to how susceptible they are to imposed quantitative analysis.

In a study by John Thibaut,[8] an attempt was made to create cohesiveness within two sociometrically homogenous groups receiving differential encouragement and actual success during the experiment. One low-status group was encouraged (and allowed) to seek group action as a means of "elevating" its status, while the other low-status group was also encouraged but not allowed to be successful in its efforts. The "unsuccessful group-action treatment" is described by Thibaut:

The low-status members are addressed in a matter-of-fact and coolly unsympathetic way, the experimenter does not address them by name but by number. The high-status team, on the other hand, is accorded sympathy, encouragement, and warmth. Moreover, the high-status team performs in all instances the more favorable functions during play.[9]

It is during a six-minute "recess" that experimental variations are introduced, such as calling the low-status group together and encouraging them to seek better treatment from the experimenter. The experimenter presumably is "programed" to exhibit a certain kind of manner which conveys sympathy, etc., toward the low-status group. The researcher relies upon post-session questionnaires and independent observers for documenting the effectiveness of the experimental treatments.

The interesting point here is the way group cohesiveness was produced by the researchers. The theoretical conceptualization of the problem and the experimental creation of social structures are both independent of any theory of the actor as a constructed social type. The researcher's interest in creating social structures leads to a model of the actor which imputes psychological forces (e.g., common-sense notions of encouragement, aspiration) to compel him to behave in certain ways. The present view prefers to leave as problematic the ways in which social action is structured by the actors' stock of knowledge, the kinds of strategies they entertain as revealed by the kinds of practical action employed, and the imputations or meanings they assign to objects and events in the social scene. Thibaut's study and the many related ones reported in the Cartwright and Zander volume do not recognize the simulation of social action as problematic; they assume that when the experimenter attempts to convey "a matter-of-fact and coolly unsympathetic way," it is clearly understood as such by the reader and the subjects participating in the experiment. We are not questioning the "success" of the treatments, as measured, for example, by differences in group performance, but whether what was intended by the experimenter was perceived and interpreted identically by the relevant subjects and would also be so interpreted by independent observers. The experimenter has relied upon meaning structures which remain unspecified to himself, the subjects, and the reader, but which produced some effects that he considered relevant to the problem at hand. The researcher apparently employed common-sense definitions of the situation successfully, but how do we identify them, what are their properties, and how do we measure them? Answers to these questions would enable us to be more precise about the properties that produce "cohesiveness" and how we might obtain expressions of direct observations which could be understood and coded according to a clearly specified set of rules. Thibaut's observations on what was communicated to the subjects and how their responses to post-session questionnaires were coded remain unexplicated and nonproblematic features of the experiment. The structural properties attributed to social action consist of the actor's patterned meanings assigned to objects and events in accordance with the researcher's theoretically derived rules of interpretation. These meanings, which remain unstated in Thibaut's study, are precisely what should interest the sociologist, for when routinely invoked in everyday situations, they provide stability and introduce change for the actor and others in concerted action. The typification of objects and events permits the actor to assign meanings to discrepant situations; it renders understandable changing or ambiguous appearances and enables the actor to maintain a stable environment in the face of confusing, disruptive, arbitrary kinds of events.

Thibaut's actor is responding to an environment made problematic by the experimenter to produce differential consequences. If we were to replicate the experiment, how would we know if we were introducing the same amount of "unsympathetic coolness," "warmth," "friendliness," or "encouragement"? One answer would be if we obtain the same or similar findings. I am not denying the importance or the relevance of Thibaut's research but asking for an explicit account of those features which he manipulated, presumably successfully, but which remain unknown to the reader and to anyone who wished to replicate the experiment. Thibaut's study and others like it are, nevertheless, useful because such success as they do achieve underlines the importance of being explicit about our conception of the structure of social action and the operations which we are introducing. We can conclude that the experiment shows that the actions of the experimenter communicated meanings which were perceived and interpreted by subjects in apparently similar ways, as intended by the researcher, and that these meanings were also shared by the observers evaluating the interaction and coding the questionnaires. This can be conceived as an experimental demonstration of a common culture which is manipulable and can be observed as such, but where we cannot always be sure of what elements generate the results. Operational procedures are present but not obvious or actually ascertainable by the reader. Even a movie and sound track of the entire experiment would not be adequate, although helpful for illustrating the results. Without a set of procedural rules by which to decide whether "cohesiveness" was occurring, when particular kinds of behavior were demonstrated, we obviously would have to rely upon our common-sense knowledge to determine the meaning of even the movie and sound track.

The same comments can be made about Harold H. Kelley's experiment on status hierarchies.[10] In this experiment the creation of status differences is formally implied in the directions given to subjects, and the results indicate that the author was successful in producing differences which can be honored as interesting and significant; but it is difficult to know precisely how the results were produced and interpreted, much less why alternative sets of directions would not be equally applicable. Is it self-evident that if persons are given certain directions which explicitly locate their position in some created hierarchy, these directions always will be understood? The important point here is that Kelley's presuppositions about basic social process remain conceptually unformulated. He has presupposed a common culture utilized implicitly. The experimental situation may be so structured that certain differences and status discrepancies may be eliminated by experimental controls, but clearly the subjects will respond to the experiment in terms with which they are accustomed to responding in everyday life. But if we do not know something about how subjects manage their everyday lives (as individuals and as generic actors) then we cannot possibly know what is motivating them to respond in the experiment.

The above discussion is intended to encourage the use of experiments for studying the basic social processes of everyday life that produce social structures. The experimental study of basic social processes is a necessary prerequisite for the kinds of studies conducted by Thibaut, Kelley, and others. In the final section of this chapter I will attempt to indicate briefly what such experiments would look like, describe two examples, and indicate further experiments it might be useful to undertake. I assume that culture, conceived as a system of action, can be studied experimentally and its basic theoretical elements clarified and measured.

✌ᔒ *Basic Social Process and the Problem of Social Order*

In a doctoral dissertation which attempts experimentally to test the invariance of what Schutz described as the stable features of social action, Harold Garfinkel exposed premedical students to a fake recording of an actual interview between a "medical school admissions interviewer" and an "applicant to the school." [11]

The "applicant" was "programed" as a "boor" and his responses were designed to violate what the experimenter considered to be relatively appropriate behavior. An appendix to the study containing the recorded interview provides the reader with a verbatim account of the properties which were violated and how this general ineptness was "programed." The experimental subjects all felt that the "applicant" would not succeed and that he had conducted himself improperly. Every point made by the subject which characterized the "applicant" in bad light was then contradicted by the experimenter who revealed information not previously given which might place the subject in a favorable light. After facing this barrage of contradictions, the student subjects were invited to hear the recording a second time. Although most of the students managed to "re-read" the "applicant" and see him now as a "successful" one (having been told he was accepted with "flying colors"), Garfinkel reports that the predicted and intended confusion (i.e., the breakdown in stable social action) did not come through as well as expected, even though there was a marked increase in "measured anxiety" between the first interview and the second. The students were able to transform the "applicant" from a boor who hadn't a chance of succeeding into a successful candidate. The results can be construed as demonstrating that the experimental situation was "realistic" and conformed to the expected results. An important merit of this experiment was that it simulated realistic conditions. Another important advantage lies in the use of ex-

perimental procedures which could be replicated easily. Two
drawbacks were the difficulty in producing or determining the
"convincing" character of the simulated interview of the applicant and the difficulties of measuring anxiety. The fact that
the study was carried out with no explicit solution to both of
these problems assumes the existence of an unstated solution
to the problem of meaning.

In seeking more precise indicators of confusion and hence
the existence of social rules (as an obverse measure of stable
order) Garfinkel turned to the study of games because games
allow for identification of some of the players' (actors') expectancies of the situation. The game contains an explicit set of rules
within which routine expectancies of play operate. Garfinkel
reasoned that by being able to nail down the "basic rules" and
"constitutive expectancies" of a game like chess, he could better
grasp the variations in expectancies and general strategies which
could operate independently of, yet also be constrained by, the
basic rules. This would permit him to show the similarities and
differences between games and real-life situations. He wished to
experimentally control real-life situations by using the game
as an approximation.

In both his early experiment with the premedical student
and later experiments with games, in particular ticktacktoe, Garfinkel was interested in subjecting Schutz' notions about the constitutive phenomenology of everyday life to experimental test.
Such demonstrations would show that invariant properties of
social order exist and can be experimentally manipulated. In
pursuing Schutz' theoretical framework, it is important to produce an experiment which would demonstrate the existence of
an invariant set of "constitutive rules" or "properties" which
are "perceivedly normal" to the users or actors for the particular
"constitutive order" of which they are part. This stresses invariant *properties* of norms or "rules," not their actual content.

The general point suggested by the work of Schutz and
Garfinkel is that when the properties of constitutive rules are violated or breached, then confusion, chaos, or an abrupt breakdown of social action will follow. The critical theoretical and
empirical point is that all events, regardless of the "game," have
their "constitutive accent." Garfinkel's work shows that such
experiments are possible, that they address the basic social proc-

esses of social structures, and that they reveal some possible foundations of an experimental sociology.

In using ticktacktoe to illustrate "constitutive rules," Garfinkel shows that when a subject is invited to play the game with the experimenter, to make the first move and the experimenter follows it by erasing the mark and moving it to another cell while making his own mark, all in a "life as usual" manner, subjects will exhibit some confusion and bewilderment such that they cannot play the game under the described conditions unless two general lines of action are followed. First, for example, the subject might pretend that the illegal move was in fact legal or pretend that a "different" game was being played, suspending for the moment any actual comment on what happened while often privately thinking that perhaps there are "good reasons for all this." Some type of "normalizing" activity occurs. Or, second, if the subject in fact tried to attend the game as if it were a "regular" ticktacktoe game, he might react with annoyance and confusion. Thus, if the actor tries to adapt to the "constitutive accent," he will not necessarily become confused and see the situation as "senseless" and chaotic. But if he attempts to remain within the original "constitutive accent," he will find it hard to perceive what has happened to him as "normal."

The difference between the experiments by Thibaut, Kelley, and others described above, and those conducted by Garfinkel, lies in the theoretical questions asked, in the kinds of basic theoretical elements specified, and in the manner in which the experimental atmosphere was created. Thibaut and Kelley assumed that some particular order of events was "normal" and they sought experimentally to discover whether the order which they conceived to be "normal" was the "correct" one. They assumed that the experimental subjects would honor their characterization of the scene as dictated by the directions given, and further, that the experimental variations would be perceived as variations of an order already constituted by their initial directions and structuring. Their results reveal considerable success. We cannot be sure, however, as to the *how* or *why* of their success. They have assumed a world taken for granted by both subject and experimenter, but the basic social processes involved remain obscure. The question of what is commonly perceived by subjects and experimenter as invariant about the social scene is not addressed explicitly. They rely upon their own common-sense knowledge of the "rules of the game" in order to conceive of the experiment, to produce the experimental results, and to analyze the findings.

Garfinkel is asking a more basic question. His work can be viewed as an inquiry into how conventional experiments in social psychology and sociology can even be conceived, much less accomplish their intent. He does not ask: How do we create and vary cohesiveness and status hierarchies experimentally? *but*: How do we create or assume the theoretical and empirical knowledge necessary to produce such structures? What are the basic features of social action? How are their stable properties to be identified and maintained? What are the operational procedures which must be utilized to both show their existence and permit their experimental manipulation? Garfinkel's strategy is to begin with a situation viewed as "normal" and then systematically attempt to create "trouble," confusion, or chaos. The procedures producing chaos would suggest obversely the elements of stable order.

In addressing a variety of procedures used by sociologists in their day-to-day research, I have tried to show the relevance of a particular theoretical position. I begin by asking whether linguistic utterances, their implied cultural meanings, and the unstated common-sense definitions of the situation which we build into experimental instructions, interview schedules, and questionnaires are understandable to all the subjects in our sample? Is the same "constitutive accent" entertained by all of the subjects? And if this is so, how is it all possible?

I have assumed that the actor must entertain some constitutive order of events and honor some "constitutive accent" if he is to maintain some relationship with his environment and fellow man. This is why the survey researcher cannot avoid the problem of "rapport." For the respondent may not choose to honor the "constitutive order" defined by the questionnaire unless the interviewer provides the interviewee with some basis for doing so. The survey researcher may think that the respondent will be satisfied that he is contributing to a "scientific study or the benefit of mankind," but this is not something to be taken for granted. Even if this were the case, it would not guarantee *rapport* or mutually understood meanings. This is especially true when for many respondents the questionnaire is actually an invasion of privacy, an intrusion into an order which may be sacred to the subject. The way in which we construct questionnaires and create experimental situations which are considered "valid," "meaningful," etc., is itself a first order of business for the sociologist to study. Experimental and field demonstrations of the properties of social order are called for.

If the experimental variations are not accepted or perceived by the subjects as intended by the experimenter, a common basic order operating for the experimenter and subject(s) may still be presumed to hold. This common order is present before the experiment, is temporarily "dropped" or "suspended" during the experiment, and is adopted again after the experiment is concluded. If the experimental order is a simulation of the common order, then the former can be understood only by references to the properties of the latter. The constitutive order or set of rules provides the actor with the basis for assigning meaning structures so that he can understand what has happened or what is happening. The experimenter's directions, therefore, define the order. Experimenting with the properties of "rules" becomes a necessary task for an experimental sociology. I will close this chapter with some brief remarks about a few of these properties and their experimental possibilities.

1. Unstated meanings assumed during interaction. We could inquire into the consequences of not holding meanings in reserve during social interaction. This would mean directing subjects to express how they feel about others, the situation, and events and any other stimuli in general throughout any experimental sequence of events. All assumptions about the self-evident nature of such properties and "accents" as rules of etiquette, authority relationships, and the like would be suspended. Customer-salesmen relations, employer-employee relations, student-teacher interactions, officer-enlisted man exchanges, could be simulated. An attempt to enforce the notion of suspending private meanings experimentally would be difficult to achieve but would show the sense in which private meanings are invariant under experimental conditions. By asking what kinds of social types, in what simulated situations, would attempt to enforce the use of private meanings and with what consequences, we obtain a

concise picture of the importance of unstated meanings and imputations held in reserve for maintaining stable social order and generating change.

Another way of exploring these meanings would be to have the actor not accept the notion that his actions will be understood by other members of the group. Every move he made, therefore, would require the most elaborate explanations as to intent, motive, purpose, etc. Further, after every statement he would have to ask whether the others understood him or not. Garfinkel suggests that if the others refused to acknowledge the subject's comments but continually asked him for further explanations, the same breakdown (confusion) of concerted stable action would arise.[12] This might be produced if the others' remarks to every expression were accompanied, for example, by a demand for operational definitions. The experimental attempts to "program" these properties would provide the basis for demonstrating both their essential and common-sense features.

2. Another property amenable to experimental study is that of the "rules" governing appropriate physical distance during social interaction. Garfinkel suggests having a shill approach the experimental subject such that the physical distance separating them is virtually nonexistent, all the while the shill is asking routine or "trivial" questions and carrying on a "normal" conversation. Physical distance is a characteristic of all social interaction. It is a property of all interpersonal exchanges although variations in it may have a wide range of consequences at different times, with different persons, in various status relationships, and in different situations. Experimentally varying physical distance would demonstrate how this property structures the norms or "rules" which are perceived to be binding upon persons in the course of interaction. This property informs the actor's definition of the situation.

3. Another property which informs the actor's definition of the situation may be found in Goffman's notion of "role distance." [13] Role distance refers to the separation between the actor's self-identification and the social role he commits himself to in the course of social interaction. If we assume that this property is a variable in all social encounters, then variations in role distance which are experimentally produced should be expected to alter the norms or "rules" governing social exchanges. The

inferred other role would include an estimation by the actor of the other's role distance and how his own subsequent self-role should be shaped accordingly. The verbal and nonverbal significations that communicate role distance provide the meaning structures for inferring the amount and type of role distance intended by the other.

A host of properties perceived and interpreted in common-sense ways are take for granted unless their elements appear distorted to the participants who then distinguish the "unusual" from the "usual." Certain behavior is considered "appropriate," for example, for persons of a given chronological age, for persons who wish to be viewed as male or female, who wish to convey "interest," "concern," "happiness," "unhappiness," "coolness," and the like. Many of these properties have an undefinable set of elements which are only negatively revealed when subjected to extreme distortions, for instance, of clothing, gesture, or language. The subleties of everyday interaction inform the actor's definition of the situation and the role-taking activity he performs. There are "rules" and properties, therefore, which operate to structure what the sociologist ordinarily calls "norms." These "rules" and properties are invariant to the actual content and type of "norms" which govern social action in particular situations. The study of these "rules" and properties provides an experimental foundation for the measurement of meaning structures basic to all sociological events.

LANGUAGE

AND MEANING

HUMAN COMMUNICATION is so complex that much of it must be reduced to automatic behavior, implicit rules, often without conscious awareness and with little or no effort. One of the most fascinating accounts of how language and meaning enter into situations which the sociologist must analyze appears in *The First Five Minutes.*[1] The authors' analysis of linguistic and paralinguistic behavior as contained in the first five minutes of a psychiatric interview serves as an excellent model for sociological analysis of interview or similar materials (e.g., the dialogue of natural settings in the field) for both substantive purposes and the study of invariant properties of social behavior. *The First Five Minutes* raises important questions such as:

What does each participant say? Why does he say it? *How* does he say it? What impact does it have on the other participant? When and how is new material brought into the picture, and by whom? What is being communicated out of awareness? How does the orientation of each participant change as the transactions continue? and why? and how do we know? and does the other participant know? and if he does, by virtue of what evidence?[2]

Knowledge about stress patterns and how they may be recorded during an interview can tell us something about a basic feature of all social process as well as something about the cultural meanings intended by the speaker with respect to some substantive issue.

A continual theme throughout the book has been the implicit and explicit assertion that measurement in sociology at the level of social process cannot be rigorous without solutions to the problems of cultural meanings. Understanding the problem of meaning requires a theory of both language and culture. In this chapter I shall outline some of the elements of language and how they are important for a theory of meaning or culture. The discussion is brief, selective, and designed to introduce sociologists to some of the issues and general literature. A comprehensive and lucid statement of the position held by many linguists today can be found in Lamb's outline:

The system presented here is called stratificational because one of its chief features is the recognition of a series of strata or structural layers in language. A language, by its nature, relates sounds (or graphs, i.e. marks on paper or the like) to meanings, and this relationship is a very complex one which turns out to be analyzable in terms of a series of code-like systems, each of which connects two neighboring strata. The topmost structural stratum, the sememic, has units directly related to meaning. These sememes may be thought of as encodable into units of the next lower stratum, which in turn are themselves encodable, and so on, until one comes out with units directly related to speech or writing (i.e. with phonemes or graphemes) which, finally, may be spoken or written as the case may be. The code relating each pair of neighboring strata is a set of *stratificational rules,* whose form is described below.

The reason for this great complexity in linguistic structure is that sounds and meanings are, by their natures, patterned separately from each other; they each have their own set of structural relationships. Phonemic systems must be adapted to speech and auditory organs, while sememic systems must be adapted to thought patterns. Moreover, the process of linguistic change affects these two strata in different ways. A close correspondence between them would therefore be impossible. The same situation is true of written languages because writing systems are based upon spoken languages, so that they tend to have close correspondence to phonemic but not to sememic systems.[3]

A basic and widely held view of linguistics is that an attempt should be made to determine "the fundamental underlying properties of successful grammars. The ultimate outcome of these investigations should be a theory of linguistic structure in which the descriptive devices utilized in particular grammars are presented and studied abstractly, with no specific reference to particular languages." [4] Chomsky is interested in a device which will separate the grammatical from the ungrammatical sequences of a language. With such a device, according to Chomsky, the grammar of the language should generate only the grammatical sequences, and the test of the adequacy of the grammar is the acceptance of the sentences it generates by a native speaker.[5]

There is a tendency for some linguists to become preoccupied with the formal features of language and on the basis of these formal features alone to devise operations which assume the properties of a closed system. This is understandable because measurement properties for closed systems may be readily arrived at, and the nasty empirical problem of what is "acceptable" to a native speaker can be minimized. Chomsky concludes:

Despite the undeniable interest and importance of semantic and statistical studies of language, they appear to have no direct relevance to the problem of determining or characterizing the set of grammatical utterances. I think that we are forced to conclude that grammar is autonomous and independent of meaning, and that probabilistic models give no particular insight into some of the basic problems of syntactic structure.[6]

Chomsky's position is an important one to note here because while he rejects the notion that grammars can be completely programed via a machine or probabilistic models, he also rejects the dependence of syntactic structure upon meaning. "A grammar does not tell us how to synthesize a specific utterance; it does not tell us how to analyze a particular given utterance. . . . Each such grammar is simply a description of a certain set of utterances, namely, those which it generates." [7] Yet the sentences generated by a grammar are expected to be acceptable to a native speaker. Thus, the grammar must generate acceptable sentences, but there may be ungrammatical sentences which are "understandable" to the native speaker, or some native speakers, or a set of native speakers forming a subculture, and so on. The formulations by Chomsky and Lamb seek, wherever possible, the advantages of a closed mathematical system. Little attention is given to the anthropologist's and sociologist's problem of connecting sound and thought patterns with cultural meanings, and with the language as it is spoken and written.

Many linguists are interested only in the correspondence between patterns of sounds, phonemic systems, linguistic structure, linguistic analysis, and the general goal of grammatical description.[8] The primary interest is in describing language in its own terms without reducing it to, say, the physiology of speech, the acoustics of sound, or the neurological elements involved. The sociologist's problem (and more obviously the anthropologist's problem, since the latter has always recognized the importance of language) is to somehow demonstrate the significance of cultural meanings, as well as gesture, intonation, and stress for how language is perceived and interpreted, chosen and delivered during the course of social action. Thus, the existence of grammatically correct sentences in a language and their use in social research do not insure that subjects being interviewed will perceive and interpret the questions asked in the same way as the interviewer. The adequacy of a theory of language is based on the understanding and usage of the "native speaker"; yet even though the "rules" governing "grammaticalness" may be clear and consistent, some "native speakers" (e.g., interviewers) may not be understood by other "native speakers" (e.g., interviewees). A sociologist may seek the advice of a linguist who passes judgment on the grammaticalness of his questionnaire, but he is still left with unsolved problems of meaning unless he also considers differences in dialect, idiomatic expressions, stress, intonation, and gestures. The "stratificational rules" mentioned by Lamb presuppose a set of cultural meanings if he considers *all* the different strata he describes to be within the linguist's domain of interest. But these presupposed meanings necessary for "acceptable" linguistic utterances remain problematic in the study of both language and social behavior.[9] The general problem is stated clearly in the following:

The code of features used by the listener does not exhaust the information he receives from the sounds of the incoming message. From its sound shape he extracts clues to identify the sender. By correlating the speaker's code with his own code of features, the listener may infer the origin, educational status and social environment of the sender. Natural sound properties allow the identification of the sex, age, and psycho-physiological type of the sender and, finally, the recognition of an acquaintance.[10]

Jakobson and Halle note that a linguist who studies an unknown language begins as a cryptanalyst until he can gradually break the code and become more and more like a native decoder. The sociologist, for example when interviewing, cannot afford to treat his own language from the perspective of a native speaker, but must adopt the position of a cryptanalyst approaching a strange language.

The linguist's strategy is to merge "casual" and "noncasual" language [11] (such as everyday speech with poetry or mathematics) and to establish a formal discipline which unifies them structurally before semantic elements of language are explored. But this strategy obscures, as Voegelin notes, the problem of linguistic selection and how selection can be significantly different in casual as opposed to noncasual utterances. Similarly Chomsky criticizes Lounsbury for taking informants' responses at face-value and assuming they automatically signify "meaning," that what is said is literally what is meant. Chomsky's point is that when Lounsbury writes "In linguistic analysis we define contrast among forms operationally in terms of difference in meaning responses," he conceives of meaning too broadly—as any response to language—especially when linguistic devices can be used which are not dependent upon the subject's definition of the situation.[12] An important question here is how semantic analysis can afford to treat as self-evident the ways (the "rules") by which subjects assign meaning to events? The anthropological field worker assumes, as does the structural linguist, he shares and understands common-sense meanings that are intended for his subjects—even those in nonliterate societies. Many of these assumptions include meanings expressing such moods as "annoyance," "happiness," and "friendliness" conveyed by voice intonations, physical distance, and general employment of common-sense cultural meanings derived from the parent society of the observer.

The following remarks by Chomsky provide one important strategy for the measurement of social events:

More generally, it appears that the notion of "understanding a sentence" must be partially analyzed in grammatical terms. To understand a sentence it is necessary (though not, of course, sufficient) to reconstruct its representation on each level, including the transformational level where the kernel sentences underlying a given sentence can be thought of, in a sense, as the "elementary content elements" out of which this sentence is constructed. In other words, one result of the formal study of grammatical structure is that a syntactic framework is brought to light which can support semantic analysis. Description of meaning can profitably refer to this underlying syntactic framework, although systematic semantic considerations are apparently not helpful in determining it in the first place. The notion of "structural meaning" as opposed to "lexical meaning," however, appears to be quite suspect, and it is questionable that the grammatical devices available in language are used consistently enough so that meaning can be assigned to them directly. Nevertheless, we do find many important correlations, quite naturally, between syntactic structure and meaning; or, to put it differently, we find that the grammatical devices are used quite systematically. These correlations could form part of the subject matter for a more general theory of language concerned with syntax and semantics and their points of connection.[13]

The strategy suggested by Chomsky has received wide support among linguists. Thus, Saporta criticizes "attempts to identify *grammaticalness* as used here with either *banality* on the one hand or *literalness of meaning* on the other. According to the view proposed by Chomsky and adopted here, such identifications seem unwarranted. For example, 'Misery loves company,' although at least as banal, is less grammatical than the synonymous 'People who are miserable love company,' owing to the different classes of nouns represented by 'misery' and 'people.' Similarly, semantic notions would seem to be irrelevant since both grammatical and ungrammatical utterances may be equally nonsensical." [14] In urging that grammaticalness, statistical notions, and semantic notions be distinguished and measured separately, Saporta notes their high intercorrelation but is not interested in how what we know in one area (meanings shared by members of the same culture) is critical for understanding another area (like grammaticalness). The example he gives is interesting because "Misery loves company" as a shorthand version of "People who are miserable love company" presupposes a rather elaborate unstated set of cultural meanings in either form of the expression. The meaning of an utterance is not completely independent of its grammaticalness, in spite of attempts to develop rules for *degrees* of grammaticalness, because of the linguist's reliance upon the common-sense cultural meanings of the native speaker. The linguist's implicit use of common-sense knowledge in constructing grammatically "correct" sentences the meaning of which he assumes will be intuitively understood, presupposes that he and the "native speaker" share a wide range of implicit common-sense meanings.

The embarrassing part of my argument for sociologists lies in my assumption that the linguist should consult the anthropologist and sociologist for the structure and dynamics of cultural meanings. Unfortunately, the sociologist (and anthropologist) is often relying upon the same unstated common-sense knowledge he has acquired as any other member of the society. The core of the problem for both linguist and sociologist can be found in the distinction between thought patterns and meanings as they are learned in a given culture, and the units of spoken and written languages (following Lamb's formulation) which can be stratified. The epistemological problem posed by the Sapir-Whorf hypothesis cannot be dismissed by the sociologist (or anthropologist) *or* linguist (as is sometimes the case), regardless of the internal consistency to be found in the structure of language and social institutions, like kinship, for example. The actor's experience of events and objects in his environment, his thought patterns and the meanings to which they are linked are communicated via casual and noncasual language and via spoken units and written ones. The weak correspondence between these two parallel systems, casual and noncasual, makes their interrelationships all the more important because in passing from one to the other form of discourse and in communication generally we always have one foot, as it were, in the common-sense world of everyday life.[15] The conditions or "rules" which enable us to pass from the casual to the noncasual presuppose that we know the structure of both and particularly the details of how they become linked.

⤠ Language and the Study of Meaning

The use of language as a tool of social research must distinguish between institutional and innovational elements.[16] "The institutional element de Saussure calls *la langue,* and the innovational element *la parole;* by definition the two together exhaust *le langage*." [17] The distinction suggests the importance of knowing something about the signs a person receives from other members of the same speech community and which contribute to his competence as a hearer of everyday conversation. *Langue*, as a system, can be studied for its structural features and its potentialities for discourse. It is a repository governed by rules that can be highly formalized. "Native speakers (excluding scholars) are ignorant of the history of their own language, which means that the history is irrelevant to the system as they know it . . ." [18] Now *langue* is the basis for *parole*, but *parole* is also the basis for change in a language because of its actual use in everyday life. Thus, *la langue* represents both the official (if there are written documents) and the traditional stock of knowledge at hand held by members of the society by which communication occurs. *La parole* is the innovational use of language whereby new definitions of the situation are created day by day. The research sociologist cannot avoid this distinction in formulating a research design, asking questions, and analyzing answers.

The fact that utterances involve words with intonational contours, and some ordering among the words means that the definition of the situation and the role-taking acts of a set of actors in verbal communication can be conceptualized crudely and subjected to preliminary empirical test. Various speech acts can be ordered syntactically into "situational utterances" and "response utterances." [19] Response utterances are usually based on a response to other utterances. "In contrast with response utterances, a situational utterance is one that is generally employed to initiate a discourse, conversation: 'How do you do?' 'I want to tell you something.' 'Do you have any books?' " [20] Ziff goes on to describe some of the "conditions" whereby "response" and "situational" utterances structure situations in social action. This is not the place to attempt a detailed analysis of all the devices and concepts which linguists and semanticists have to offer sociologists. I wish here simply to suggest possible strategies which measurement in sociology might follow and the relevance of linguistic studies to furthering the development of such measurement. The tools and concepts of the linguist and semanticist suggest possible operational procedures for pinpointing cultural meanings and the structure of social action. [21]

Another related viewpoint can be found in Wittgenstein's

observations about meaning: that the meaning of a word is to be understood through its use, where meaning is use.[22] Ziff's analysis provides balance in this discussion; it is consistent with Chomsky's remarks cited earlier. Ziff stresses the importance of both syntactic structures and situational conditions which alter meaning. Including the syntactic emphasis is an important argument against the view that meaning is a situational fiction because use changes continuously.

৵৳ *Meaning and Measurement*

Although the methods of structural linguists facilitate measurement strategies for the general problem of meaning, there have been some specific attempts to measure meaning directly which deserve comment. The following from Lounsbury is relevant:

(1) Semantic features may be recognized in more than one way in a language. Some may be recognized overtly, with separate phonemic identities, while others may be recognized covertly, merged with other semantic features in various jointly and simultaneously shared phonemic identities.

(2) For a single semantic feature there is sometimes a mixing of the two manners of linguistic recognition: some features emerge, so to speak, at some points to find separate identity in the segmental structure of a language, but are submerged at other points, being identifiable only as possible contrasts between various already irreducible segments.

(3) There are two possible ways of treating these "submerged" categories in linguistic description: (a) they may be given morphemic status, perhaps by forcing the segmentation as far as it can be pushed and then by resorting to portmanteaus where segmentation is impossible; or (b) they may be given special submorphemic status as "components."

(4) The description of the componential structure of contrasting forms is an important part of linguistic analysis, whether or not the contrasts have any correlates in the segmental structure of forms.[23]

Lounsbury is interested in the "semantics of reference, rather than of linguistic distributions; the components are to be semantic features rather than distributional features." [24] Lounsbury shows the importance of relating knowledge about a group's ethnography, in his case the use of kinship terms and their place in the

wider social structures, to an understanding of the meaning of
the society's kinship classifications and thereby to formulate
hypotheses about social behavior which can be documented by
observation. The analysis of kinship terms is informed by some
knowledge of day-by-day routines. The overt structure of terms
may correspond to behavioral acts, while abstract "rules" and unstated meanings may inform the usage to which terms are put.

The idea of applying componential analysis to cultural
forms (as opposed to linguistic forms) is the basis for Ward
Goodenough's interest in "developing an empirical science of
meaning" [25]:

The aspect of meaning to be dealt with is signification as distinct from
connotation. What is meant by these terms will become clear in the
course of the discussion. Suffice it to say at this point that the signifi-
catum of a linguistic form is composed of those abstracted contextual
elements with which it is in perfect association, without which it cannot properly occur. Its connotata are the contextual elements with
which it is frequently but less than perfectly associated. Significata are
prerequisites while connotata are probabilities and possibilities. Only
the former have definitive value.[26]

Goodenough's interests are directly relevant to problems important to sociologists concerned with social action as defined by
Weber. The following description shows how cultural meanings in common-sense situations may be studied, at least by first
approximation to what is practiced and enforced.

Now let us suppose that the language under study is a written one, and
that the notation used by those who are literate in it is partially
phonemic, but not perfectly so. There are some phonemes which are
written with more than one symbol and some which are written with
the same symbol, e.g. the identical phonemes of English *see* and *sea*
and the different phonemes of English *read* in the expressions *will read*
and *have read*. Let us suppose, furthermore, that it is the linguist's job
not only to determine what the phonemes of the language are but to
show how they relate to the symbols conventionally used for writing it.
To do this he would have to get a literate speaker to read him a text
written in the conventional alphabet. He would have to record this text,
as it was read, in a phonetic notation and derive the phonemes in the
prescribed manner. He would then have to draw up a phonemic transcription of the text, compare it with the text as written conventionally,
and compare both with the text as recorded phonetically in order to

make a precise statement of what are the phonological elements in the language for which the conventional symbols stand.

It is the situation just described which is analogous to the one facing the semantic analyst. While he aims to find the conceptual units out of which the meanings of linguistic utterances are built, he has the conventional symbols of speech which more or less stand for these units (or combinations of them) already given him. He must acquire an informant who knows how to use these symbols. The procedure is to note what speech symbols the informant uses in what contexts, and at the same time to describe these contexts by means of a notation which makes as many discriminations as conveniently possible. Such a notation is analogous to the phonetic notation of the linguist.[27]

Goodenough's work extends the methods applied to the study of syntactic structures to the study of meaning, thereby providing potentially measurable bases for theories of social organization which assume a congruence between role relationships and the everyday categories signified by the terms of kinship, friendship, religion, etc. The mathematics presupposed is founded upon a base of set-theoretic axioms. There is probably a close correspondence, especially in societies small in scale, between social organization as described normatively—that is, its institutionalized features—and the closed features of set-theoretic axioms. These "formalized" features of social organization, then, correspond to *la langue* of de Saussure. But, as Goodenough indicates in the opening page of his paper, he is not interested in *la parole*, even though obtaining information from informants may include elements from both *la langue* and *la parole*. Goodenough assigns the connotative features of meaning a minor role in his work. The anthropologist traditionally describes kinship systems in their formal aspects, not in their practiced and enforced character. This is not to deny a description of the latter in ethnography as a whole, but the method of obtaining information from a key informant is itself often an obstacle to learning what is practiced and enforced, much less the innovational features of social organization and language. Goodenough suggests, of course, that there are other dimensions of meaning which he does not touch in his paper. This is not to criticize him for what he did not do, but to argue that these other dimensions, especially those of social interaction as appearance, gesture (which he mentions), and status relationships as

expressed in interaction (which he also mentions) are not amenable, as currently conceived, to measurement by the same mathematical assumptions. Further, that present linguistic and semantic
methodological devices for measuring meaning will have to reflect the problematic character of *la parole*. Goodenough's work
is suggestive as a guide to discovering the "natural logic" of common-sense meanings even though the measurement procedures
are not applicable.

Before closing this section it is important to note another
method for measuring meaning which presupposes, and treats as
self-evident, the relationship between social organization and *la
langue*. Further, the innovational or situational determinants of
social organization and language are ruled out by the method.
Consider the following:

The meaning of "meaning" for which we wish to establish an index is
a psychological one—that process or state in the behavior of a sign-
using organism which is assumed to be a necessary consequence of the
reception of sign-stimuli and a necessary antecedent for the production
of sign-responses. Within the general framework of learning theory,
we have identified this cognitive state, *meaning,* with a representational
mediation process and have tried to specify the objective stimulus and
response conditions under which such a process develops.[28]

The actual measurement device, the "semantic differential," is
similar to attitude-scaling techniques and is described as follows:

The semantic differential is essentially a combination of controlled
association and scaling procedures. We provide the subject with a concept to be differentiated and a set of bipolar adjectival scales against
which to do it, his only task being to indicate, for each item (pairing of
a concept with a scale), the direction of his association and its intensity
on a seven-step scale. The crux of the method, of course, lies in selecting the sample of descriptive polar terms.[29]

Osgood's mediation process is a hypothetical construct. As Roger
Brown has remarked: "It could be entirely cortical without in-
validating behavioral implications. The theory is not to be
judged on the evidence for fractional implicit responses but by
the success with which it predicts—together with the rest of
Osgood's learning theory—overt behavior. I have found that this

success cannot, at present, be given anything approaching a conclusive evaluation. . . . Finally, behavioral meanings are found cheek-by-jowl with imaginal meanings inside the organism —neither revealed in action nor available to introspection." [30]

✑ *Sociological Theory and Meaning*

The discussion of method and measurement has stressed the importance of invariant conditions constituting the structure of common-sense acts. Wittgenstein's discussion of the similarity between language and a game shows that learning a set of abstract rules enables one to act appropriately in spite of the contingencies which surround play. [31] The "rules" governing everyday life are discussed in much of Wittgenstein's work and his discusion of them underlines Schutz' insistence that the study of categories employed by the man in the street should be the first task of sociology. For example: "If we look at the example in S1, we may perhaps get an inkling how much this general notion of the meaning of a word surrounds the working of language with a haze which makes clear vision impossible. It disperses the fog to study the phenomena of language in primitive kinds of application in which one can command a clear view of the aim and functioning of the words." [32] Wittgenstein continues with a discussion of "language-games" and provides further theoretical support for the notion of common-sense "rules" and acts. His discussion of "boundary" is particularly relevant:

For how is the concept of a game bounded? What still counts as a game and what no longer does? Can you give the boundary? No. You can *draw* one; for none has so far been drawn. (But that never troubled you before when you used the word "game.")
"But then the use of the word is unregulated, the 'game' we play with it is unregulated." . . . It is not everywhere circumscribed by rules; but no more are there any rules for how high one throws the ball in tennis, or how hard; yet tennis is a game for all that and has rules too. . . . To repeat, we can draw a boundary—for a special purpose. Does it take that to make the concept usable? Not at all! (Except for that special purpose.) [33]

Wittgenstein notes further that the concept "game" has

blurred edges and that indistinct pictures or notions are often what is needed. The point made by Schutz that discourse in everyday life is punctuated by its taken-for-granted and often ambiguous character is relevant here. The necessity to place the word "rules" in quotation marks when using it to describe common-sense activities is nicely put by Wittgenstein:

in philosophy we often *compare* the use of words with games and calculi which have fixed rules, but cannot say that someone who is using language *must* be playing such a game.—But if you say that our languages only approximate to such calculi you are standing on the very brink of a misunderstanding. For then it may look as if what we were talking about were an *ideal* language. As if our logic were, so to speak, a logic for a vacuum.—Whereas logic does not treat of language —or of thought—in the sense in which a natural science treats of a natural phenomenon, and the most that can be said is that we *construct* ideal languages. But here the word "ideal" is liable to mislead, for it sounds as if these languages were better, more perfect, than our everyday language; and as if it took the logician to show people at last what a correct sentence looked like. . . .

And is there not also the case where we play and—make up the rules as we go along? And there is even one where we alter them—as we go along.

I said that the application of a word is not everywhere bounded by rules. But what does a game look like that is everywhere bounded by rules? whose rules never let a doubt creep in, but stop up all cracks where it might? —Can't we imagine a rule determining the application of a rule, and a doubt which it removes—and so on?

But that is not to say that we are in doubt because it is possible for us to *imagine* a doubt. I can easily imagine someone always doubting before he opened his front door whether an abyss did not yawn beyond it; and making sure about it before he went through the door (and he might on some occasion prove to be right)—but that does not make me doubt in the same case.

A rule stands there like a sign-post. —Does the sign-post leave no doubt open about the way I have to go? Does it show which direction I am to take when I have passed it; whether along the road or the footpath or cross-country? But where is it said which way I am to follow it; whether in the direction of its finger or (e.g.) in the opposite one? —And if there were, not a single sign-post, but a chain of adjacent ones or of chalk marks on the ground—is there only *one* way of interpreting them?—So I can say, the sign-post does after all leave no room for doubt. Or rather: it sometimes leaves room for doubt and sometimes not. And now this is no longer a philosophical proposition, but an empirical one.[34]

Wittgenstein's comments about philosophy—that it seeks to clarify our use of words, for instance, or to clarify the "state of mathematics that troubles us"—are important for sociology inasmuch as he appears to say that language is not in perfect correspondence either with formal logic or with everyday life meaning. Language and "game" have rules, but these rules are not literal rules in the sense of exhausting a set of possibilities or determining a set of possible outcomes. As he states, we get entangled in our own rules. But this means that we have "rules" not rules because we want to know how this entanglement and the conditions surrounding such activities are both sources of data and barriers to precise measurement. The problematic features of everyday life cannot be explained by formal logic or by any system isomorphic with its axioms. The language we adopt for describing the realities of life always runs the risk of entanglement with what we mean. The logic of everyday activities in which the social object under study is embedded must be related to the logic of the observer's theory such that the two systems are both distinct and yet interrelated. Wittgenstein is telling us that the transformations which relate one system to another and the language which describes each system taken separately and both systems taken together will never be perfect. There can be general congruence but not perfect correspondence.

Moving on to more concrete ground, we note among the various features of "rules" governing language one, the study of idiom formation, which shows the imperfection of syntactic structure and meaning and which is empirically crucial for any understanding of social action. "An idiom is a grammatical form —single morpheme or composite form—the meaning of which is not deducible from its structure." [35] As Hockett notes, idioms are continually being introduced into all languages under various sorts of conditions for its survival. The fact that idioms are not deducible from their structure becomes an obvious limitation on the completeness with which a language can be described even though certain patterns are favored in particular languages. [36] For the present interest the following is critical:

It is a remarkable fact that a speaker may say something that he has never before said or heard, to hearers to whom the utterance is equally

novel, and yet be completely understood without anyone being aware
of the novelty. Indeed, this is a daily occurrence. The way in which
it comes about is basically simple: the new utterance is a nonce-form,
built from familiar material by familiar patterns. . . .

However, the mere occurrence of a nonce-form for the first time
does not in itself constitute the creation of a new idiom. An additional
ingredient is required: something more or less unusual either about the
structure of the newly-produced nonce-form, or about the attendant
circumstances, or both, which renders the form memorable. As we go
about the business of living, we constantly meet circumstances which
are not *exactly* like anything in our previous experience. When we
react via speech to such partially new circumstances, we may produce
a phrase or an utterance which is understandable only because those
who hear it are also confronted by the new circumstances. Alternatively,
an individual may react to conventional circumstances with a bit of
speech which is somewhat unconventional—again being understood because of context. Given any such novelty, either of expression or of
circumstances or of both, the event installs special meaning into the
linguistic form which is used, and the latter becomes idiomatic. . . .

The total context, linguistic and nonlinguistic, in which a nonce-
form takes on the status of an idiom is thus the *defining context* for the
idiom.[37]

Idiom formation and "naming" are not new to any field researcher, but the fact that to understand them requires a knowledge of both linguistic and nonlinguistic features which can aid
him in explaining and predicting social events cannot be overlooked. Their meaning and linguistic form can be approximated
or addressed directly by techniques already mentioned. They are
basic to any understanding of the actor's interpretation of an
environment of objects.

The fact that meanings are employed which are not represented in the manifest data, for instance interview protocols, does
not mean that we are required to posit hypothetical constructs
to explain their role in social action. What is required is an
explicit conceptualization of how these meanings are inferred
and acted upon by actors in social scenes.

In constructing a model of the actor we assume that there
are imperfect correspondences between *la langue* (institutional)
and *la parole* (innovational) features of language; between normative, idealized, or formal social organization and the social
organization which is practiced and enforced; between language

structure and meaning; between the perceived object, the meaning attached to it, the acts whereby object constancy is achieved, and the physical description of the object; between the rules of the game and "rules" of everyday life; and finally, between the social scene, as perceived and interpreted by its members at some point in time as a world taken for granted and known in an unquestioned way, and the world which can become problematic in the course of interaction because of potential and actual contingencies.

The social researcher must add to his methodology the theory and methods necessary for an analysis of the "ethnography of speaking" if field research and experimental techniques are to reflect everyday life.[38] Recent work has shown that the analysis of speech, gestures, and physical appearance can be important research tools for studying social solidarity, social distance, role distance, authority relationships, and general social organization.[39]

THEORETICAL

PRESUPPOSITIONS

THE CONCERN with the theoretical presuppositions of method and measurement throughout all of the earlier chapters of this book has probably provoked a number of questions on the part of the reader as to precisely what I have been assuming about sociological theory. The present chapter will discuss some theoretical issues without any attempt to give them a critical foundation. While I think it essential to discuss the bearing of theoretical assumptions on the measurement of sociocultural events, no attempt is made to present the foundations of sociological theory. I assume general familiarity with the two major theoretical traditions—the classical view which includes Comte, Spencer, Marx, Weber, and Durkheim, and the social psychological view in the tradition of Baldwin, Freud, Cooley, Mead, and Thomas—which continue to generate sociological research and theorizing. I further assume—as suggested by Dennis Wrong's excellent paper [1]—that any views on method and measurement presuppose a certain kind of actor; accordingly I shall present some details on the kind of actor my views presuppose. Since my primary concern is with method and measurement at the level of social process or of what Max Weber called "social action," I feel the major burden of this chapter should be directed to the structure of social action and, in particular, the "rules" governing social conduct.

✑§   *The Problem*

The problem of order as posed by Hobbes—or for the sociologist the problem of social order—remains a common concern for both classical theorists of society and those who adopt the social psychological view. Although the classical sociologist conceives of society as a unitary organization (which can be broken down by institutions, e.g., religion and kinship) and of societies as related to each other in terms of their "stages" of development, those who adopt the sociopsychological point of view are also concerned with the problem of order in relation to the initiation, maintenance, alteration, and destruction of face-to-face social relationships. Sociologists have tended to focus on either the one or the other level of analysis for both conceptual and empirical reasons. While both are necessary levels of analysis, little work is done to show their relationship. One way of demonstrating their relationship is to describe the measurement problems that arise when theoretical and research problems call for both levels of analysis.

Hobbes, who saw the human situation as one in which every man is the enemy of every other, where life is "solitary, poor, nasty, bruitish and short," [2] was able to conceive of the relationship of man to man in society through the development of and belief in the social contract. The social contract is an important point of departure for considering both the classical and the social psychological views of social order because it represents the formal conditions which must be followed if a state of war is to be avoided and order and security maintained. By specifying the kinds of social action which obtain under a state of war—the absence of social contract and sovereign authority—Hobbes implicitly assumes some form of social action that must obtain under both war and social contract. But the form of social action which must obtain under social contract, the normative elements necessary for its effective maintenance, depends on the fulfillment of both explicit and unstated conditions. The explicit conditions are often explained in terms of a society's laws. An understanding of the unstated conditions requires a solution to the problem of meaning because these implicit conditions presuppose man's perception and interpretation of rules of conduct which are shared with his fellow man but which are followed and enforced differentially. The differential interpretation and perception of rules of conduct (their practiced and enforced character) require an explicit theory of social action; where social action, as defined by Max Weber, consists of "all human behaviour when and insofar as the acting individual attaches a subjective meaning to it. [and] . . . takes account of the behaviour of others and is thereby oriented in its course." [3] While Weber did not elaborate his definition of social action, his work presumably builds on the concept.

The classical theorists opposed the reduction of social life to psychological laws or explanations of human conduct. Although his early work included material on the problem of alienation, Marx directly challenged the reduction of legal, political, and social structures to psychological concepts about human nature.[4] Marx's point is that society cannot be explained by reference to man's unique personal motives, his hopes, fears, and needs, but that these factors are the product of life in society. For Marx it is the social, economic, and political conditions of life which determine man's personal characteristics in group activity. Man's characteristics and behavior can be studied and explained by examining group life. The problems of society cannot be reduced to those of "human nature." Freud also stressed the importance of norms in understanding general social conduct and in particular social control in his writings on the internalization of social norms. The development in Freud's thought from stress on biological to psychological to social and cultural conditions underlines the problem of meaning in the study of social action.[5]

Durkheim stressed the notion that society and social life are not to be explained by the psychological constitution of the individual; rather, sociology has its own proper level of abstraction which cannot be reduced to that of individual psychology, but must be studied in terms of observables at its own level. Thus, the regularities to be found in the "social suicide-rate" imply the existence of collective tendencies which are "exterior" to the individual and cannot be explained by reference to individual psychology. Each individual's behavior, his private and public feelings, his hopes and fears, are influenced by forms of collective life which transcend the individual and which can be studied and understood without reference to the particular consciousness of concrete persons. All forms of collective life (e.g., religion, law, morals, political institutions, customs, teaching practices), have their reality independent of the individual consciousness of the persons carrying out these precepts that the group prescribes and proscribes, and they can accordingly be studied independently. But, as Durkheim notes, not all social consciousness (as opposed to individual consciousness) achieves externalization and materialization. There is much— the greater part—which is diffused and "at liberty." He cautions that we must not take the sign for the thing signified. In a footnote he makes the following important point:

We do not expect to be reproached further, after this explanation, with wishing to substitute the exterior for the interior in sociology. We start from the exterior because it alone is immediately given, but only to reach the interior. Doubtless the procedure is complicated; but there is no other unless one would risk having his research apply to his personal feeling concerning the order of facts under investigation, instead of to this factual order itself.[6]

Thus, even though there is much of collective life which is not fixed or clearly formulated, say, in the form of written rules or laws, study of the precepts involved must consider them as external to "each average individual taken singly." Although we may obtain information from individuals about the "interior" workings of social consciousness and are interested in the social constraints which control and provide meaning to these "interior" workings, it is the way we act under the pressure of the collectivity that is of primary interest to the sociologist.

That part of collective life which is not fixed or clearly formulated in written rules and laws is discussed by Durkheim with reference to organic and contractual solidarity. He notes that contractual relations multiply as social labor becomes divided.[7] He criticizes Spencer for failing to see that noncontractual relations develop at the same time. Durkheim points out that we would have a precarious solidarity if socio-legal relationships were based only upon the agreed terms of contracts. More specifically:

It forces us to assume obligations that we have not contracted for, in the exact sense of the word, since we have not deliberated upon them in advance. Of course, the initial act is always contractual, but there are consequences, sometimes immediate, which run over the limits of the contract. We co-operate because we wish to, but our voluntary co-operation creates duties for us that we did not desire.[8]

In addition to the unstated conditions of contractual relations there are customs—rules which are not sanctioned by any code but nevertheless binding upon us—which reflect traditional experience and can be independent of contractual relations.[9]

In his conceptual and empirical work on suicide, Durkheim makes continual reference to the influence of marital status, religion, age, country, race, seasonal variation, etc., while using neat cross-tabulations to show how the data he has lead to explanatory concepts like "collective ideas and practices," "suicidal tendency," "widowhood," "bachelorhood," "collective sentiments," the "integration of religious society," the "integration of domestic society," the "integration of political society," and the like. Parsons notes that Durkheim initially used two sets of social facts in his empirical work: legal codes and statistics of suicide; but that social facts then became relegated to what Parsons calls a "residual category" and Durkheim's conceptual scheme shifted to that of a cognitive framework which stressed the "actor's knowledge of the situation of his action." [10] Parsons states that Durkheim confused levels of abstraction by not discriminating between "society," the "individuals," and the emergent properties that are formed when the elements are integrated as a whole. But Parsons makes it clear that Durkheim also means that "society cannot in principle exist except as a synthetic product of the association of individuals." [11]

My interest in Durkheim's changes in conceptual and methodological positions as described by Parsons is critical for its emphasis upon social action for studying the problem of social order. Parsons notes that the meaning of constraint changes for Durkheim and signals a change in his conceptual and methodological perspective. The problem of social control becomes identified with constraint as the moral authority of a system of rules. Social structure becomes a common system of normative rules which are also dependent upon common moral rules or values. The exteriority of constraint in a cognitive sense changes to the notion of norms which are "internal" to the actor. The

actor, according to Durkheim, then becomes "identified" with
these norms in the same sense, Parsons notes, as with Freud's
notion of the "introjection" of norms in the formation of a
superego.[12]

Parsons' work is important because he demonstrated a con-
vergence in the study of social action by Durkheim and Weber,
for example, the relation between legitimacy in agreements and
the noncontractual elements of contract. Another important connection, states Parsons, can be found in Durkheim's and Weber's
interpretation of constraint as moral authority.[13] Parsons' principal concern was to study the emergence of a theory of social
action in the works of Marshall, Pareto, Durkheim, and Weber,
and to develop a generalized theory of action. Weber's work is
given final consideration because Parsons felt he came closest to
formulating an explicit theory of action, but with some
limitations.

Thus his explicit systematic theorizing tended to run off in a direction
different from that of the main present interest, that of a systematic
classification of structural ideal types of social relationship. But in spite
of these methodological limitations it has been possible to elicit by
analysis a definite scheme of the structure of a generalized system of
action which appears at the most strategic points of Weber's work and,
though he did not clearly recognize its logical nature, this scheme was
absolutely essential to Weber's specific results both empirical and
theoretical.[14]

Weber's "theorizing . . . in a direction different" from a concern
with a generalized theory of action is important for an understanding of the problem of measurement in sociology and for a
clarification of subsequent theory in the structure of social action.
It is the relation of ideal social types to social action which is
important for measuring social process and social structure. Parsons, of course, was not concerned with the methodological
problems of measuring social action, and therefore would not be
expected to be interested in the relationship between the
observer's and actor's social categories, measurement categories
and social action.

To close this section, I want to stress my concern with linking the measurement of social action to inferences about social
structure. The study of social structure by collecting social facts

such as births, deaths, age, marital status, and divorce does not pose a serious measurement problem. Thus, demographers interested in demonstrating the decline or growth of populations can do so without serious problems of measurement. When sociologists become interested in accounting for and interpreting the trends in fertility within and between cultures, the examination of the social facts *per se* can provide useful data for clarifying and pointing the way to the kinds of social action inherent in a particular kind of society, for example, the study of differential fertility in families in what Durkheim calls "domestic society." The measurement problems in studying social facts in relation to social action, however, are difficult and often insoluble at our present state of knowledge. The sociologists who have devoted extensive efforts to the empirical study of social action are usually labeled "social psychologists" by the theoreticians following the classical tradition. The study and measurement of social action involve such concepts as attitudes, role-taking, and norms. Sociologists who follow classical theorists, although sometimes accepting "sociological social psychology" as an integral part of sociology, would, on the whole, consider the study of social process in terms of attitudes, role-taking, and norms as a reduction of sociology to psychology.[15] The sociologist who bases his work on the classical theorist would probably view the study of social action as acceptable to the extent that the emphasis were upon normative and nonnormative [16] factors, particularly on how nonnormative conditions act as constraints upon the actor's group-shared motives, on how they affect his stock of knowledge at hand, and enter into his role-taking in daily life situations and his life plans. Although the forms of ownership and the control of productive means may be considered as nonnormative factors *per se,* they assume normative significance inasmuch as the actor's behavior takes them into account as conditions for coming to terms (happily or unhappily) with his environment, and as their emergence, transformations, and stability constitute part of the total sociocultural complex. The social conflict and constraint between the nonnormative order and the dominant values and norms of the social order are empirically relevant at all levels of analysis. My interest has been in the measurement problem of social action as it includes the conditions of both the factual and the social order, and the research methods that sociologists have typically employed to study social action.

The remainder of the chapter will briefly outline the elements of social action which presumably the methods discussed earlier seek to describe and measure. Weber's definition of social action is taken to mean that cultural meanings (as group-shared properties) orient, guide, and modify social relationships and interpersonal exchanges in the course of face-to-face interaction and secondary communications. It is assumed that such concepts as role-taking can be studied and explained without reference to some underlying hypothetical continuum of individual attitudes (as psychologically defined). An understanding of the structure of social action is assumed to begin and end with the conceptualization and observation of a culturally defined scene of action. The study of social action, then, is not reducible to the psychological motivations or attitudes of the individuals making up some group or collectivity, but social action is to be explained by the norms, values, or ideologies that are binding upon the members of a group and that transcend any particular actor taken as a psychological entity. The study of society at the level of social action and the study of comparative social structures as collectivities both take factual and normative conditions as their point of departure. The two levels of analysis are linked, though often not explicitly, for instance, in the sociological study of population growth and decline in relation to the social action leading to increased fertility based on such normatively regulated factors as illegitimacy, religious beliefs about the desired number of males in a family, ignorance of contraceptive methods, and so on. Other examples might include the comparative study of industrialization and how cultural expectations and ideologies influence the implementation of rationality in industrial organizations at the level of managerial decision-making. Another example can be found in Bendix' discussion of Marx's belief in reason. Bendix points out that Marx did not "explain why some 'bourgeois ideologists have raised themselves to the level of comprehending the historical movement' in accordance with the principles of scientific socialism, although this conflicts with their bourgeois class interest." [17] At the level of social action, class conflict becomes a study of differential perception of one's environment and how culturally defined ideologies or belief systems emerge, achieve stability, become altered, or are destroyed.

✍ *Some Elements of Social Action*

I now turn to the discussion of some of the elements of social action which are presupposed in my earlier remarks on method and measurement. I will hereafter, unless specifically noted, refer to sociological theory, and sociological method and measurement, in a generic sense, but actually I intend their use as they refer to the study of social action. I shall, therefore, avoid continual references to theory, method, and measurement "at the level of social action," but assume that the reader will realize that it is implied each time.

A basic goal of sociology is the search for and measurement of invariant properties of social action within the context of a changing social order. One of the first to emphasize the importance of face-to-face contacts, especially in intimate social relationships between persons in "primary groups," was Charles Horton Cooley.[18] In stressing the social nature of the self, Cooley also underlined the importance of contingencies that arise in face-to-face social interaction. Following the tradition of Cooley's work George Herbert Mead devoted considerable attention to how the individual is able to anticipate the perspective of the other during the course of communication. He explicitly noted that communication involves the conveyance of *meaning*.[19] Mead's extensive discussion of role-taking testifies to the necessity of including and studying the mutual modification of social action inherent in taking the role of the other. The concept of role-taking presupposes the notion of meaning or "subjective" meaning used by Weber and Mead. There is a tendency in contemporary sociological research to accept the importance and properties of meaning in role-taking as given, rather than pushing its conceptualization beyond the work of Weber and Mead. This is as true of Parsons as it is of Weber and Mead. It is also true of Cooley's notion of the "looking-glass self" and Thomas' "definition of the situation." All of these notions presuppose that meanings, their generation, transmission, and understanding, according to some set of standards, are matters which can be accepted as self-evident. Thus, for Mead, meaning arises out of the sequences of social interaction in which the actor finds himself and is part of the action scene in the form of physical and verbal (and nonverbal) responses and gestures.[20] Although it is clear that meanings are being communicated continuously in the course of interaction, their properties have not been objects of sociological study. Yet it is clear that Mead presupposes an order of events governed by rules of conduct ("the rules of the game") which make up the notion of the "generalized attitude" of the group.[21] The "rules of the game" are always invoked in one form or another to account for ways in which actors evaluate each other's conduct and how role-taking is achieved. Thus, while sociologists would probably all agree that the actor is oriented to rules of conduct, they seldom indicate the structure of such "rules" or how they inform the actor about the nature of his environment. Stated another way, how does the actor go about making sense of his environment in socially acceptable ways? Each time we make reference to taking the role of the other, the actor's "definition of the situation," "the generalized other," the "reflexive self," etc., we presuppose a solution to the problem of meaning.[22]

Talcott Parsons, who has written extensively on the conceptualization of social action, refers in his earlier work to the elements of social action as actor, norms, ends, and means. Later he elaborates these elements in describing the actor as a system of action *per se* (called the personality system), the social system as a network of interactive relationships among actors, the pattern variables as invariant structural features of the actor's experience, and cultural patterns (the notion of culture later changed to a system of action).[23] Parsons explicitly refers to the role of expectations in the interaction of ego and alter, the contingent character of choosing alternative courses of action, the "stability of meaning" observed by ego and alter, and the role of culture in providing a shared symbolic system or "ways of orienting."[24]

Although Parsons' use of concepts like "expectations," "stability of meaning," and "ways of orienting" is intended to deal with the problem of subjective meaning, these concepts subsume a variety of interpretive rules for assigning meanings to events and objects. What is lacking is a model of the actor which permits us to distinguish between the possible interpretive rules used by the actor and researcher for deciding the import or meaning of each other's gestures and verbalizations (or their absence). The researcher cannot assume that he and the actor enjoy the same community of subjective meaning structures for assigning cultural significance to an event or object. But what enables the researcher to transcend this community of meaning and assign scientific significance to the interpretive rules employed by the actor? [25] The first step is the formulation of a general model which permits the researcher to recognize the possible differences between how the scientist goes about assigning meanings to events and objects he studies and how the actor being studied accomplishes the same objectives. The next step requires some specification of the "rules" which orient the actor's perception and interpretation of his environment. Some comment on the notion of norms is in order here.

If norm is taken to mean a "directive to action" then we can assume that some set of "rules" or "standards" constitutes the ingredients to be identified. The actor, somehow, decides what is expected or appropriate by perceiving and interpreting the social scene which becomes the object of his interest. My discussion is concerned not with the assignment of meanings to specific events or objects in particular situations but rather with the general or invariant properties which can be said to characterize the "rules" or "standards" whereby meanings are assigned to events or objects. A more detailed discussion of norms ("rules" or "standards") is required because the role-taking process or a role consists of norms.

◆§   *Norms and Subjective Meaning*

Many sociologists follow the tradition developed by Sumner in his work *Folkways*.[26] A recent account of this position is contained in Robert Bierstedt's *The Social Order*.[27] According to Bierstedt, norms refer to ways of "doing" as opposed to ways of "thinking." Social order therefore becomes synonymous with the existence of norms. Norms for Bierstedt are rules or standards with which we are *expected* to conform. They guide our conduct in society, are usually taken for granted, and we are seldom aware of them except when they are violated.[28] The emphasis placed by Bierstedt (and all sociologists) upon the expected or "appropriate" properties of norms in given situations raises the following question: How can we say that social order is constituted by norms which refer to what is expected or appropriate? If social order means a normative order consisting of standards which are shared, does it not also mean that the stability of the order lies in the existence and enforcement of some properties whose violation would lead to temporary or sustained disruptions, disorganization, or chaos?

Norms are characterized as discrete sets of rules (folkways, mores, and laws which are cross-cut by communal norms—binding upon the entire society—and associational norms applicable only to certain groups) which persons in a given society are expected to honor. While acknowledging the constitutive character of norms for social order, Bierstedt explicitly states that the motivated character of norms is for the psychologist to determine. Yet there are two kinds of culture, the "ideal" and the "real"; in the former, persons conform to the same degree, while in the latter there are many degrees of actual conformity.[29] We can summarize the view of norms exemplified by followers of Sumner (e.g., Bierstedt) as follows:

1. Although the differential perception, interpretation and motivation to comply with norms determine the extent to which and how norms are binding upon persons in a given society, the study and conceptualization of such properties are the domain of the psychologist.

2. Conceived as three disjoint sets, folkways, mores, and laws are believed to be "out there" in some unambiguous and explicit manner. Yet there are many groups in society with norms that differ or conflict. The "ideal" and degrees of "real" conformity can apparently be conceptualized and studied without concern for the differential perception, interpretation, and motivation to comply with them.

Another view of norms, found in Robin Williams' *American Society*,[30] begins with a characterization of culture as the basis for an elaborate network of "rules" that orients the actor in various situations. Williams points out that persons in everyday life seldom know what determines their conduct or what will follow from it and usually only become aware of "what happened" after some sequence of events has occurred, remaining unaware of the "causes" and "consequences" of what has taken place.[31]

Cultural norms (which include culturally approved goals and means for their attainment) are learned and shared. They range from "technical or cognitive" types, through "conventional" (custom and etiquette) types, "esthetic" standards, to "moral" norms. All norms, according to this formulation, have some prescriptive or proscriptive quality to them. Williams describes four "major dimensions" to norms: their *distribution* (knowledge of them, acceptance or agreement with them, and their application to everyone or particular persons); *enforcement* ("externally" by punishment or reward, by enforcing agency or group or community, by the consistency and source of authority for enforcement, or through "internalization"); *transmission* (learned in primary or secondary relations and these relations may reinforce what is learned); and *conformity* (amount of conformity or deviance, extent of deviance or nonconformity to them).[32]

Williams notes that the empirical properties of norms are inferred from testimony by persons or indirectly by their descriptions of approved and disapproved conduct for situations and by observation of their spontaneous behavior in everyday life. The *after the fact* ways of ascertaining the existence and nature of norms, i.e., from asking persons or observing their actions, require a theoretical framework which can take both the actor's *and* the observer's perspectives into account. This can become a difficult problem if we recall that the actor, according to Williams, usually does not know what happened until after the act, or event is over. The difficulty is compounded when we observe that the meaning of the norm can shift depending upon variations in time, place, emotional needs, intergroup and interpersonal exchanges, and a variety of situational pressures and interests.[33] Whatever exists "out there" as a norm can only be known *after the fact* and its very "existence" may be altered, depending upon the various qualifications mentioned above. In short, the influence of the norm "out there" depends upon the actor's definition of the situation. Williams clearly states the problematic character of norms in his discussion of "Institutional Variation and the Evasion of Normative Patterns." He explicitly points out the causal role of nonnormative conditions and individual differences in perception and interpretation of norms,[34] and also claims that the sociologist should treat the differences in perception and interpretation as "given facts" and leave the task of explaining them to the psychologist and social psychologist. To summarize Williams:

1. Norms are proscriptive and prescriptive, and detected *after the fact* where the sources of data are the actor and/or observer.

2. Any given norm is subjected to an unknown number of contingencies such as how the actor defines the situation, the time period involved, the place, "situational pressures," and the like.

3. The actor may not be consciously aware of the norms— which may be "internalized"—that are involved in any given social scene, but they are, nevertheless, "directives to action."

4. Normative variation occurs because of nonnormative factors and individual differences in perception and interpretation. These contingencies or differences are not sociological variables but to be explained by psychological and social psychological theories of perception.

A critical and major problem is posed by the conceptions of norms formulated by Bierstedt and Williams: How can norms be described or imputed to an environment of objects unless we make the actor's differential perception and interpretation of them, and his general definition of the situation, the basic properties of the concept? To attempt to investigate norms through questioning of actors or observing social interaction presupposes a social reality which has stable and uniform properties. Patterns of responses may enable us to infer the existence and substantive properties of norms, but these patterns do not tell us how the actor perceives the role of the other and then shapes his self-role accordingly. They do not explain the differential perception and interpretation of norms and their practiced and enforced character in everyday life. The sociologist's ideal concepts of the existence, structure, and alterations of norms are abstractions from the actors' differential perceptions, interpretations of them and motivations to comply with them over time. It is difficult to imagine any discussion of norms apart from the abstraction procedures from actual social processes. Social norms as ideal disjoint sets are abstractions made by the sociologist and documented by the common-sense knowledge he has of them. But if Williams' conception of norms is meaningful, then social roles (as norms) should be given similar problematic status. If role-taking requires that the actor infer the role of the other as a condition for shaping his self-role in subsequent interaction, then differential perception, interpretation, and motivation to comply with normatively defined roles during interaction are variables for deciding what the actor's environment consists of and how his environment structures social action.

Formal legal "rules," "rules" of etiquette and those governing work activities provide boundary conditions for the structure of social action, but it is the informal and unstated conditions of the contract, to repeat Durkheim's notion, which makes for the binding character of such "rules." Thus, it is the unstated "rules" which inform the actor as to what is "appropriate" or "expected" *affect* on the part of others and himself (e.g., the *voice intonation* necessary to convey "anger," "pleasure," etc., the *gestures* which should accompany particular occasions, and so on). "Typical," and often unstated conceptions about what is appropriate and expected provide the actor with an implicit model for evaluating and participating in (practiced and enforced) normative behavior. An empirical issue which sociology has barely touched is how the actor manages the discrepancies between the formally stated or written rules, his expectations of what is expected or appropriate, and the practical and enforced character of both the stated and unstated rules. On this issue depends the precise identification of fundamental units of social analysis and the determination of their measurement properties.

A Working Model for Norms

The contingencies of differential perception and the actor's knowledge about rules of conduct can be of interest to the sociologist without relying upon neurophysiological or psychological states. The actor's thoughts which are a result of his unique psychological make-up are of interest to the social scientist only insofar as they can be explained by reference to a common culture; although they are not irrelevant to the social scientist, he assigns them residual status. The working model I shall describe is adopted from game-theoretic notions. The notion of a game as described by Garfinkel has been used by many theoretical and empirically oriented social scientists because it provides a useful point of departure for understanding "norms" as usually depicted by sociologists, and it generates a model which avoids the discrepancies found in current conceptions.[35]

Garfinkel chooses to work with games as illustrative of stable situations because they allow the researcher to describe a sequence of social events in which each player is provided with some kind of scheme for knowing what he and the other players are doing and intending. The basic rules of a game indicate what will be considered "normal" for those players who seek to abide by the rules.[36] Basic rules are defined by three properties which are called "constitutive expectancies." (1) the "constitutive expectancies" provide a set of boundary conditions within which each player must make decision choices regardless of personal likes and dislikes, plans and consequences for himself or others. The choices are independent of the numbers of players, patterns of moves or territory of play. (2) Each player assumes a norm of reciprocity with respect to the alternatives which are binding on each other. (3) The players assume that whatever they expect of each other is perceived and interpreted in the same way.[37]

Garfinkel notes that "constitutive expectancies" may be assigned to a particular set of possible events and not to others and may be said to provide the *"constitutive accent"* for this particular set of events. The related set of possible events to which "constitutive expectancies" are assigned is given the label *"constitutive order of events of the game."* [38] A game for Garfinkel, then, is defined by its rules to which "constitutive expectancies" are attached. He notes that it is possible to produce a new game by removing the "constitutive accent" from one set of possible events and assigning them to another set. In addition to the basic rules, there are two other types of rules which are critical features of any game. Garfinkel calls them "rules of preferred play" and "game furnished conditions."

"Rules of preferred play" are distinguished from basic rules by the discretion provided the player with respect to compliance on his part. The player defines "correct procedure" within the limits of the basic rules, but the "preference rules" tend to operate independently of the basic rules. The independence stems from various kinds of traditional play, "efficiency" procedures, aesthetic preference, and the like, which are open to the player.[39] *Game furnished conditions* help to fill out how the game tends to be played and correspond to each set of basic rules. The players' decisions are always constrained by them and they are independent of whether the player wins or loses. They describe the general characteristics of the game but are invariant to any particular state of the game because they always enter into each decision. Garfinkel finds a good example of the game furnished conditions in chess where the basic rules provide a situation of perfect information at all times. A different game with different basic rules may not provide for such conditions. Thus in poker the situation is quite different and the game furnished conditions are such that every decision contains a varying amount of uncertainty.

The foregoing analysis enables us to distinguish changing conditions of play and to specify which rules are in "focus" during any given state of the game. The notion of basic rules as a set of invariant properties allows the observer to describe the standards which will serve as definitions of correct or "normal" play. These rules can be specified before actual play and make it possible to manipulate the game scene so as to predict the consequences for the game of players not conforming to them. But do game conditions and rules provide us with an adequate model for characterizing and studying "rules" of conduct in everyday life? As a preliminary answer to this question it might be useful to specify what I see as the advantages of using the game model for understanding norms and role-taking.

1. The game model enables the researcher to speak cogently about the different kinds of "rules" the actor honors in his perceived environment.

2. Understanding of the conditions and rules of the game permits *a priori* specification of what will be "strange" or "unusual" and therefore what might be called "expected" and "proper."

3. Knowing something about the properties of the constitutive rules would permit sociologists to specify properties which contribute to the stability of social action.

4. Ability to specify or identify constitutive rules and preference rules would enable the researcher to make use of them in
experiments to discover the nature and consequences of given
kinds of social interaction.

5. The notion of "constitutive accent" enables the researcher
to understand how the social scene or the definition of the situation changes over time.

6. The game model provides us with a basis for specifying
how the actor infers the role of the other, according to what
"rules," and how he shapes his self-role accordingly. This
requires some analysis of the problem of cultural meanings in
everyday life and how they are situationally attached to objects,
facts, and events over time.

Garfinkel notes that if we extend the notion of constitutive
properties to everyday life then current concerns with the moral
status of norms, their legal status, or customary usage are not the
critical problems the sociologist should address *initially,* rather
he should be primarily concerned with how "norms" define what
Garfinkel calls "perceivedly normal" events. The sociologist
could then talk about "normally organized environments" and
"socially disorganized environments" within the same framework
i.e., without judging the latter (negatively) within a moral context. Garfinkel's proposal that perceived events have a constitutive
structure requires a more detailed explanation.

The pivotal concept employed by Garfinkel for considering
the bases of social action in everyday life is that of "*trust.*" A
basic question here is: How do members of a group or society
perceive and interpret their everyday lives? How do objects,
events, and facts come to be seen as "normal," "making sense,"
"understandable"? The notion of "trust" explains the compliance of persons to a "constitutive order of events." This order,
however, is neither perceived explicitly nor known uniformly by
any given population. The ambiguity of "rules" together with
the differential perception, interpretation, and motivation to
comply with them suggest that the actor must "trust" his environment in the face of uncertainty, but also suggests a basis for
social change. Further information may or may not be forthcoming and may or may not clarify the social scene. The notion
of "trust" implies that the actor must "accept" and rely upon definitions of the situation which are potentially problematic and

for which explicit rules do not exist. If the "constitutive accent" honored by the actors can be specified conceptually and defined operationally under experimental conditions, then we would have a basis for describing what might be "perceivedly normal." A model of norms and role-taking would have to break down "perceivedly normal" into a set of elements which would constitute variable conditions whereby the actor makes "sense" of his environment.

The notion of *perceivedly normal events* directs the researcher's attention to (1) the *typicality* of everyday events and their *likelihood* of occurrence, (2) the ways in which they *compare* with events in the past and suggests how future events might be evaluated, (3) the actor's assignment of *causal significance* to events, (4) the ways events fit into an actor's or society's typical *means-end* relationships, and (5) the ways events are deemed necessary to an actor's or society's *natural* or *moral* order.[40] How the actor perceives his environment is rooted in a culturally defined world. Practiced and enforced norms or rules of conduct would vary by *typicality, comparability, likelihood, causal significance, means-end schema,* and the nature of the *natural* or *moral order*. Role-taking would depend upon the same variables. The role-taking process forces the actor to decide, during the course of interaction, the nature of the other role under uncertainty conditions. It is difficult to find a game which provides rules that cover all the possibilities that can or may arise. During the course of interaction the actors often silently agree to follow some set of explicit and/or implicit rules during social interaction. There is the further problem that the timing of moves, their duration, and the like are not matters over which the player has complete control. All of these problems in games, however, turn out to be features, as Garfinkel shows, that the sociologist would subsume under a more precise "definition of the situation." He proposes that the notion of "constitutive accent" may be an integral feature of all kinds of domains of events, from games through science, from everyday life to dreaming.

The differences between games and everyday life point to the difficulties which the sociologist may expect to encounter when he seeks to measure behavioral states which reflect norms and to study the process of role-taking. One critical difference lies in the fact that in games timing provides a delimited context in which success and failure is to be decided, for accomplished play is what Garfinkel calls "an encapsulated episode." [41] The outcomes of games, then, are not at all dependent on the development of later situations *"outside"* the conditions of play. In everyday life matters may not be decided for an indefinite time period. Or they may be re-decided time and time again. Another point is that it is misleading to speak of "rules" and "norms" in the same way that one can talk about basic and preferential rules in a game. The term "rule" when used in everyday life does not carry the same precision and meaning that it does in a game. This is because events in everyday life do not have the absolute bounded conditions which can be found in games. When a basic rule is violated in the game it terminates play or disrupts "normal events of play" sufficiently so that the player is confused and must resort to some kind of "normalizing." [42] In everyday life, however, it is difficult to find violations of "rules" or "norms" which produce clearly measurable instability in the social order. So-called "rules" in everyday life are continually violated, often systematically, including the mores, without our being able to demonstrate an immediate or even shortrange clear-cut threat to the stability of the social order. We usually argue that if such violations continued systematically over time with a large number of participants the social order would "fall apart"; this argument, however, does not specify "how long?" and "how many participants?" or "what would be the nature of the instability?" Further, we have no way of knowing what *new* forms of social order would emerge. Garfinkel's answer to this dilemma is to concentrate on the *properties* of perceivedly normal events and the constitutive order of such events, not on "rules or norms" *per se*. Social "rules" or "norms" do not have the bounded conditions of basic rules of play in a game; their time structure is basically different.

Their difference in time structure can be explained by the invariant properties of rules in a game as opposed to those in everyday life. Basic rules in a game have a calculable character because they are sufficiently bounded to permit unambiguous decisions as to when something "strange," "unusual," or basically "wrong" has occurred. In everyday life laws are "broken" and very elaborate procedures are used to clarify what invariably becomes an ambiguous problem. This is true of our determination of violations of rules of law; the police, witnesses, the jury, the judge, the defense and prosecuting attorneys, the victim, and the accused may all very seriously entertain judgments which taken together are at once contradictory, overlapping, and vague. The situation is compounded when we are confronted with judgments on unclear nonlegal matters: evaluations of another's character, of affect, of physical attractiveness, of art objects, of marriage partner, and the like. I would like to view the "rules" of everyday life as essentially "noncalculable" in the sense of conventional measurement because of the discrepancy between their ideal description and their practiced and enforced character. The "noncalculability" is not to be found merely in the actor's judgments, but also in the observer's model of the actor. This is not to say that a precise model of the actor's judgments is impossible, but that conventional measures which are, for example, found in two-valued logic, ordinal scales, and mathematical game theory do not adequately depict everyday decisions. In order to pursue this point further we should examine the role-taking process more closely. We should decide how the actor infers the role of the other and the properties which make up the time structure of everyday decisions.

◄§ *Role-Taking and Meaning*

To say that the boundary conditions of everyday decisions are "noncalculable" is a misleading characterization of the structure of everyday decisions. I am asserting that existing measurement systems do not take into account the problematic features of these decisions. In order for them to do so it would be necessary to extend existing measurement systems to include the measurement of judgments which are subject to the contingencies of the changing definitions of the situation imputed to the social scene by the actor. The difficulties inherent in the conceptual problem can be illustrated by discussion of Thomas C. Schelling's book *The Strategy of Conflict* [43] where explicit attempts are made to show the influence on choices in games of strategy of what is termed "irrational" behavior. What Schelling calls "irrational"— an inconsistent value system, faulty calculation, poor communication, random or haphazard influences—are common occurrences in everyday life and are not subject, with our present knowledge, to literal measurement by conventional devices. But Schelling's discussion is not sufficiently detailed to handle the nuances of the role-taking process or how the actor defines the situation and shapes his self-role. The notion of a game of strategy wherein each player bases his choice on what he expects of the other player is basic to role-taking, but how the scene comes to be defined and the self-role shaped in subsequent interaction is not clear. Although Schelling's formulation underlines the "noncalculable" character of everyday judgments or decisions if conventional measurement systems are used, his work takes for granted precisely those features of the social system which the sociologist must make problematic. For example, suggesting that an experimenter add "cooperative" and "uncooperative" players, orient the players to "consistent or inconsistent value systems," he presupposes that norms and values are clear-cut and easily specified and that the role-taking process is not seriously affected by their differential perception, interpretation, and motivated compliance.

But what are the apparent difficulties here? What elements of role-taking require more precise formulation if the measurement problems are to be clarified? Ward Edwards illustrates the problematic features of role-taking for experimental situations where the experimenter and subject presumably share the same language and employ terms assumed to be clear and unambiguous. He remarks:

Many of the instructions most commonly used in psychological experiments are at best ambiguous and at worst internally contradictory. For example, consider a speeded intelligence test. Its instructions say: "Answer as many questions as you can. You have 10 minutes for this part of the test." What is the subject supposed to do? Should he make certain that each answer is correct, thus minimizing errors but dealing with relatively few questions? Should he answer as many questions as possible guessing when he does not know the answer? Or should he adopt some compromise between these strategies; and if so, what compromise? The instructions do not say. In fact, the instructions tell him to perform an impossibility; they say that he should simultaneously maximize the number of questions answered and minimize the number of errors. These instructions are internally inconsistent. A computing machine would reject as insoluble a problem presented with such in-

structions. Human beings, more tractable and less logical, perform such
tasks every day. The only way they do so is to provide some kind of
self-instruction which supersedes the impossible instructions.[44]

Edwards further points out how the same problems arise in
other experimental situations where time, number of correct
responses, and number of incorrect responses are involved. He
notes that inconsistent or ambiguous instructions are "most
likely to arise when perfect performance is specified as ideal
(e.g., all questions should be answered correctly) but no information is provided which would enable the subject to evaluate the
relative undesirability of various kinds of deviations from
perfection." [45] In order to avoid inconsistent and ambiguous
instructions to subjects Edwards suggests that the experimenter
specify the optimal strategy to the subject even though experiments have shown that subjects will seldom follow this strategy
if revealed to them. He hypothesizes that removal of internal
contradictions will reduce experimental error and make the
experiment easier to interpret. The most interesting part of
Edwards' paper lies in his remarks about the role of evaluative
criteria used by the experimenter and subject. He raises the issue
of the consequences of differential criteria between experimenter
and subjects and points to the obvious problem of deciding the
import or meaning of the experimental results. He notes that
"Money is probably the most universally used and understood
evaluative dimension in our culture; almost all subjects will
understand the statement: 'Your purpose in this experiment is to
go home with as much money as possible.'" [46] Edwards' paper
points unambiguously to the problem of defining the situation
such that the experimenter knows the properties of the environment of objects which both he and the actors under study must
perceive and interpret in the same way and toward which they
are expected to exhibit complementary motivated compliance.
Subjects should be informed as to the evaluative criteria with
which they are expected to comply. The researcher in formulating an experiment or constructing a questionnaire to measure
role-taking must have some way of conceptualizing the actor's
environment and how the actor is culturally motivated to perceive and interpret it. But Edwards' argument presupposes that
the *meaning* of the evaluative criterion, in his case money, is

sufficiently clear and patterned so that the experimenter's research will not be confounded by cultural variables which are necessary considerations in psychological experiments. But if this is true for psychological experiments, is it not equally true for sociological experiments and surveys? How can we possibly know what our substantive findings *mean* if we have not settled the problem of evaluative criteria raised by Edwards? An understanding of the way the actor infers the other role presupposes that the problem of how he assigns meaning to his environment is solved. But the nature of the inferred role of the other is a problem seldom addressed by sociologists. (For example, how does the subject decide the meaning of questionnaire items?) Such research would require that the sociologist provide a solution to the problem raised by Edwards in another way; namely, by specifying how the actor assigns cultural meanings in role-taking and indicating the invariant and variable properties of these cultural meanings.

✍ *Meaning and Communication*

For present purposes meaning will be taken to refer to the interpretation of some sign according to some standard.[47] Following Alfred Schutz, the things signs stand for are to be decided by reference to four types of orders.[48] Schutz breaks up the "rules" or "standards" indicated by Kecskemeti into different kinds of orders or ways in which signs can be analyzed by the observer. This constitutes a model by which the observer can order the meanings assigned to events by the subjects under study. In everyday life, Schutz argues, we tend continuously to substitute one order for another, but we will often focus upon one order, while rendering the others arbitrary or contingent. The interesting point here is that what may be an important sign or symbol of something for some actor or group, may be quite irrelevant for some other actor or group.[49] The different kinds of orders by which objects, facts, and events are interpreted can be characterized by four basic forms of "appresentational" relations (i.e., linking signs to the things to which they refer) employed by the actor for transcending the world within his actual reach. The four are marks, indications, signs, and symbols. The first three transcend the world within the actor's reach, but are "appresentational" relations found in the world of everyday life. The fourth transcends the world within the actor's reach and also provides the basis for transcending the world of everyday life. These four forms of "appresentational" relations provide us with a model for understanding communication between persons. Stated another way, these sign-signatum relations are necessary ingredients for role-taking, for they tell us how the actor comes to assign meanings to objects and events in his environment.

The actor experiences the world within his reach as part of his unique biographical situation, and this "involves a transcending of the Here and Now to which it belongs." [50] The actor, therefore, approaches the role-taking situation with a background of conventions or ignorance [51] which precedes his abstractions from the immediate objects and events in his visual field. Schutz notes that one way in which we find our way in the world, especially on occasions when we re-enter some part of it from which we have been absent, is to *mark* certain objects. The mark, e.g., the notation on the margin of a book, the brief comment on an appointment pad, serves as a subjective reminder for the interpreter when some object returns within his reach (or he returns within reach of the object or event). The mark transcends the experienced world of the actor's Here and Now and represents an arbitrary selection of certain objects to remind the actor of something. The mark on the book is paired with its referential meaning—"important point made by the author."

Another form of pairing by appresentation which helps the actor transcend the world within his actual reach Schutz calls *indication*. Schutz notes that what he calls indications cover what are frequently subsumed under the term "natural signs." [52] The indication, like the mark, does not presuppose intersubjectivity, and is described as follows:

The indicating member of the pair is not only a "witness" for the indicated one, it does not only point to it, but it suggests the assumption that the other member exists, has existed, or will exist. Again the indicating member is not perceived as a "self," that is, merely in the apperceptual scheme, but as "awakening" or "calling forth" appresentationally the indicated one. It is, however, important that the particular nature of the motivational connection remains opaque. If there is clear and sufficient insight into the nature of the connection between the two elements, we have to deal not with the referential relation of indication but with the inferential one of *proof*. The qualification contained in the last statement eliminates, therefore, the possibility of calling the footprint of a tiger (recognized as such) an indication or "sign" of his presence in the locality. But the halo around the moon indicates coming rain, the smoke fire. . . ." [53]

A *sign* for Schutz designates "objects, facts, or events in the outer world, whose apprehension appresents to an interpreter cogitations of a fellow man." [54] Objects, facts, and events which are interpreted as signs must, states Schutz, directly or indirectly refer to the bodily existence of another actor. The simplest case is that of face-to-face relationships, but distances in space or time are also included; yet this does not mean that actual perception is required, for the actor may recollect or fantasy the object, fact, or event. Further, the interpretation of an object, fact, or event as a sign for someone's cogitations does not necessarily mean that the communicator intended the cogitations interpreted by another party, or that the interpreter was intended as the recipient of the cogitations. Finally, the two actors involved do not have to be known to one another. It should be clear, however, as Schutz notes, that communication or role-taking between persons requires that they share a similar system of relevances. "To be successful, any communicative process must, therefore, involve a set of common abstractions or standardizations." [55] The basis for common abstractions or standardizations is provided by the vocabulary and the syntactic structure of everyday language. Unfortunately, sociology textbooks neglect material on language and meaning, and theories of role-taking treat language and meaning as self-evident. The ways in which the actor in everyday life and the sociologist who observes him achieve common abstractions or standardizations remain unclear.

The final appresentational form which Schutz discusses is *symbols*. He defines the symbolic relationship

as an appresentational relationship between entities belonging to at least two finite provinces of meaning so that the appresenting symbol is an element of the paramount reality of everyday life. (We say "at least two" because there are many combinations such as religious, art, etc., which cannot be investigated within this paper.) [56]

Thus far the appresenting and the appresented members of the pair of any sign-signatum relation as well as the interpreter belong to the reality of everyday life, whereas symbolic appresentation transcends the finite province of meaning found in everyday life. In higher symbolic forms only the appresenting member refers to everyday life, while the appresented member has its reality in some other province of meaning such as the world of science, fantasy, and the like.

The four types of couplings described by Schutz, and the marks, indications, signs, and symbols he discusses, all presuppose some basic features of everyday life to which he has given considerable attention. Any discussion of the analytic elements of social interaction in general, and of role-taking in particular, requires an explicit reference to the total social situation within which role-taking occurs. The following elements of the social situation relevant to role-taking, though not exhaustive, are presented as essential to Schutz's scheme:

1. *The reciprocity of perspectives.* The connection between the sign and the signatum assumes that (1) in everyday life the actor takes for granted that he and the other actors would have the same experience if they were to change places; and (2) the actor assumes ". . . that the differences originating in our private systems of relevances can be disregarded for the purpose at hand and that I and he, that 'We' interpret the actually or potentially common objects, facts, and events in an 'empirically identical' manner, i.e., sufficient for all practical purposes." [57] Our worlds overlap. "The two fluxes of inner time, yours and mine, become synchronous with the event in outer time . . ." [58] and permit our actors a basis for communicating with one another. The reciprocity of perspectives tells us that the accuracy of role-taking assumes common experiences which makes such activity contingent upon the interpretations, in the course of interaction, placed upon objects, events, and facts by the actors concerned.

2. *The actor's stock of knowledge at hand.* Schutz notes that the greatest part of the actor's knowledge is socially derived from others. Knowledge is socially distributed and the stock of knowledge at hand differs for different actors.[59] The actors in everyday life, in order to communicate about matters which are socially approved and taken for granted, must make certain assumptions

about *what* his neighbor knows and *how* they both know the "same" fact.[60] The actor's stock of knowledge, therefore, becomes a variable in how the actor infers the role of the other and how his self-role is managed.

3. *Typification.* Socially distributed knowledge taken for granted in everyday communication is exchanged within a context whereby the actor typifies both his own and the other's behavior.[61] Typical social roles and typical expectations are assumed in the exchange of socially distributed and socially approved knowledge. "Socially approved knowledge consists, thus, of a set of recipes designed to help each member of the group to define his situation in the reality of everyday life in a typical way." [62] The reader will note, as does Schutz, that these preceding remarks are to be traced, explicitly or implicitly, to the writings of Simmel and Durkheim in their concern with individual and collective consciousness, Cooley in his notion of the "looking glass self," and G. H. Mead in his concepts of the "generalized other," the "I" and the "me." [63] What is lacking in their writings, however, is the clear-cut focus and variable status which Schutz assigns to the world of everyday life as the basis for our understanding of objects, facts, and events. He does this by showing the kinds of couplings which link signs with their signatum, and how marks, indications, and signs are the "appresentational" references which structure this understanding. Symbols, as higher forms of appresentational references, are anchored in this reality of everyday life, but also structure our understanding of objects, facts, and events which transcend our experience of everyday life. The realities which transcend everyday life, such as science, art, fantasy, and poetry, cannot be understood without reference to daily life. Schutz notes that the world of everyday life, as a set of subjective meaning structures which is socially approved and taken for granted, corresponds to Thomas' notion of the definition of the situation. The problem of subjective meaning then, requires that communication accomplished by the role-taking process be given variable status according to the ways in which actors *can* and *do* exchange sign-referent relationships with one another. The foregoing discussion can be elaborated as follows:

1. Assume that the definition of the situation means the

same thing as the "constitutive accent" described earlier. The constitutive accent for a particular set of events provides the "sense of reality" which Schutz attributes to William James' theory of many sub-universes conceived as different realities.

2. The problem of meaning enters the picture immediately for

In order to free this important insight from its psychologistic setting we prefer to speak instead of many sub-universes of reality of *finite provinces of meaning* upon each of which we may bestow the accent of reality. We speak of provinces of *meaning* and not of sub-universes because it is the meaning of our experiences and not the ontological structure of the objects which constitutes reality.[64]

A given set of experiences is called a finite province of meaning if it shows a "specific cognitive style." A particular reality or social world as a finite province of meaning, like the notion of "constitutive order of events," enables the observer to specify the properties of the environment of objects to which the actor responds.

3. The cognitive style or constitutive order of events or accent of reality, as conceptualized by the observer, is a model for deciding how the actor makes sense of his experiences in the course of social interaction. Stated another way, the model provides a basis for deciding, from the actor's point of view, the "strangeness," the "usual" or "normal" features of his visual field and private thoughts, i.e., the basis for inferring the other role.

4. Schutz speaks of shifting from one finite province of meaning to another as a "shock." For example:

There are as many innumerable kinds of different shock experiences as there are finite provinces of meaning upon which I may bestow the accent of reality. Some instances are: The shock of falling asleep as the leap into the world of dreams; the inner transformation we endure if the curtain in the theater rises as the transition into the world of the stage-play; the radical change in our attitude if, before a painting, we permit our visual field to be limited by what is within the frame as the passage into the pictorial world; our quandary, relaxing into laughter, if, in listening to a joke, we are for a short time ready to accept the fictitious world of the jest as a reality in relation to which the world of our daily life takes on the character of foolishness; the child's turning toward his toy as the transition into the play-world; and so on.[65]

These different finite provinces of meaning—the world of dreams, art, imageries, religious experience, various types of mental illness, science, etc.—have their peculiar cognitive style.

5. Each cognitive style, like the rules of the game or the constitutive order of events, has its consistency and compatibility of experiences, its basis for deciding what is perceivedly normal, unusual, and the like, and provides for something like a set of boundary conditions. Schutz hypothesizes that the term "finite" is intended to convey the impossibility of speaking in terms of a transformation formula which would enable the actor to relate one province to another.

6. According to Schutz, "The passing from one to the other can only be performed by a 'leap,' as Kierkegaard calls it," which manifests itself in the subjective experience of a shock." [66] This amounts to radical modification of our mental set or attention to objects and events around us.

7. The cognitive style of any finite province of meaning or constitutive order of events is oriented by a set of "rules" which provides the actor with the basis for deciding the mental set or attitude which is appropriate and necessary, the kind of spontaneity required, a particular time perspective, a particular form of experiencing one's self, and the kind of intersubjective world of communication and social interaction operative. The notion of multiple realities is for Schutz a basis for generating a typology of finite provinces of meaning or different social worlds.

᪉ *Philosophical Background*

My interpretation of Schutz' and Garfinkel's material on the nature of "rules" governing conduct in everyday life and the properties of such "rules" (or at least some of them), assumes several concepts borrowed from the philosophy of Edmund Husserl. The problem of meaning is central to Husserl's work and a brief mention of the phenomenological movement is essential for informing the reader as to some of the background and motivation for writing this book.[67] A variant of the Sapir-Whorf hypothesis appears in Husserl's writings when he refers to language as constitutive of experience and that any understanding of how persons communicate with each other requires an understanding of the language used, but an understanding whereby the analyst can transcend the problem of multiple realities only to the extent that he treats the actor's everyday world (as well as his own everyday and scientific world) as objects of inquiry. At the same time, and as noted in the last chapter, cultural meanings are not synonymous with linguistic utterances, but require the study of common-sense categories of experience and their linguistic counterparts.

An important notion is that of "intentionality" as developed by Husserl and described by Aron Gurwitsch.[68] Consider the following:

To be aware of an object means that, in the present experience, one is aware of the object as being the same as that which one was aware of in the past experience, and as the same as that which one may expect to be aware of in a future experience, as the same as that which, generally speaking, one may be aware of in an indefinite number of presentative acts.[69]

The phenomenon of object constancy refers, therefore, to different perceptual acts which the actor treats as identical. The meaning of a gesture or set of acts for the actor cannot be decided by a literal description of the object as perceived by an "objective" observer using independent methods or his own judgment. Intentionality refers to the correspondence between the experience and awareness of an object and the acts in which the object is embedded. The correspondence is not one-to-one, however, and the same stimuli which are used to produce an experience and awareness of some object in a subject do not necessarily produce the same experience and awareness in another subject. Therefore a distribution of responses to identical stimuli does not necessarily reveal the nature of object constancy. Yet constancy may be achieved, the same meanings imputed, when different stimuli are presented to different subjects. The conditions under which object constancy occurs are critical because exact measurement may never be achieved particularly by simple operational procedures tied to the assumption that identical stimuli or acts produce the same experience and awareness of objects in subjects. This is to say that the relationship between language and meaning requires reference to contingencies which are outside of formal or structural arrangements.

Operational procedures for measuring meaning must take into account the fact that the actor's awareness and experience of an object are determined not only by the physical object as it is presented or given but also by imputations he assigns to it. The notion of intentionality and meaning can be clarified by reference to the concept of "horizon." [70] The following comments by Kuhn describe Husserl's notion of "inner horizon" in relation to intentionality:

The frame of a picture, though forming no part of it, helps to constitute its wholeness. Similarly, the horizon determines that which it frames. The fact that the object is framed by a horizon is relevant to its mode of appearance. Its way of being is essentially a "being within." Hence horizon as a guiding notion enables us to reveal shades of meaning cast on the object by its environment. . . .

"Horizon" is but another name for the totality of organized serial potentialities involved in the object as *noema,* that is, as the intended object of an "intentional" act. The "ray of consciousness" illuminates a small central sphere, the sensuous substratum immediately given to our visual, auditory, olfactory, or tactual perception. Around this focus there is a halo of potential perceptions shading off the meaning of the focal center. Nucleus and horizon together compose the percept or, more generally speaking, the "object in mind." [71]

There corresponds to the "inner horizon" an "outer horizon" which means that the object is not isolated, but is related to other objects and the meanings attached to them, and to wider meanings attached to the same and related objects. "Furthermore, both the outer and the inner horizon are inextricably interwoven with the *temporal horizon.* The present perception of the object before me is the link in a chain of successive perceptions each of which either had or will have a presence of its own. Accordingly, the apprehension of the thing points both ways: to the immediate and remote past on the one hand, to the immediate and the distant future on the other. The temporal characters of the 'stream of consciousness,' the remembrance of the past as well as the expectancy of coming things, inform the present apprehension." [72] The actor, therefore, comes to each social act and may reflect upon it in terms of a framework of expectations within which he locates the typical elements of experienced objects.

⮗ *Conclusion*

I have assumed throughout the book that the nature of collective life—its social institutions such as kinship and bureaucratic organization, its ecological arrangements, both the areal distribution of living conditions (residence and work) and the physical distance which in part determines the formation of primary or secondary relations, and general norms and values which are explicit—is then the distinct subject matter of sociology and it provides us with a set of boundary conditions which we assume determines or sets limits upon social conduct and life in general. But a large part of collective life is also problematic to define because of its essentially oral tradition and because even its formally stated written tradition is subject to the differential perception and interpretation of actors variously distributed in the social structures. Thus, what is written about policy, ideology, values, norms, and even scientific knowledge about natural events and objects does not describe what determines the actor's conduct because of problematic features in the social action scene. The oral tradition which characterizes institutional norms and values and ideologies can be viewed as policy statements that are sometimes perceived as explicit, but they are frequently implicit and unstated although conversation or concrete action may make them explicit. Thus, the very questionnaire items posed about implicit values, norms, and ideologies may crystallize some of their relatively amorphous properties. I have focused on the unstated, including both stable and problematic, features of social action because they are the most difficult to measure by means of methodological devices available to the sociologist. I have argued that because of their dependence for stability on the actor's perception and interpretation of them, the measurement of the stated and formal features of everyday life (even after assuming that social institutions and ecological arrangements delimit the forms of collective life) and, especially, the unstated conditions of everyday life are sufficiently indeterminate to raise serious questions about the measurement systems now in use. I have also implied that some forms of everyday life may never be measured very precisely because of the innovative elements in social action.

Our actor is a constructed type in the sense used by Max Weber. We are in the business of constructing an actor and subtypes which we imagine to be gifted with consciousness.[73] But this consciousness is restricted precisely to those theoretical features which hopefully are relevant to operational procedures and empirical confirmation by observation. To this fictitious consciousness the observer assigns typical cultural motives for achieving future action and typical cultural motives imputed to others for understanding their action. In addition we construct what Schutz calls "course-of-action types" (i.e., typical patterns of behavior) which we impute to anonymous others we do not know. These course-of-action types include invariant motives which presumably govern the others' actions. Schutz continues:

Yet these models of actors are not human beings living within their biographical situation in the social world of everyday life. Strictly speaking, they do not have any biography or any history, and the situation into which they are placed is not a situation defined by them but defined by their creator, the social scientist. He has created these puppets or homunculi to manipulate them for his purpose. A merely specious consciousness is imputed to them by the scientist which is constructed in such a way that its presupposed stock of knowledge at hand (including the ascribed set of invariant motives) would make actions originating therefrom subjectively understandable, provided that these actions were performed by real actors within the social world. But the puppet and his artificial consciousness is not subjected to the ontological conditions of human beings. The homunculus was not born, he does not grow up, and he will not die. He has no hopes and no fears; he does not know anxiety as the chief motive of all his deeds. He is not free in the sense that his acting could transgress the limits his creator, the social scientist, has predetermined. He cannot, therefore, have other conflicts of interests and motives than those the social scientist has imputed to him. He cannot err, if to err is not his typical destiny. He cannot choose, except among the alternatives the social scientist has put before him as standing to his choice.[74]

The model of the actor outlined by Schutz enables the social scientist to make explicit the inner horizon of ("subjective") social action as defined by Weber. The construction of typical motives, roles, cues, constancies, unstated meanings, and so forth permits their possible manipulation under experimental or quasi-experimental conditions.

The sociological observer, therefore, who fails to conceptualize the elements of common-sense acts in everyday life, is using an implicit model of the actor which is confounded by the fact that his observations and inferences interact, in unknown ways, with his own biographical situation within the social world. The very conditions of obtaining data require that he make use of typical motives, cues, roles, etc., and the typical meanings he imputes to them, yet the structures of these common-sense courses of action are notions which the sociological observer takes for granted, treats as self-evident. But they are just the notions which the sociologist must analyze and study empirically if he desires rigorous measurement. The distributions he now constructs relegate such notions to a taken-for-granted status or to some latent continuum. Therefore, the observations which go to make up a distribution of, say, types of cities, responses to questionnaire items, or occupational prestige categories are only half of the picture. The distribution merely represents the "outer" horizon for which operational procedures have been devised. Yet the "meaning" of the distribution relies upon common-sense knowledge which includes the observer's typification of the world as it is founded in his own biographical situation, *and* his formalization of the actor's typification which is inextricably woven into his response. *Both sets of typifications must be objects of sociological inquiry.*

The inner horizon of idiomatic expressions, course-of-action motives, institutional and innovational language, and the like remain unclarified in the sociologist's distributions. The observations which are coded into dichotomies, fourfold tables, ordinal scales, zero-order correlations, and distributions in general reveal only half of the story; the "bottom half" has been taken for granted, relegated to a "latent continuum," yet informs the observer's description and inferences about the "top half" represented by "rigorous" measurement devices. It is the lack of explicit conceptualization and observation on the "bottom half" which makes measurement in sociology metaphorical and not literal. The difficulty is to be found in the lack of adequate conceptualization and the use of measurement axioms which do not correspond to the structure of social action.

Conventional measurement systems may have a moderate correspondence with the institutional features of everyday life (in spite of the potentially problematic character of differential perception and interpretation which is a built-in property of institutional structures). But the use of conventional measurement models with their deterministic axiomatic assumptions for the formal properties of such institutions as kinship, legal and corporate structures, does not mean that the structure of social action should be studied with the same model. The recipes of everyday life consist of a set of analogies which are constantly being masked, altered, and created during the course of interaction. The study of cultural meanings, with their invariant and innovative properties, remains empirically open. Our methods often follow the assumptions of the measurement systems we would like to use, and we are led into their application without asking whether alternative modes of measurement are possible or even demanded because of the structure of events under study. After going through an elaborate set of methodological decisions (where many unstated presuppositions are built-in each time), we assume that the fourfold tables or quantitative measures somehow stand on their own independently of the procedures by which they were produced. The quantitatively expressed results necessarily reify the events under study, but our interpretations of them—even after the usual formal apologies and cautions about their generality and precision—are treated as positive findings which are fictitiously assumed to be replicable and valid. All of this tends to make social research something of a closed enterprise rather than an open search for knowledge relative to a given era.[75]

NOTES

INTRODUCTION

1. R. M. MacIver, *Social Causation,* Boston: Ginn, 1942, pp. 20-21.

2. Max Weber, *The Theory of Social and Economic Organization,* trans. by A. M. Henderson and Talcott Parsons, New York: Oxford University Press, 1947, p. 88. For two excellent discussions of Weber's work and their importance for theory and method in sociology, see Peter Winch, *The Idea of a Social Science,* London and New York: Routledge and Kegan Paul and Humanities Press, 1958, especially chapters II, IV, and V; and John Rex, *Key Problems of Sociological Theory,* London: Routledge and Kegan Paul, 1961, especially chapters I, V, VI, IX, and X. Rex's book contains a lucid discussion of differences in the substantive foundations of social theory and research. My own discussion bearing upon sociological theory in the chapters that follow will seldom deal with the kinds and varieties of substantive theoretical issues raised by Rex, but will be concerned primarily with "basic theory" which I presume would underlie all of the various substantive theories he describes.

3. Everyday language and the syntax and meaning associated with common-sense vocabularies are basic to routine communication in daily life. The critical assumption is that persons employing such language assume they know what each is talking about by definition. More precise definitions are given in Chapters 2 and 9.

4. See the interesting paper by James F. Short, Jr., Fred L. Strodtbeck, and Desmond S. Cartwright, "A Strategy for Utilizing Research Dilemmas," *Sociological Inquiry,* 32 (Spring 1962), 185-202.

5. One important attempt to treat behavior in small groups with formal models can be found in J. Berger, B. P. Cohen, J. L. Snell, and M. Zelditch, Jr., *Types of Formalization in Small Group Research,* Boston: Houghton Mifflin, 1962. Unfortunately, the question of whether the models developed distort the basic or substantive properties under study is not adequately addressed in this book.

6. Literal measurement refers to an exact correspondence between

the substantive elements and relations under study and the ordered elements and relations of the measurement system. Measurement by fiat is an arbitrary or forced correspondence between elements, relations, and operations.

7. Ernest Nagel, *The Structure of Science,* New York: Harcourt, Brace, 1961, especially Chapter VI, "The Cognitive Status of Theories."

CHAPTER I

1. The terms metaphorical or synecdochical and their use here were suggested by Harold Garfinkel. A synecdochical usage here refers to the practice by sociologists of allowing theoretical and empirical statements to stand for a larger whole without specifying how the part fits in with the rest of the theory or the rest of the findings. In the present context it means that measurement theories are frequently used such that they "stand for" an appropriate demonstration of a correspondence between the elements of the theory presupposed and the empirical elements generated by the measurement system, when in fact no such correspondence has been accomplished. Instead, the one is presented alone. This is especially the case when data are analyzed without any specification of how the theory contributes to the interpretation that follows. The procedure is to concentrate upon the method of analysis and to assume that the rest is somehow taken care of without further effort on the part of the researcher. In the case of metaphorical usage, mathematical systems are frequently used by sociologists as analogous to some theoretical system or a measurement theory is used which bears a "likeness" to data gathered rather than a demonstrable correspondence between its elements, relations, and the operations permitted. The critical point here is that sociologists, in their research, often juxtapose theoretical statements alongside of empirical ones and expect the reader to demonstrate the correspondence which is only implied by the researcher who does not specify precisely what elements, relations, and operations are related.

2. See Herbert Hochberg, "Axiomatic Systems, Formalization, and Scientific Theories," and May Brodbeck, "Models, Meaning, and Theory," in L. Gross (ed.), *Symposium on Sociological Theory,* Evanston: Row, Peterson, 1959.

3. Hochberg, *ibid.,* p. 424.

4. *Ibid.,* pp. 424-425.

5. Brodbeck, *op. cit.,* pp. 376-378.

6. Hans Zetterberg, *On Theory and Verification in Sociology,* New York: Tressler Press, 1954.

7. Hochberg, *op. cit.,* pp. 376-378.

8. The terms "explicit" and "implicit" theories were suggested by Hochberg in personal communications.

9. See Herbert Simon, "A Formal Theory of Interaction in Social

Groups," *American Sociological Review,* 17 (April 1952), 202-211. Joseph Berger, Bernard P. Cohen, J. Laurie Snell, and Morris Zelditch, Jr., *Types of Formalization in Small-Group Research,* Boston: Houghton Mifflin, 1962.

 10. Warren Torgerson, *Theory and Method of Scaling,* New York: Wiley, 1958; C. West Churchman and P. Ratoosh, *Measurement,* New York: Wiley, 1959.

 11. Norman Campbell, *What is Science?* New York: Dover, 1952, p. 110.

 12. Ernest Nagel, "Measurement," *Erkenntnis,* 2 (1931), 313-333.

 13. S. S. Stevens, "Mathematics, Measurement, and Psychophysics," in S. S. Stevens (ed.), *Handbook of Experimental Psychology,* New York: Wiley, 1951, p. 1.

 14. Clyde Coombs, "Theory and Methods of Social Measurement," in L. Festinger and D. Katz (eds.), *Research Methods in the Behavioral Sciences,* New York: Dryden, 1953, p. 472.

 15. Torgerson, *op. cit.,* pp. 14-15.

 16. T. W. Reese, "Application of the Theory of Physical Measurement to the Measurement of Psychological Magnitudes with Experimental Examples," *Psychol. Monogr.,* 55:3 (1943), 8.

 17. Reese, *ibid.,* pp. 9-10.

 18. C. West Churchman, "Why Measure?" in Churchman and Ratoosh, *op. cit.,* p. 84.

 19. Coombs, *op. cit.,* pp. 471-472.

 20. Torgerson, *op. cit.,* pp. 21-22, italics in the original.

 21. Coombs, *op. cit.,* pp. 486-487.

 22. Paul F. Lazarsfeld, "Evidence and Inference in Social Research," in D. Lerner (ed.), *Evidence and Inference,* New York: The Free Press of Glencoe, 1959, p. 108.

 23. *Ibid.*

 24. *Ibid.,* p. 109.

 25. *Ibid.*

 26. *Ibid.,* p. 112.

 27. *Ibid.,* p. 113.

 28. *Ibid.,* p. 115.

 29. Paul F. Lazarsfeld and Allen H. Barton, "Qualitative Measurement in the Social Sciences," in D. Lerner and H. D. Lasswell (eds.), *The Policy Sciences: Recent Developments in Scope and Method,* Stanford: Stanford University Press, 1951, p. 155.

 30. *Ibid.,* p. 156.

 31. *Ibid.*

 32. *Ibid.,* pp. 156-157.

 33. *Ibid.,* p. 160.

 34. *Ibid.,* p. 166.

 35. *Ibid.*

 36. *Ibid.,* p. 167.

 37. *Ibid.*

38. The notion of language as a "grid" is taken from Kenneth L. Pike's work. See his *The Intonation of American English,* Ann Arbor: University of Michigan Press, 1945; *Language in Relation to a Unified Theory of the Structure of Human Behavior,* Glendale: Summer Institute of Linguistics, 1955.

39. The reader will recognize that my use of the notion "grid" is another way of stating the Sapir-Whorf hypothesis. Further comments and their consequences can be found at the end of the chapter and throughout the book.

40. Logical equivalence assumes that the following laws of logic hold: reflexive law (A is equivalent to A); symmetric law (A is equivalent to B means that B is equivalent to A); and the transitive law (A is equivalent to B and B is equivalent to C means that A is equivalent to C). Two finite sets (M and N) are said to be equivalent to each other " . . . if their elements can be related so that to every element of M there corresponds one and only one element of N, and conversely." Joseph Breuer, *Introduction to the Theory of Sets,* H. F. Fehr (trans.), Englewood Cliffs, N. J.: Prentice-Hall, 1958, p. 13.

41. *British Journal of Sociology,* XI (March 1960), 10-23.

42. Herman Weyl, *Philosophy of Mathematics and Natural Science,* Princeton, N. J.: Princeton University Press, 1949, p. 15.

43. *Ibid.,* p. 24.

44. *Ibid.,* pp. 50-54, 65. See also Weyl's chapter, "The Ghost of Modality," in M. Farber (ed.), *Philosophical Essays in Memory of Edmund Husserl,* Cambridge: Harvard University Press, 1940, pp. 278-303.

45. "The Ghost of Modality," *loc. cit.,* p. 278.

46. *Ibid.,* p. 287, italics in original.

47. *Ibid.,* p. 299.

48. *Ibid.,* p. 303. For one type of application of modal logic to the study of the formal properties of norms, cf. A. R. Anderson and O. K. Moore, "The Formal Analysis of Normative Concepts," *American Sociological Review,* 22 (February 1957), 9-17.

49. Harry Hoijer (ed.), *Language in Culture,* Chicago: University of Chicago Press, 1954, pp. 93-94. Copyright 1954 by Robert Redfield. See also B. J. Whorf, *Language, Thought and Reality,* edited by J. B. Carroll, New York: Wiley and the Technology Press, 1956.

50. "Social Control in Modern Science," unpublished Ph.D. dissertation, Department of Sociology, University of California, Berkeley, 1963.

51. See Felix Kaufmann, *Methodology of the Social Sciences,* New York: Oxford Univ. Press, 1941, for a discussion of the corpus of a science.

CHAPTER II

1. Arthur J. Vidich, "Participant Observation and the Collection and Interpretation of Data," *American Journal of Sociology*, LX (January 1955), 355.

2. Benjamin D. Paul, "Interview Techniques and Field Relationships," in A. L. Kroeber *et al.*, *Anthropology Today*, Chicago: University of Chicago Press, 1953, pp. 430-431.

3. *Ibid.*, p. 431.

4. Morris S. Schwartz and Charlotte Green Schwartz, "Problems in Participant Observation," *American Journal of Sociology*, LX (January 1955), 344.

5. For an informative account of total participation, the reader should consult W. F. Whyte's *Street Corner Society*, Chicago: University of Chicago Press, 1955, especially the methodological appendix.

6. *Ibid.*, p. 300.

7. John P. Dean, "Participant Observation and Interviewing," in John T. Doby (ed.), *Introduction to Social Research*, Harrisburg, Penn.: The Stackpole Co., 1954, p. 233, emphasis in the original.

8. Schwartz and Schwartz, *op. cit.*, p. 347.

9. *Ibid.*, p. 350.

10. Raymond L. Gold, "Roles in Sociological Field Observations," *Social Forces*, 36 (March 1958), 217.

11. *Ibid.*, p. 219.

12. *Ibid.*, p. 221.

13. Schwartz and Schwartz, *op. cit.*, pp. 345-346.

14. Vidich, *op. cit.*, p. 360.

15. Howard S. Becker, "Problems of Inference and Proof in Participant Observation," *American Sociological Review*, 23 (December 1958), 652-653.

16. *Ibid.*, p. 657.

17. *Ibid.*, p. 660.

18. Alfred Schutz, "Concept and Theory Formation in The Social Sciences," *Journal of Philosophy*, LI (April 1954), 266-267.

19. *Ibid.*, p. 270.

20. *Ibid.*, p. 267. For further details on this point the reader should consult the following: Alfred Schutz, "The Problem of Rationality in the Social World," *Economica*, 10 (1943), 130-149; "On Multiple Realities," *Philosophy and Phenomenological Research*, 5 (1945), 533-575; "Common-Sense and Scientific Interpretation of Human Action," *Ibid.*, 14 (1953), 1-38; Harold Garfinkel, "The Rational Properties of Scientific and Common Sense Activities," *Behavioral Science*, 5 (January 1960), 72-83.

21. Schutz, "Common-Sense and Scientific Interpretation . . . ," *op. cit.*, p. 31.

22. *Ibid.*

23. See Felix Kaufmann, *Methodology of the Social Sciences,* New York: Oxford University Press, 1941, for a discussion of procedural rules.

24. The point is discussed in a paper delivered at the Fourth World Congress of Sociology, Milan, Italy, 1959, entitled "Common Sense Knowledge of Social Structures." The reader can find this point discussed in a paper by Karl Mannheim, "On the Interpretation of Weltanschauung," in *Essays on the Sociology of Knowledge,* London: Routledge and Kegan Paul, 1952.

25. Melville Dalton, *Men Who Manage,* New York: Wiley, 1959.

26. See Kaufmann, *op. cit.,* for a discussion of this point.

27. Dalton, *op. cit.,* p. 277.

28. *Ibid.*

29. *Ibid.,* pp. 279-280.

30. *Ibid.,* pp. 280-281.

31. Erving Goffman, *The Presentation of Self in Everyday Life,* Garden City, N.Y.: Doubleday and Co., 1959, pp. 1, 3. Copyright 1959 by Erving Goffman. Reprinted by permission of Doubleday and Co., Inc.

32. *Ibid.,* p. 249.

33. Alfred Schutz, "Common-Sense and Scientific Interpretation . . . ," *op. cit.,* p. 27.

34. Schutz, "Common-Sense and Scientific Interpretation . . . , " *op. cit.,* pp. 31-32.

35. Schutz, "Concept and Theory Formation . . . , " *op. cit.,* pp. 266-267.

36. John P. Dean, "Participant Observation and Interviewing," *op. cit.,* pp. 225-252.

37. *Ibid.,* p. 235.

38. *Ibid.,* p. 236.

39. Erving Goffman, *The Presentation of Self in Everyday Life, op. cit.,* pp. 145-149.

40. The reader should note that the work of H. G. Barnett, *Innovation,* New York: McGraw-Hill, 1953, is especially relevant here. Barnett's interest in the cultural types who are more likely to produce cultural change requires that he make use of types of actors discussed by Dean and Goffman.

41. The reader is encouraged to consult the informative account of these points in W. F. Whyte's *Street Corner Society, op. cit.*

42. Howard S. Becker and Blanche Geer, "Participant Observation and Interviewing: A Comparison, *"Human Organization,* 16, No. 3 (Fall, 1957), 28-32; Martin Trow, "Comment on Participant Observation and Interviewing: A Comparison," *ibid.,* pp. 33-35.

43. See Beatrice B. Whiting (ed.), *Six Cultures,* New York: Wiley, 1963.

44. Abraham Wald, *Sequential Analysis,* New York: Wiley, 1947.

CHAPTER III

1. R. K. Merton, M. Fiske, and P. Kendall, *The Focused Interview*, New York: The Free Press of Glencoe, 1956; H. Hyman *et al.*, *Interviewing in Social Research*, Chicago: University of Chicago Press, 1954; R. L. Kahn and C. F. Cannell, *The Dynamics of Interviewing*, New York: Wiley, 1957.

2. W. J. Goode and P. K. Hatt, *Methods in Social Research*, New York: McGraw-Hill, 1952, p. 186.

3. *Interviewing in Social Research, op. cit.*, p. 20.

4. *Ibid.*, p. 30.

5. *Ibid.*, p. 32.

6. R. B. MacLeod, "The Phenomenological Approach to Social Psychology," *Psych. Review*, LIV (1947), 193-210.

7. *Interviewing in Social Research, op. cit.*, p. 36.

8. *Ibid.*, p. 37.

9. Goffman, *The Presentation of Self in Everyday Life*, New York: Doubleday, 1959.

10. *Interviewing in Social Research, op. cit.*, p. 40.

11. *Ibid.*, p. 44.

12. *Ibid.*, p. 46.

13. *Ibid.*, p. 47. Emphasis in original.

14. *Ibid.*, pp. 47-48.

15. *Ibid.*, p. 52.

16. *Ibid.*, p. 53. Emphasis in original.

17. *Ibid.*, p. 53. Emphasis in original.

18. *Ibid.*, p. 55. Emphasis in original.

19. *Ibid.*, p. 57. Emphasis in original.

20. *Ibid.*, pp. 63-64.

21. *Ibid.*, p. 66. Emphasis in original.

22. *Ibid.*, p. 69. Emphasis in original.

23. *Ibid.*, p. 80.

24. Kahn and Cannell, *Dynamics of Interviewing, op. cit.*, p. 26.

25. *Interviewing in Social Research, op. cit.*, pp. 59, 63-64.

26. Kahn and Cannell, *op. cit.*, pp. 34-38.

27. *Ibid.*, p. 59.

CHAPTER IV

1. Herbert Hyman, *Survey Design and Analysis*, New York: The Free Press of Glencoe, 1955, pp. 27- 28, italics in original.

2. See W. V. Quine's discussion of "passing show" in *Word and Object*, New York: Technology Press and Wiley, 1960, pp. 2-8.

3. Bert F. Green, "Attitude Measurement," in Gardner Lindzey (ed.), *Handbook of Social Psychology*, Reading, Mass.: Addison-Wesley, 1954, Vol. I, p. 336, italics in original.

4. *Survey Design and Analysis, op. cit.*, pp. 29-59.

5. See C. W. Hart, "Some Factors Affecting the Organization and Prosecution of Given Research Projects," *American Sociological Review* 12 (1947), 514-519.

6. See Louis Schneider, "The Category of Ignorance in Sociological Theory," *American Sociological Review*, 27 (August 1962), 492-508.

7. D. Krech, "Public Opinion and Psychological Theory," *International Journal Opin. Attitude Research*, 2 (1948), 85-88.

8. *Survey Design and Analysis, op. cit.*, p. 193.

9. *Ibid.*, p. 194.

10. *Ibid.*

11. "How Long is a Generation?" *British Journal of Sociology*, XI (March 1960), 10-23.

CHAPTER V

1. Sociological demographers like Vance have asked for more theory, while others like Gutman claim adequate theories exist for organizing present knowledge. See Rupert B. Vance, "Is Theory for Demographers?" in J. J. Spengler and O. D. Duncan (eds.), *Population Theory and Policy*, New York: The Free Press of Glencoe, 1956, pp. 88-94. Robert Gutman, "In Defense of Population Theory," *American Sociological Review*, 25 (June 1960), 325-333.

2. O. D. Duncan and L. Schnore, "Cultural, Behavioral, and Ecological Perspectives in the Study of Social Organization," *American Journal of Sociology*, 65 (September 1959), 132-146. See also the "Comment" by Peter H. Rossi and the "Rejoinder" by Duncan and Schnore, *ibid.*, pp. 146-149 and pp. 149-153, respectively.

3. George C. Homans, "Social Behavior as Exchange," *American Journal of Sociology*, 63 (May 1958), 597-606, and *Social Behavior*, New York: Harcourt, Brace and World, 1961.

4. William Petersen, *Population*, New York: Macmillan, 1961.

5. *Ibid.*, p. 297.

6. Alfred Schutz, "The Problem of Rationality in the Social World," *Economica*, X (May 1943), 136.

7. Petersen, *op. cit.*, pp. 297-298.

8. *Ibid.*, p. 298.

9. *Family Planning, Sterility, and Population Growth*, New York: McGraw-Hill, 1959.

10. *Ibid.*, p. 119.

11. Petersen, *op. cit.*, p. 240.

12. Frank W. Notestein, "The Population of the World in the Year 2000," in J. J. Spengler and O. D. Duncan (eds.), *Demographic Analysis*, New York: The Free Press of Glencoe, 1956, p. 37.

13. *Ibid.*, pp. 38-43.

14. *Ibid.*, p. 38.

15. *Ibid.*, p. 39.

16. *Ibid.,* p. 40.
17. *Ibid.,* p. 43.
18. Alfred Schutz, "The Problem of Rationality in the Social World," *op. cit.,* pp. 142-143.
19. Harold Garfinkel, "The Rational Properties of Scientific and Common Sense Activities," *Behavioral Science,* 5 (January 1960), p. 76.
20. *Ibid.,* pp. 73-75. The reader will notice that these characterizations of "rational" common-sense action imply some kind of calculation, but the actual form of calculation is notably absent. The accent is on being "reasonable," "explicit," and "efficient." While these features are rewarded in everyday life, they do not have the precision inherent in the canons of ideal scientific inquiry or in the requirements for programing a computer.
21. *Ibid.,* p. 82.
22. Petersen, *op. cit.,* p. 180, italics in original.
23. *Ibid.,* p. 182, italics in original.
24. *Ibid.,* p. 182.
25. *Ibid.,* pp. 182-183.
26. Cf. W. S. Robinson, "Ecological Correlations and the Behavior of Individuals," *American Sociological Review,* 15 (June 1950), 351-357.
27. G. W. Barclay, *Techniques of Population Analysis,* New York: Wiley, 1958, pp. 93-94.
28. See M. Kramer *et al.,* "Application of Life Table Methodology to the Study of Mental Hospital Population," reprinted from *Psychiatric Research Reports* No. 5, American Psychiatric Association, Washington, D.C., June 1956. M. Kramer *et al.,* "A Method for Determination of Probabilities of Stay, Release, and Death, for Patients Admitted to a Hospital for the Mentally Deficient: The Experience of Pacific State Hospital During the Period 1948-1952," *Am. J. Mental Deficiency,* 62, 1957.

CHAPTER VI

1. This chapter leans heavily upon Louis Gottschalk, Clyde Kluckhohn, and Robert Angell, *The Use of Personal Documents in History, Anthropology and Sociology,* New York: Social Science Research Council, 1947; Bernard Berelson, *Content Analysis in Communicative Research,* New York: The Free Press of Glencoe, 1952; and Dorian Cartwright, "Analysis of Qualitative Material," in L. Festinger and D. Katz, *Research Methods in the Behavioral Sciences,* New York: Holt, Rinehart & Winston, 1953, pp. 421-470; and Ithiel De Sola Pool (ed.), *Trends in Content Analysis,* Urbana, Ill.: University of Illinois Press, 1959.
2. Louis Gottschalk, "The Historian and the Historical Document," in Gottschalk, Kluckhohn, and Angell, *op. cit.,* p. 9. Italics in original.
3. *Ibid.*

4. *Ibid.,* pp. 25-26.

5. *Ibid.,* p. 27.

6. *Ibid.,* p. 32.

7. *Ibid.,* pp. 48-54.

8. *Ibid.,* pp. 68-69, italics in original.

9. Bernard Berelson, *Content Analysis in Communicative Research, op. cit.*

10. *Ibid.,* p. 16.

11. *Ibid.*

12. D. Cartwright, "Analysis of Qualitative Material," *op. cit.,* p. 424.

13. Berelson, *op. cit.,* p. 17.

14. *Ibid.,* p. 17.

15. *Ibid.*

16. Clyde Coombs, "Theory and Methods of Social Measurement," in L. Festinger and D. Katz, (eds.), *Research Methods in the Behavioral Sciences,* New York: Dryden, 1953, p. 471.

17. Berelson, *op. cit.,* p. 19.

18. *Ibid.*

19. *Ibid.,* p. 20.

20. Cartwright, *op. cit.,* p. 444.

21. Reported in Pool, *Trends in Content Analysis, loc. cit.*

22. Alexander L. George, "Quantitative and Qualitative Approaches to Content Analysis," in *ibid.,* pp. 7-32.

23. George F. Mahl, "Exploring Emotional States by Content Analysis," in *ibid.,* pp. 89-90.

24. *Ibid.,* p. 105.

25. Sol Saporta and Thomas A. Sebeok, "Linguistic and Content Analysis," in *ibid.,* pp. 135-137. Within the quote from Saporta and Sebeok there is a quote from Z. S. Harris, "Distributional Structure," *Word,* 10 (1954), 146-162.

26. Ithiel De Sola Pool, "Trends in Content Analysis Today: A Summary," in *ibid.,* p. 226.

CHAPTER VII

1. See Donald T. Campbell, "Factors Relevant to the Validity of Experiments in Social Settings," *Psychological Bulletin,* 54 (July 1957), 297-312; "Quasi-Experimental Designs for Use in Natural Social Settings," unpublished manuscript. Campbell's papers are useful for experiments in both natural and laboratory settings. His work offers a comprehensive coverage of the problems of conducting experiments in natural social settings. See also J. Berger, B. P. Cohen, J. L. Snell, and M. Zelditch, Jr., *Types of Formalization in Small Group Research,* Boston: Houghton Mifflin, 1962.

2. See Leon Festinger's discussion in "Laboratory Experiments," in

L. Festinger and D. Katz (eds.), *Research Methods in the Behavioral Sciences,* New York: Dryden, 1953, pp. 136-172.

3. See Alfred Schutz, "Concept and Theory Formation in the Social Sciences," *The Journal of Philosophy,* LI (April 1954), 266-267.

4. S. E. Asch, "Effects of Group Pressure upon the Modification and Distortion of Judgments," in H. Guetzkow (ed.), *Groups, Leadership and Men,* Pittsburgh: Carnegie Press, 1951, pp. 177-190.

5. M. Sherif, "An Experimental Approach to the Study of Attitudes," *Sociometry,* 1 (1937), 90-98.

6. F. P. Kilpatrick and W. H. Ittelson, "The Size-Distance Invariance Hypothesis," *Psychological Review,* 60 (1953), 223-232; A. Ames, Jr., *An Interpretive Manual for the Demonstrations in the Psychological Research Center, Princeton University: The Nature of Our Perceptions, Prehension, and Behavior.* Princeton: Princeton University Press, 1955; Egon Brunswick, *Perception and the Representative Design of Psychological Experiments.* Berkeley: University of California Press, 1956.

7. An essay which shows the relation and importance of cultural variables for survey research and its application to problems of substantive interest to sociologists can be found in Bennett M. Berger, "How Long is a Generation?" *The British Journal of Sociology,* XI (March 1960), 10-23.

8. John Thibaut, "An Experimental Study of the Cohesiveness of Underprivileged Groups," in D. Cartwright and A. Zander (eds.), *Group Dynamics,* Evanston and New York: Harper & Row, 1953, pp. 102-120.

9. *Ibid.,* p. 107.

10. "Communication in Experimentally Created Hierarchies," in Cartwright and Zander, *op. cit.,* pp. 443-461.

11. Harold Garfinkel, *The Perception of the Other: A Study in Social Order,* Doctoral dissertation, Harvard University, 1952. This experiment is briefly reported in a revised version of a paper read at the annual meetings of the American Sociological Association, Washington, D.C., 1957, entitled "A Conception of and Experiments with 'Trust' as a Condition of Stable Concerted Action."

12. Garfinkel, "Common Sense Knowledge of Social Structures," paper read at the Fourth World Congress of Sociology, Milan, Italy, 1959.

13. Erving Goffman, *Social Encounters,* Indianapolis: Bobbs-Merrill, 1961.

CHAPTER VIII

1. Robert E. Pittenger, Charles F. Hockett, and John J. Danehy, *The First Five Minutes,* Ithaca, New York: Paul Martineau, 1960.

2. *Ibid.,* p. 210. Italics in original.

3. Sidney M. Lamb, *Outline of Stratificational Grammar,* Berkeley:

Associated Students of the University of California Bookstore, 1962, p. 3. Italics in original.

4. Noam Chomsky, *Syntactic Structures,* The Hague: Mouton and Co., 1957, p. 11.

5. *Ibid.,* p. 13.

6. *Ibid.,* p. 17.

7. *Ibid.,* p. 48. See the lucid discussion by Hilary Putnam, "Some Issues in the Theory of Grammar," in *Structure of Language and its Mathematical Aspects,* Proceeding of Symposia in Applied Mathematics, XII (1961), 25-42.

8. See Lamb, *op. cit.,* pp. 4-8.

9. See the important work of Ludwig Wittgenstein, *Philosophical Investigations,* trans. by G. E. M. Anscombe, Oxford: Blackwell, 1953; J. L. Austin, *Philosophical Papers,* J. O. Urmson and G. J. Warnock, (eds.), London: Oxford University Press, 1961, particularly Chapter 3, "Other Minds," and Chapter 6, "A Plea for Excuses"; and Stanley Cavell, "Must We Mean What We Say?" *Inquiry,* 1 (Autumn 1958), 172-212.

10. Roman Jakobson and Morris Halle, *Fundamentals of Language,* The Hague: Mouton and Co., 1956, p. 11. See also Basil Bernstein, "Some Sociological Determinants of Perception," *British J. Sociology,* 9 (1958); "A *Public* Language: Some Sociological Implications of a Linguistic Form," *British J. Sociology,* 10 (1959); "Language and Social Class," *British J. Sociology,* 11 (1960); "Linguistic Codes, Hesitation Phenomena and Intelligence," *Language and Speech,* 5 (January-March 1962); and "Social Class, Linguistic Codes and Grammatical Elements," *Language and Speech,* 5 (October-December 1962).

11. C. F. Voegelin, "Casual and Noncasual Utterances within Unified Structure," in Thomas A. Sebeok (ed.), *Style in Language,* New York: The Technology Press and Wiley, 1960, pp. 57-68.

12. Chomsky, *op. cit.,* pp. 97-100. Cf. Floyd G. Lounsbury, "A Semantic Analysis of the Pawnee Kinship Usage," *Language* 32 (January-March 1956), 154-194.

13. Chomsky, *op. cit.,* pp. 107-108.

14. Sol Saporta, "The Application of Linguistics to the Study of Poetic Language," in Sebeok, *Style in Language, op. cit.,* p. 92. Italics in original.

15. See Alfred Schutz, "Symbol, Reality, and Society," in Lyman Bryson, Louis Finkelstein, Hudson Hoagland, and R. M. MacIver (eds.), *Symbols and Society,* New York: Harper, 1955, especially pp. 147-189. Schutz' views on meaning are presented in the following chapter.

16. This distinction is due to Ferdinand de Saussure, *Cours de Linguistique Generale,* Charles Bally and Albert Sechehaye (eds.), Paris: Payot, fourth edition, 1949. My use of de Saussure's notions is taken from Rulon S. Wells, "De Saussure's System of Linguistics," in Martin Joos (ed.), *Readings in Linguistics,* Washington, D.C.: American Council of Learned Societies, 1957, pp. 1-18.

17. Wells, *loc. cit.,* p. 9. Italics in original.

18. *Ibid.,* p. 9.

19. Paul Ziff, *Semantic Analysis,* Ithaca, New York: Cornell University Press, 1960, pp. 79-80.

20. *Ibid.,* p. 80.

21. For specific examples the reader might consult N. Chomsky, M. Halle, and Fred Lukoff, "On Accent and Juncture in English," in M. Halle *et al.* (eds), *For Roman Jakobson,* The Hague: Mouton and Co., 1956, pp. 65-80. Also N. Chomsky, *Syntactic Structures, op. cit.,* Chapter 7, "Some Transformations in English"; Roger Brown and Albert Gilman, "The Pronouns of Power and Solidarity," in Sebeok, *Style in Language, op. cit.,* pp. 253-276.

22. L. Wittgenstein, *Philosophical Investigations, op. cit.*

23. Floyd G. Lounsbury, "A Semantic Analysis of the Pawnee Kinship Usage," *op. cit.,* pp. 161-162.

24. *Ibid.,* p. 162.

25. Ward Goodenough, "Componential Analysis and the Study of Meaning," *Language,* 32 (January-March 1956), 195-216.

26. *Ibid.,* p. 195.

27. *Ibid.,* p. 196. Italics in original.

28. C. E. Osgood, G. J. Suci, and P. H. Tannenbaum, *The Measurement of Meaning,* Urbana: University of Illinois Press, 1957, p. 9. Italics in original.

29. *Ibid.,* p. 20.

30. Roger Brown, *Words and Things,* New York: The Free Press of Glencoe, 1958, p. 102.

31. Wittgenstein, *Philosophical Investigations, op. cit.,* pp. 15-50.

32. *Ibid.,* p. 4.

33. *Ibid.,* p. 33. Italics in original.

34. *Ibid.,* pp. 38-40, italics in original.

35. Charles F. Hockett, "Idiom Formation," in M. Halle *et al.* (eds.), *For Roman Jakobson, op. cit.,* p. 222.

36. *Ibid.,* p. 222. See also, Hockett's *A Course in Modern Linguistics,* New York: Macmillan, 1958, Chapters 17-19.

37. Hockett, "Idiom Formation," *loc cit.,* p. 223, italics in original.

38. See Dell H. Hymes, "The Ethnography of Speaking," in *Anthropology and Human Behavior,* publication of the Anthropological Society of Washington, D.C., 1962.

39. See in addition to previously cited materials the following: C. H. Ferguson and J. J. Gumperz (eds.), *Linguistic Diversity in South Asia,* Bloomington, Indiana: Research Center in Anthropology, Folklore and Linguistics, 1960; J. J. Gumperz, "Speech Variation and the Study of Indian Civilization," *American Anthropologist,* 63 (October 1961), 976-988; Gregory P. Stone, "Appearance and the Self," in A. M. Rose (ed.), *Human Behavior and Social Processes,* Boston: Houghton Mifflin, 1962, pp. 86-118.

CHAPTER IX

1. Dennis Wrong, "The Oversocialized Conception of Man in Modern Sociology," *American Sociological Review,* 26 (April 1961), 183-193.

2. Thomas Hobbes, *Leviathan* (edited with an introduction by Michael Oakeshott), Oxford: Blackwell, 1960, pp. 82-93.

3. Max Weber, *The Theory of Social and Economic Organization,* A. M. Henderson and Talcott Parsons (trans.), New York: Oxford University Press, 1947, p. 88.

4. See K. R. Popper, *The Open Society and Its Enemies,* Vol. II, London: Routledge and Kegan Paul, 1957, pp. 88-99; Sidney Hook, *Towards the Understanding of Karl Marx,* New York: John Day Co., 1933, pp. 90-101, 147-186.

5. See Sigmund Freud, *The Ego and the Id,* Joan Riviere (trans.), London: Hogarth Press, 1950; *Civilization and Its Discontents,* New York: Doubleday Anchor, 1958.

6. Emile Durkheim, *Suicide,* John A. Spaulding and George Simpson (trans.), New York: The Free Press of Glencoe, 1951, p. 315.

7. Emile Durkheim, *The Division of Labor in Society,* George Simpson (trans.), New York: The Free Press of Glencoe, 1947, p. 206.

8. *Ibid.,* p. 214.

9. For a detailed discussion of the importance of the unstated conditions of social contracts, see Talcott Parsons, *The Structure of Social Action,* New York: The Free Press of Glencoe, 1949, Chapter VIII.

10. *Ibid.,* p. 366.

11. *Ibid.,* pp. 367-368.

12. *Ibid.,* pp. 385-389.

13. *Ibid.,* pp. 660-662.

14. *Ibid.,* p. 716.

15. One sociologist, Paul Lazarsfeld, has devoted the major part of his life work to the study of attitudes in behavior and in particular to the methodological problems involved in their measurement. In an unpublished paper ("Some Historical Notes on the Study of Action," 1957), he explicitly argues that Weber's untranslated work shows that he would reduce the study of collectivities to the actions of individuals and actually consider the study of concrete social action to be the task of the psychologist. Lazarsfeld documents, through a careful analysis of Weber's untranslated empirical materials, that Weber sought to keep his interest in "empirical psychology" separate from his work in sociology. The critical question is whether the concept of social action requires, both conceptually and empirically, the *necessary* use of psychological concepts like attitudes (which are equated to drives, needs, habits, etc.).

16. See David Lockwood, "Some Remarks on 'The Social System,'"

British Journal of Sociology, 7 (June 1956), 136, for a useful discussion of the difference and importance of both normative and nonnormative factors in the study of social order. Lockwood uses the term "substratum" to refer to nonnormative conditions which can influence social action. He gives the example of Marx's theory of social stratification as based on "the differentiation of competing economic interest groups in the society on the basis of productive relations" (p. 138), where the nonnormative conditions refers to the "factual organization of production, and the powers, interests, conflicts, and groupings consequent on it" (pp. 137-138). Lockwood's statement (that "Every social situation consists of a normative order with which Parsons is principally concerned, and also of a factual order, or substratum. Both are 'given' for individuals; both are part of the exterior and constraining social world" [p. 139]) about Parsons is probably one that most sociologists would agree with, though it is not clear that Parsons' work excludes the nonnormative conditions of social action, particularly as they become part of the actor's environment of action.

17. Reinhard Bendix, *Social Science and the Distrust of Reason,* Berkeley and Los Angeles: University of California Publications in Sociology and Social Institutions, Vol. I, No. 1, 1951, p. 18.

18. C. H. Cooley, *Human Nature and Social Order and Social Organization,* New York: The Free Press of Glencoe, 1956.

19. G. H. Mead, *The Philosophy of the Present,* Chicago: Open Court, 1932, pp. 83-84.

20. G. H. Mead, *Mind, Self and Society,* Chicago: University of Chicago Press, 1934, p. 78.

21. G. H. Mead, *The Philosophy of the Act,* Chicago: University of Chicago Press, 1938, p. 192.

22. One widely quoted attempt to extend Mead's work can be found in Ralph H. Turner, "Role-Taking, Role-Standpoint, and Reference-Group Behavior," *American Journal of Sociology,* LXI (January 1956), 316-328. Turner's formulation seeks to break down the role-taking process so that it would be more conducive to operational procedures; but subjective meaning is not assigned variable status. Turner chooses to leave unexplained the way in which the actor comes to assign significance to his environment, preferring to deal with the way in which the inferred other-role provides the conditions for the enactment of the self-role. He thus assumes the given existence of an environment of objects, a social order, which is already highly structured, and which he chooses to "build-on" for particular conceptual and operational purposes. But this is a social order with unstated properties. How the actor comes to infer the role of the other is critical in how this other-role facilitates the enactment of the self-role.

23. Talcott Parsons and Edward A. Shils (eds.), *Toward a General Theory of Action,* Cambridge: Harvard University Press, 1951. Talcott Parsons, *The Social System,* New York: The Free Press of Glencoe, 1951. The notion of culture as a system of action is discussed in Par-

sons' "Introduction, Culture and the Social System," in T. Parsons, E. Shils, K. D. Naegele, and J. R. Pitts (eds.), *Theories of Society,* Vol. II, New York: The Free Press of Glencoe, 1961.

24. See *Toward a General Theory of Action, op. cit.,* pp. 15-16.

25. The notion of a community which the researcher must somehow transcend if he is to do more than employ the same commonsense concepts and rules as the actor is described by Alfred Schutz and Harold Garfinkel. Using Schutz' work as the point of departure, Garfinkel refers to this problem as "seeing the society from within" in "Common Sense Knowledge of Social Structures," paper read at the Fourth World Congress of Sociology, Milan, Italy, 1959.

26. William Graham Sumner, *Folkways,* Boston: Ginn and Co., 1906.

27. R. Bierstedt, *The Social Order,* New York: McGraw-Hill, 1957.

28. *Ibid.,* p. 175.

29. *Ibid.,* p. 199.

30. R. M. Williams, *American Society,* New York: Knopf (rev. ed.), 1960.

31. *Ibid.,* pp. 23-25.

32. This classification is based upon Williams' earlier edition of *American Society* and an article which incorporates and expands the original formulation. Cf. Richard T. Morris, "A Typology of Norms," *American Sociological Review,* 7 (October 1956), 610-613. See Williams, *op. cit.,* pp. 26-27.

33. Williams, *American Society, op. cit.,* p. 34.

34. *Ibid.,* p. 377 and especially footnote 4.

35. I shall rely primarily on Harold Garfinkel's paper "A Conception of and Experiments with 'Trust' as a Condition of Stable Concerted Action," revised and expanded paper read at the annual meetings of the American Sociological Association, Washington, D.C., 1957. Another fascinating view with many similar features can be found in the challenging papers by O. K. Moore and A. R. Anderson. See "Some Puzzling Aspects of Social Interaction," *The Review of Metaphysics,* XV (March 1962), 409-433; "The Structure of Personality," *ibid.,* XVI (December 1962), 212-236; and "The Formal Analysis of Normative Concepts," *American Sociological Review,* 22 (February 1957), 9-17.

36. Garfinkel, "A Conception of and Experiments with 'Trust' . . . ," *op. cit.,* p. 5. The reader should note that Garfinkel's formulation, as far as I can tell, does not explicitly allow for the possibility of sustained conflict over time because he is not actually addressing substantive conflict *per se,* but the stable features of everyday and game situations which must hold even if there is substantive conflict among the participants. Thus, some basic order or set of rules are presumed to be present which allow for substantive conflict or harmony. Substantive conflict (e.g., continual arguments and disagreements) is not ruled out, but simply not an issue of the paper.

37. *Ibid.,* pp. 5-6.

38. *Ibid.,* p. 6, emphasis in the original.

39. *Ibid.,* pp. 7-8.

40. *Ibid.,* p. 2.

41. *Ibid.,* pp. 27-28.

42. *Ibid.,* p. 23. Garfinkel presents findings from studies of the game ticktacktoe which supports this position. The results are most striking for children between the ages of five and eleven for whom a violation of a basic rule produces bewilderment. Adults tend to shift their perspectives and treat the violation as "amusing" or a "different" game or distrust the experimenter's character.

43. Thomas C. Schelling, *The Strategy of Conflict,* Cambridge: Harvard University Press, 1961.

44. Ward Edwards, "Costs and Payoffs are Instructions," *Psychological Review,* 68 (July 1961), 275-276.

45. *Ibid.,* p. 276.

46. *Ibid.,* p. 281.

47. Paul Kecskemeti, *Meaning, Communication, and Value,* Chicago: University of Chicago Press, 1952, pp. 7-9.

48. Alfred Schutz, "Symbol, Reality, and Society," in L. Bryson, L. Finkelstein, H. Hoagland, and R. M. MacIver (eds.), *Symbols and Society,* New York: Harper, 1955. Schutz' paper contains a detailed discussion of how couplings occur between signs and their signatum.

49. *Ibid.,* p. 150.

50. *Ibid.,* p. 156.

51. See the excellent article by Louis Schneider, "The Role of the Category of Ignorance in Sociological Theory: An Exploratory Statement," *American Sociological Review,* 27 (August 1962), 492-508.

52. Schutz, *op. cit.,* p. 159.

53. *Ibid.,* pp. 158-159. Italics in original.

54. *Ibid.,* p. 166.

55. *Ibid.,* p. 170.

56. *Ibid.,* p. 189.

57. *Ibid.,* p. 163.

58. *Ibid.,* pp. 164-165.

59. See Schneider, "The Role of the Category of Ignorance in Sociological Theory," *op. cit.*

60. Schutz, "Common-Sense and Scientific Interpretation of Human Action," *Philosophy and Phenomenological Research,* 14 (September 1953), p. 10.

61. *Ibid.,* pp. 11-14.

62. Schutz, "Symbol, Reality, and Society," *op. cit.,* p. 194.

63. Cf. Schutz, "Common-Sense and Scientific Interpretation of Human Action," *op. cit.,* pp. 13-14.

64. Alfred Schutz, "On Multiple Realities," *Philosophy* and *Phenomenological Research,* V (June 1945), 551, italics in the original.

65. *Ibid.,* p. 553.

66. *Ibid.,* p. 554.

67. An excellent recent source book is Herbert Spiegelberg, *The Phenomenological Movement, A Historical Introduction,* 2 volumes, The Hague: Nijhoff, 1960. Another excellent general overview is contained in Richard Schmitt, "In Search of Phenomenology," *The Review of Metaphysics,* XV (March 1962), 450-479.

68. "On the Intentionality of Consciousness," in Marvin Farber (ed.), *Philosophical Essays in Memory of Edmund Husserl,* Cambridge: Harvard University Press, 1940, pp. 65-83.

69. *Ibid.,* p. 66, italics in original.

70. Helmut Kuhn, "The Phenomenological Concept of 'Horizon,' in M. Farber, *loc. cit.,* pp. 106-123.

71. *Ibid.,* pp. 107-108, 112. Italics in original.

72. *Ibid.,* p. 113. See also the excellent application of Husserl's concepts to literary criticism by H. D. Hirsch in "Objective Interpretation," PMLA (Publications of the Modern Language Association), LXXV (September 1960), 463-479.

73. My discussion follows closely that of Alfred Schutz, "Common-Sense and Scientific Interpretation of Human Action," *op. cit.,* pp. 1-38.

74. *Ibid.,* p. 32.

75. See Felix Kaufmann, *Methodology of the Social Sciences,* New York: Humanities Press, 1958.

INDEX

actor, constitutive accent and, 206; experience of time in, 118; in experimental environment 163; inner states of, 111, 116, 193; knowledge of world and meaning in, 104, 126, 162, 215-216; model of, 62, 114; point of view and perception of, 20; psychological makeup of, 203-204; rationality of, 126; in role-taking situation, 213; rules and, 203; variables of, in everyday world, 118-120
American Society, 200
Ames, A., 235
Anderson, A. R., 228, 249
"appresentational" relations, 212-213
Asch, S. E., 96, 158-159, 235
attribute space, 25
"attributes," 15; error and, 29
Austin, J. L., 236
autokinetic effect, 158
axiomatic systems, 8

background information, in questionnaire, 108
Baldwin, J. M., 189
Barclay, George W., 137, 233
Barnett, H. G., 230
Barton, Allen H., 19-23, 227
Becker, Howard S., 47-49, 66, 69-70, 229, 230
Bendix, Reinhard, 196, 239
Berelson, Bernard, 146, 149, 151, 233
Berger, Bennett, 31, 235
Berger, J., 225, 227, 234
Bernstein, Basil, 236
Bierstedt, Robert, 197-200, 202, 240
birth rates, measurement problems in, 29-30, 194-195; social process and, 129
births, "accidental," 127; demographic method and, 121
Breuer, J., 228

Brodbeck, May, 226
Brown, Roger, 183, 237
Brunswick, Egon, 235
bureaucracy, 36, 126, 135

Campbell, Donald T., 234
Campbell, Norman, 10-11, 127, 227
Cannell, C. F., 76, 94-99, 231
Cartwright, D., 147, 150-151, 162, 225, 233
Cavell, Stanley, 236
channels, formal and unofficial communication, 54-55
"cheater interviewer," 115
Chomsky, Noam, 173-176, 180, 236
Churchman, C. West, 10-12, 227
classification, multiproperty type of, 25
classification categories, 28-29
classification problems, 20-21
clock time, 27, 110, 114, 118
coding, theory and, 116-120
Cohen, B. P., 225, 227, 234
"cohesiveness," 161-163, 168
common sense, interpretation and, 52-53; in interviewing, 79; in scientific observations, 61, 88
common-sense meanings, in everyday life, 111
common-sense rules, language and, 184
communication, complexities of, 172-173; meaning and, 212-218
communication materials, connotive and denotive, 149
Comte, Auguste, 189
constitutive accent, norms and, 205-206
content analysis, 143-156; measurement in, 144; procedures in, 147-148
contradiction, law of, 31
Cooley, C. H., 189, 216, 239